Counseling
and
Self-Esteem

RESOURCES FOR
CHRISTIAN COUNSELING

RESOURCES FOR CHRISTIAN COUNSELING

(*Other volumes forthcoming*)

Counseling
and
Self-Esteem

DAVID E. CARLSON

RESOURCES FOR
CHRISTIAN COUNSELING

—————— General Editor ——————

Gary R. Collins, Ph.D.

WORD PUBLISHING

Dallas·London·Vancouver·Melbourne

3/10/10

COUNSELING AND SELF-ESTEEM, Volume 13 of the Resources for Christian Counseling series. Copyright © 1988 by Word, Incorporated. All rights reserved. No portion of this book may be reproduced in any form, except for brief quotations in reviews, without written permission from the publisher.

Unless otherwise indicated, all Scripture quotations in this volume are from the New American Standard Bible, copyright © 1977 by the Lockman Foundation. Used by permission. Scriptures indicated NIV are from the New International Version. Copyright © 1983 International Bible Society. Used by permission of Zondervan Bible Publishers. Scriptures indicated KJV are from the King James Version.

Permission to quote the following
 "The Lament," by Marcia Esther Allen, "Value" by Carol Hass, © 1986, is gratefully acknowledged.

Library of Congress Cataloging-in-Publication Data

Carlson, David E., 1938–
    Counseling and self-esteem.

    (Resources for Christian counseling; v. 13)
    Bibliography: p.
    Includes index.
    1. Self-respect. 2. Counseling. 3. Pastoral
counseling. I. Title.   II. Series.
BJ1533.S3C37 1988   253.5   87-34080
ISBN 0-8499-0479-X

Printed in the United States of America

01239 AGF 9876543

CONTENTS

5

EDITOR'S PREFACE

A MISSIONARY RECENTLY DESCRIBED a challenging conference in Central America where the participants discussed ways to help the poor become self-sufficient. Back home the next Sunday, the missionary heard his pastor condemn self-sufficiency, calling it a sin and the fastest way to destruction.

As he left the church that morning, the missionary wondered, "Is self-sufficiency virtuous or is it sinful?" Clearly the conference leaders and the pastor were using the same word, *self-sufficiency*, but giving it different meanings. The conference was devoted to helping people gain skills so they could be productive and no longer dependent on handouts. The pastor was criticizing something else: a godless, humanistic,

7

self-serving type of self-sufficiency that ignores God, boosts human potential, and declares that humans are solely responsible for their own destinies.

This missionary story about self-sufficiency reminded me of the debate that currently swirls around discussions of the self. While some counselors seek to build self-esteem, a positive self-concept, and self-sufficiency in their counselees, other counselors emphasize self-denial, self-sacrifice, and self-abasement. While some books proclaim the importance of self-respect and "feeling good about ourselves," other writers attribute most contemporary human problems to selfish and self-centered opinions of ourselves.

In this book, David Carlson shows how much of the debate over self-sufficiency and self-esteem comes because we confuse terminology. We assume, in error, that self-esteem always means self-absorption or self-worship. We conclude erroneously that humility is the same as humiliation or that self-denial involves self-degradation. Basing his conclusions on the Bible, the author shows instead that committed believers who sincerely seek to obey the Scriptures should and can have healthy self-concepts built on their relationships to Jesus Christ.

By considering the problem of low self-esteem, this book considers an issue that lies at the core of a great deal of counseling. An in-depth discussion of the self-concept fits well into the Resources for Christian Counseling series. Each of these books is intended to deal with some topic that is likely to come up in your counseling. Written by counseling experts, each of whom has a strong Christian commitment and practical counseling experience, these volumes are intended to be examples of accurate psychology and careful use of Scripture. Each is intended to have a clear evangelical perspective, careful documentation, a strong practical orientation, and freedom from the sweeping statements and undocumented rhetoric that sometimes characterize books in the counseling field. Our goal is to provide books that are clearly written, practical, up-to-date overviews of the issues faced by contemporary Christian counselors. All of the Resources for Christian Counseling books have similar bindings and together they will comprise a complete encyclopedia of Christian counseling.

I am especially pleased to have a book by David Carlson in the series. When authors were being selected, we thought first of those who had written previously and had demonstrated their abilities to communicate on paper. Dave Carlson had written some helpful articles but since he had never tackled a book, his name was not among those who immediately came to mind when this series was launched. But I have known for a long time that Dave can communicate. He has an excellent reputation as a competent counselor and I have often heard him speak. We have taught at the same academic institution for a number of years, attend the same church, and live in the same community within two or three blocks of each other. When Dave gave a series of lectures on self-esteem at our church, I concluded quickly that he was the person to do this book in the series.

In reading the pages that follow, you quickly will discover an author with sensitivity and a depth of understanding that comes from many years of counseling experience. This book deals effectively and biblically with the problem of self-esteem, but it does more. The author shares his own counseling methods and clearly introduces us to the basics of neuro-linguistic programing, a new and effective approach to helping people. Readers are shown how to stimulate a Christ-honoring self-esteem in themselves, in their counselees, in families, and in their churches. Illustrated with a variety of practical and interesting case histories, this book is likely to be a helpful and much-consulted addition to your counseling library.

Somebody once said that all of us grow up wounded. Our past hurts, rejections, failures, and the abusive criticisms that come from others leave millions with deep inferiority feelings and shattered self-concepts. Dave Carlson has shown in a practical and biblically based way how we can bind up the psychological and spiritual wounds of those who come to us for counseling. I hope you will find this book to be as stimulating, thought-provoking, and genuinely helpful as it has been to me.

Gary R. Collins, Ph.D.
Kildeer, Illinois

INTRODUCTION

ALL OF US HAVE STRUGGLED WITH OUR SENSE OF WELL-BEING. Because of failures, challenges, and the criticisms of others, we have doubted ourselves. Most of us have wondered about our value and significance and importance to God, to the church, to our families, and to society. Amazingly, many people survive life's rejections fairly well. Others carry the pain and paralysis of self-doubt, inferiority, insecurity, and inadequacy into each aspect of life. The popularity of secular and religious self-help books shows that hurting people are searching for a sense of well-being and self-esteem.

Many fine books and articles have been published on the subject during the last ten years. But the topic of self-esteem, or self-love, has generated considerable debate and controversy within the Christian community. This controversy may grow out of a fear that self-love will lead to narcissism and pride in the individual Christian. Some Christians think we cannot believe in both human dignity and human depravity. I hope this book will help to dispel such fear through an accurate discussion of the biblical teaching on self-love.

Self-love, as I understand the concept biblically and psychologically, includes the following: (1) accepting myself as a child of God who is lovable, valuable, capable; (2) being willing to give up considering myself the center of the world; (3) recognizing my need of God's forgiveness and redemption. Christian self-esteem results from translating "I am the greatest, wisest, strongest, best" to "I am what I am, a person made in God's image, a sinner redeemed by God's grace, and a significant part in the body of Christ."

Like other Christian books on self-esteem, this text examines a biblical and theological basis for self-esteem. Unlike other volumes on the subject, this text identifies steps to building self-esteem, developing and placing them within an integrated, therapeutic framework. While these chapters are specifically directed to ministers and professional counselors, laypeople can use this counseling approach to build their own self-esteem as they read this book and practice its exercises. Laypeople are encouraged to consult with pastors or professional counselors who can aid them in this process.

Counseling strategies represent a balanced use of biblical principles and psychological concepts. A unique feature of the counseling approach in this book is its balanced use of cognitive, affective, and behavioral modalities and techniques. Clients are encouraged to use what they hear, see, feel, and do as sensory resources in building self-esteem. The helper, minister, or counselor is encouraged to move beyond a counseling style of proclamation and learn how to "process" with his or her counselees. Pastors are encouraged to make a distinction between their preaching and their pastoring (counseling), because church members seeking counseling have not successfully translated sermons into practical daily life. The pastor, in such cases, will need to help parishioners uncover their resistance to change as well as develop resources through which they can understand and live out a sermon's applications. Merely rehearsing the sermon will frustrate both the preacher and the person seeking help because this process will lead to failure. As the helper reads this book and practices its exercises, he or she will learn what can be done when the usual approaches (preaching, teaching, counseling) are ineffective.

Professional counselors are encouraged to add sensory modalities and techniques (auditory, visual, kinesthetic, and behavioral) to their favored approach. They are encouraged to view what looks like failure in counseling (theirs or clients') as feedback which can be utilized constructively to help achieve desired goals.

Counselors and ministers may be confronted by frustrated people who have developed a relationship with Jesus Christ but who suffer from self-criticism and even self-punishment. For reasons that this book will explore, though the Christian's greatest need (salvation) has been met, the Christian may miss the fulfillment of a basic human need—the knowledge, vision, feelings, and actions that affirm his or her value as a person.

In summary, then, this book is primarily addressed to ministers and counselors who desire to learn how to build self-esteem in their congregations and clients. Second, it may be useful to anyone who struggles with self-esteem. Whatever problems people face, self-esteem is frequently a fundamental and contributing issue. Third, you the helper will hopefully do your own growth work and build your own self-esteem before you attempt to help others. Fourth, this material may be used as a textbook in counseling since it teaches and demonstrates the use of content and process in counseling. (*Content* is defined as the "what" in counseling, the facts and substance of what is said, thought, and acted. *Process* is defined as the "how," "sequence," and "timing" of the helper's interventions as well as the way counselees talk to themselves and others, view themselves and their world, become aware of and express their feelings, and choose to act.) Counseling exercises are included to aid in the understanding of process and to develop skills in processing.

Chapter 1, "Self-Esteem: A Psycho-Theological Definition," defines self-esteem and compares biblical and nonbiblical conceptions of self-esteem. The reader is encouraged to review his or her ideas of self-love as they are contrasted with those of Scripture.

Chapter 2, "Self-Esteem: A Psycho-Theological Process," defines and illustrates how the four sense modalities (auditory/hear, visual/see, kinesthetic/feel, and behavioral/do) are the core elements of a practical counseling methodology and an integrated (psychological/theological and cognitive/affective/behavioral) counseling strategy. It introduces suggestions for developing self-knowledge, self-acceptance, self-love, and self-sharing consistent with Christian humility and service. Written exercises to help people discover and accept who they are may be duplicated for use in counseling. A counseling situation illustrates negative and positive sensory cycles and how they relate to spiritual cycles. The chapter concludes with six exploratory questions, useful in any counseling situation, which emphasize the use of process in helping.

Chapter 3, "Teaching People to Build Self-Esteem: A Twelve-Step Process," begins by identifying five common stages in the process of change. It shows why taking the twelve steps is impossible unless people are in stage three because of the ways in which low self-esteem affects personal adjustment, relationships, and approaches to life. This chapter discusses how low self-esteem leads to a vicious circle of poor performance, distorted perceptions, unrealistic expectations, and unhappy personal and social life. The body of the chapter discusses twelve ways to build self-esteem, drawing heavily on biblical data and clinical experience. The emphasis in this chapter is on growth and process, encouraging the helper to be persistent and patient while walking, talking, and picturing himself and his clients through the twelve steps.

Chapter 4 focuses on "Teaching People Their Sensory Process in Developing Self-Esteem." Counselees characteristically repeat problem-solving approaches, even though these approaches are not working, rather than try different methods. Teaching clients how they listen, look, act, and feel during problem-maintaining efforts is a first step in learning new patterns of coping.

Chapter 5, "Teaching Counselors the Sensory Process: A Counseling Illustration," demonstrates how to utilize the counselee's self-talk, self-pictures, self-actions, and self-feelings. The chapter introduces two new counseling methods: (1) how to identify and utilize a person's sensory predicates (hear, see, feel, do) and (2) how to observe his or her eye positions and movements. Predicates and eye scans tell the helper how the client is processing information and what primary sensory modalities he or she uses. These also enhance the development and maintenance of rapport. Scripture illustrates the sensory process and predicates.

Chapter 6, "Teaching Parents to Build Self-Esteem in Their Children," illustrates how to use the four modality processes within the family. Clinical experience suggests that children find trusting in Christ difficult unless they are esteemed by significant people in their lives. Illustrations of how a therapeutic relationship can prepare the way for a spiritual relationship with Christ are followed by seven specific ways to build self-esteem in the family. This chapter gives special attention to how parents' self-esteem affects children's self-esteem and stresses the importance of parents' response to real feelings, legitimate needs, and cherished values in both their children and themselves.

Chapter 7, "Teaching People to Be Their Own Nurturing Parents," develops the process of self-talk, self-concept, self-confidence, and self-action. Learning to nurture self, an adult developmental task, helps supplement whatever parenting deficits a person suffered in childhood. This chapter presents an over-all strategy for building self-esteem in oneself and in others by paying attention to the auditory, visual, kinesthetic, and behavioral modalities.

Chapter 8 is "Teaching Counselees to Nurture Themselves Through Recognizing and Accepting Feelings." Talking about feelings is not the same as experiencing and expressing them. This chapter focuses on the process of helping people identify and express their feelings. A feeling-recognition exercise is introduced as a tool to assist counselees to know what they feel; what physical sensations accompany emotions; when, where, and with whom they experience the feeling; and what they do to express the emotion.

Chapter 9, "Teaching Counselees to Experience God as Their Nurturing Parent," is one of the counselor's most important helping tasks. Experiencing the helper as a loving, caring, understanding person is frequently the human relationship through which persons can experience God as nurturing parent. This chapter introduces ways the helper can present God as nurturing parent, utilizing the counselee's sense modalities to build self-esteem through God's words, God's perspectives, God's feelings, and God's actions—all revealed in Scripture.

Chapter 10, "Teaching the Church to Build Esteem in Its Troubled Families," addresses the challenge of esteeming others despite their troubled personal, marital, and family lives. Parents and pastors benefit from learning that God had trouble with his family, too, a concept supported by biblical illustrations of troubled families that precede a discussion of why God didn't blame himself. Next, the chapter identifies constructive steps that God took when his family got into trouble. The last half of the chapter deals with how the church, friends, and family can respond positively to families in trouble.

Chapter 11, "Helping People Change: The Answer Is Not the Solution," recognizes that answers are easier for the helper than they are for the helpee. Self-esteem is acknowledged to be a basic human need and at the same time a basic problem to many personal and interpersonal difficulties. The chapter concludes with encouragement to the counselor and pastor to remember that the helping event needs be turned into a helping process.

I hope this book will accomplish these three goals: (1) provide the pastor and counselor with an understanding of self-esteem as a fundamental ingredient to one's spiritual, emotional, and social health; (2) teach accurate, biblical views of self-esteem, and (3) teach counseling strategies that can be used for building self-esteem and for dealing with other counseling problems.

I realize full well that both females and males enter into the counseling process. Also, it is my purpose to avoid language that refers to only one gender in my writing. But the English language does not make this easy. Therefore, in some examples, I will use only one gender although both male and female are represented.

I am convinced that in the preparation of a manuscript an author needs at least three resources: a good word processor, a good editor, and a good marriage. I am grateful to have all three.

I express my appreciation to my personal editorial assistant, LaVone Holt; to those clients whose counseling sessions are used in these chapters to illustrate the helping process (these stories are told either with the clients' permission or with names and situations altered to protect their identities); and to my professional associate and neighbor Gary Collins for inviting me to write for this series.

CHAPTER ONE

SELF-ESTEEM
A PSYCHO-THEOLOGICAL DEFINITION

IMAGINE THAT WE ARE CHATTING over a cup of coffee when I ask, "If you could change something about yourself, what would it be?" Take a moment to register your first responses. Now compare your reactions to typical responses which include change in hair color, amount of hair, its curl, or straightness; height, weight, and shape of body; personality characteristics and emotional responses; spiritual maturity and victory over habitual sin; improved relationships with family, friends, the opposite sex; greater intelligence or improved performance. Since you are reading a counseling book, no doubt you desire to improve as a counselor.

Society defines self-esteem through most of these answers.

Early in life, we learn that people who are bright, beautiful, popular, talented, wealthy, or productive are valued and loved. We measure ourselves by these values, usually to our loss of esteem. Equally unfortunately, we measure others by these values, usually to their loss of esteem. A vicious cycle continues; our children are measured by these values, compare themselves by these values, and, in turn, measure friends, siblings, and parents by these values. Some of us win in this process, but many of us lose esteem. This cycle then repeats itself in following generations unless those people learn to incorporate new values.

What are these new values? *I am lovable, valuable, and capable because God created, redeemed, and empowers me.* Self-esteem based on one's confidence of being made in God's image, restored to God's image, and equipped by his Spirit is solid and unchanging. It lacks the fickle and unpredictable responses of society. Self-esteem rooted in God's Word, in his perspective, in his feelings, and in his actions is lasting. Positive, biblical self-esteem, distinct from worldly esteem, does not compromise a person's own moral code to enhance pleasure, power, position, prestige, or privileges; nor does it deny that human beings have broken God's moral code. Any attempted deception of self, others, or God is challenged as a lie that demands confession (1 John 1:8–10).

Self-esteem is used broadly in this book. Specifically, it means the positive value we put on ourselves. *Self-love* includes the affection, care, and commitment we express to ourselves. *Self-concept* is the image we have of ourselves. *Self-confidence* is the trust and belief we have in ourselves, reflecting security and absence of self-doubt. *Self-acceptance* is respect, dignity, and approval of our personhood. It does not approve our sinful behavior, but acknowledges imperfections and regards humanness as positive. Self-esteem and self-love, used interchangeably in this book, include all the meanings described above.

SELF-ESTEEM: WHAT I LIKE AND DON'T LIKE ABOUT ME

Come back to our imaginary coffee chat. May I ask you to think of three qualities or characteristics you like about yourself? Pause and reflect: What is it that you like about you? Take a moment to write your answers in the chart provided below.

When asking others this question, I often get a long silence or an embarrassed smile. Some people cannot think of anything good about themselves. If they do remember positive qualities, they hesitate to express them for fear of being viewed as arrogant.

Now pause to reflect on three qualities or characteristics you don't like about you. Write these observations in the chart below. Although many people find that listing negative characteristics is easier than listing the positive, you may not wish to admit negative qualities either to anyone else or to yourself.

Now compare what you like and don't like about yourself with what you first said you wished to change. Write these answers in the chart. What new answers have you found? (This chart may be reproduced for clients to complete during the counseling session, used by the counselor as an interviewing guide, or sent home to complete.)

WHAT I LIKE ABOUT ME	WHAT I DON'T LIKE ABOUT ME	WHAT I WANT TO CHANGE ABOUT ME
1.	1.	1.
2.	2.	2.
3.	3.	3.

As you work with people, you will find these three questions useful in accessing their self-esteem levels. Anticipate their reluctance to talk about their strengths. Many times they will be more aware of their negative qualities. Part of your task as a counselor, therefore, is to help people build self-esteem by discovering their positive characteristics.

Self-Esteem: Two Definitions

I understand self-esteem as *the willingness to give up being the center of my world and accept myself as God's creation: lovable, valuable, capable, forgivable, and redeemable.* (See the Appendix for additional definitions.)

All of us are born with self-centeredness. Our natural tendency is to say, see, and feel that we are the center of the world. Self-centeredness has two primary roots, spiritual and psychological. Its spiritual root is the result of sin. As such, each of us must face his selfish impulses to be a god. We want to be all-powerful, all-knowing, irresistible, indispensable, and immortal. These five fantasies are our legacy from Adam and Eve's temptation (original sin) in the Garden of Eden. To give up self-centeredness is to surrender our desire to be God's equal. It is to accept ourselves as God's creation, redemption, and expression of himself.

The second root of self-centeredness is psychological. As children we grow through a self-centered stage when only our needs count. We want the world to center around us so we can have what we want when we want it. As babies, we need attention, respect, understanding, echoing, and mirroring if we are to develop a healthy self.[1] When our development is healthy, we outgrow the narcissistic stage. We come to value others as much as we value ourselves. We allow others to need us as much as we need them. If our development is not healthy, we stay stuck in the stage of grandiosity. That is, we admire ourselves for the same reasons our parents admire us, for our qualities of beauty, cleverness, success, and achievement. We remain trapped in narcissism when self-esteem depends on admiration and when self-respect depends on outstanding capabilities and performance. People are free from grandiosity when their self-esteem is based on the legitimacy of their own feelings and needs and not on the possession of personal qualities or achievements.

If our development is not healthy, it may take a second negative form, martyrdom. The narcissist says, "Only I count." The martyr agrees: "Only you count." The self-sacrificing person may look humble, but the martyr has as big a self-esteem problem as the proud person does. To the martyr, personal needs and feelings do not count. Such persons have learned that to be loved by others, they must accommodate to others' needs and deny their own feelings. That is, the child is not loved for who he or she is, but for being good, undemanding, and willing to serve.

A third common expression of narcissism, depression, is often the reverse side of grandiosity. "Depression can be understood as a sign of the loss of self and consists of a denial of one's own emotional reactions and feelings," notes Alice Miller.

Depression often results when a person is not free to experience the very earliest feelings, such as fright, anger, sadness, discontent, pain, hunger, or loneliness, without being rejected, ridiculed, or punished.

Alice Miller observes this narcissistic developmental process as follows:

> . . . a child trained in accordance with his parents' needs may never experience [spontaneous pleasure in sharing and giving], even while he gives and shares in a dutiful and exemplary way, and suffers because others are not as "good" as he is. Adults who were so brought up will try to teach their children this same altruism as early as possible. . . . It usually does not occur to the parents that they might need and use the child to fulfill their own egoistic wishes. They often are convinced that they must teach their child how to behave because it is their duty to help him along on the road to socialization. If a child brought up this way does not wish to lose his parents' love (and what child can risk that?), *he must learn very early to share, to give, to make sacrifices, and to be willing to do without and forego gratification—long before he is capable of true sharing or of the real willingness to "do without" (italics mine).*[2]

Obviously, then, being willing to give up oneself as the center of the world requires human and divine relationships that respect, affirm, and understand a person for who he or she is. Nobody surrenders spiritual pride and emotional egoism without the help of loving people. We do not surrender to God without experiencing God's love for us just as we are. He makes no demands on us to be better behaved, more attractive, or more achieving before he accepts us, loves us, and cares for us (Romans 5:8). And this is our challenge as Christian counselors: to be God's representatives of love and acceptance without demands and judgments, and to provide a relationship in which clients experience being at the center, being noticed, and being understood when they try to express their feelings. We who are counselors need to develop our talents without depending on counselees for self-esteem, knowing that we do not need their comfort or their smiles. For those we counsel this means: "I can be sad or happy whenever anything makes me sad or happy. I don't have to look cheerful for someone else, and I don't have to suppress my distress or anxiety to fit other people's needs. I can be angry, and no one will die or get a headache because of my anger. I can rage and smash things without 'losing' myself or my counselor."[3]

A second way to define self-esteem is $S.E. = E.I. - R.S.$ Self-Esteem equals Ego Ideal minus Real Self. All of us have dreams of what we would like to be. We create these images as we play and daydream. We fantasize about who we can be—professional athlete, star entertainer, famous scientist, successful preacher. These ego ideals motivate us to behave in ways that will make the dreams a reality.

Some of us approach our ego ideal more closely than others do, but we all fail to achieve that ego ideal. When we compare who we have become (the real self) to our ego ideal, the result is our self-esteem level. If we are compassionate to ourselves, the comparison is more motivating than damaging because that comparison provides a goal to strive for rather than a measure of failure. On the other hand, people who are perfectionists damage themselves by comparing their real selves to their ego ideals. If anything less than achieving the ego ideal is intolerable, the result is lowered self-esteem and increased self-hate.

Levels of Self-Esteem

The following diagram[4] helps to describe the various levels of self-esteem. Notice that healthy self-esteem differs from two unhealthy types of self-esteem with their unrealistic appraisal of the self and superior/inferior perspective of others. Self-esteem does not occur in a relational vacuum. It involves *a value, a feeling,* and *a perspective* of the person in relation to others. That is, how valuable am I compared to others? Do I feel as positive toward myself as I do toward others, and do I see myself as equal to others? Answers to these questions determine our attitudes and actions toward ourselves and others. Positively we experience this comparison as love and compassion toward ourselves and/or others; negatively we experience this comparison as prejudice and hatred toward ourselves and/or others.

TYPES OF SELF-ESTEEM	SELF-APPRAISAL	OTHER APPRAISAL
healthy self-esteem	realistic	I am equal to others
pride	unrealistic	I am superior to others
low self-esteem	unrealistic	I am inferior to others

Dimensions to Self-Esteem: An Exercise

The purpose of this exercise is to increase our self-awareness. Ask each question and write the first thoughts that come to mind. Responses may also have a context of who, when, where. Feel free to identify this awareness. Here are some examples: "I feel happy when I am with Bob, but sad when I am with Joe." Or, "I am a pretty good speaker, but my writing is not as well-developed." Or, "I am worth as much as my brothers as long as I don't disappoint my parents." "I see myself as a loving husband and irritable father." "I like my voice when I am relaxed, but dislike it when I am tense." "I am patient with and compassionate toward myself."

The following chart may be reproduced to use with clients in written form or used by the counselor as an interview guide.

DIMENSIONS TO SELF-ESTEEM	WHEN	WHERE	WHO
Feelings: What do I feel toward me? (emotions)			
Beliefs: What do I believe about me? (convictions)			
Values: How much do I value me? (worth)			
Perceptions: How do I see myself? (images)			
Conversations: How do I sound to myself? (self-talk)			
Actions: How do I act? (behaviors)			

Criteria of Healthy Self-Esteem

How do I know when my self-esteem is healthy? One way of knowing is to identify the level of esteem in the chart above. Do I compare myself positively with others, or do I tend to evaluate myself as superior/inferior to others?

Another way of knowing whether we have healthy self-esteem is to assess ourselves by considering the following criteria: First, *humility is not the same as humiliation.* Humility is recognizing who we are as created by God. It is being content with who we are, acknowledging that we are God's children, who have worth and are loved even though we have gone astray. Humility is the experience of knowing, accepting, loving, and sharing who we are while recognizing and appreciating who others are. Humility is accepting our strengths as well as our weaknesses.

In contrast, humiliation is a sense of shame and embarrassment. It is being discontented with who we are. It is a sense of worthlessness, the horrible experience of feeling bad about who we are. It is often accompanied by a sense of powerlessness to change the self or a fear of pride. Of course, pride, considering ourselves better than others, is condemned in Scripture. Yet, to our surprise, we will find no encouragement to think of ourselves as inferior, inadequate, or insecure. When we consider ourselves negatively, we confuse humility with humiliation.

Second, *putting off the sinful nature is not the same as putting down self.* The apostle Paul writes about "putting off" the old man and "putting on" the new man (Eph. 4:20–32). Notice the positive difference between the phrases "putting off" or "putting on," and "putting down." While Scripture does not use the phrase "put down self," some Christian music expresses this negative idea. For example, ". . . put my human nature down" is a phrase in André Crouch's song "My Tribute," and ". . . such a worm as I" comes from the hymn, "At the Cross," by Isaac Watts. My point here is that recognizing and accepting our sinfulness is not the same as putting our-selves down. When John Newton wrote, "Amazing grace! How sweet the sound that saved a wretch like me!" he was expressing an accurate assessment of his slave-trading life. He was not putting himself down; rather, he was recognizing his depravity and the overwhelming grace of God that had rescued him from his sin.

While these hymn phrases sound spiritual and biblical, they are, in fact, antibiblical when they are used to teach self-abasement. Describing the sinful human condition is not the same as condemning or depreciating the person. Paul addresses this problem of self-effacement in Colossians 2:18, 23: "Let no one keep defrauding you of your prize by delighting in self-abasement and the worship of the angels. . . . These are matters which have, to be sure, the appearance of wisdom in self-made religion and self-abasement and severe treatment of the body, but are of no value against fleshly indulgence." Some people in the church at Colossae believed that self-abasement would lead to humility. Paul perceived the opposite effect, commanding them to stop putting themselves down because that process leads to arrogant self-righteousness rather than to a vibrant spiritual life.

This encouraging message needs to be proclaimed in our churches as they distinguish between "putting oneself down" and "putting off the old man." This distinction was good news to the people Paul addressed in Ephesians 4:23, 24: ". . . be renewed in the spirit of your mind, and *put on the new self,* which in the likeness of God has been created in righteousness and holiness of the truth" (italics added). Now that is good news to those of us who desire to be what God wants us to be! With Christ's power we can put off our sin, selfishness, sensuality, impurity, greediness, and futility (see Ephesians 4:17–19), and put on the righteousness and holiness which are God's likeness. It is good news to those of us who fear we cannot be what God wants us to be, and it is good news to those of us who are being less than God wants us to be. "Achieve, Arise, Conquer! This feeling, this longing for the abrogation of every imperfection, is never absent" in human beings.[5]

Third, *self-denial is not equivalent to self-degradation.* Self-denial is a biblical concept, but self-degradation is not.[6] Self-denial means that I am willing to put off my sinful, selfish desires and behavior. It does not mean that I am going to put myself down or psychologically annihilate myself. Self-denial does not mean that I become nothing, no one, nonexistent. It does mean that I am willing to let Christ come into my life and empower me to represent his redemption and grace. Self-denial means that I set aside my sinful, selfish desires for the benefit of myself, others, God, and his kingdom.

Is this the way the concept of self-denial is taught in the church? In the past, at least, self-denial has often been represented as self-degradation. As we read in Colossians 2:18, this was a problem in the New Testament church. We need to be careful that we represent and teach the biblical view of self-denial. To aid us in this endeavor, reflecting on Galatians 2:20 is instructive. "*I* have been crucified with Christ; and it is no longer *I* who live, but Christ lives in *me;* and the life which *I* now live in the flesh *I* live by faith in the Son of God, who loved *me,* and delivered Himself up for *me*" (italics added). The I's and me's have been emphasized to draw attention to this reality: when Christ comes to live in us he replaces the "crucified self" with a "resurrected self." Although the old self has died with Christ, we need to affirm that we still have a self, an identity, a personhood that has been reclaimed, renewed, and resurrected by Christ.

Fourth, *unworthy is not the same as worthless.* Theologically, we are unworthy of God's love, mercy, and grace. However, to confuse this teaching with worthlessness is inaccurate and emotionally damaging. The Bible clearly teaches that we are of immense value and worth to God. He was willing to sacrifice his Son for our salvation. We were "bought with a price" (1 Cor. 6:20). With God's value of us in mind, we will desire to be what God wants us to be—a reflection of his image.

Fifth, *self-love is not the same as selfishness.* Selfishness is an attitude and behavior that puts my needs before your needs at your expense. Self-love is an attitude and behavior that considers you and your needs to be as important as mine, but it also means that my needs and feelings are as important as yours and that when I give them up, I do so voluntarily and graciously for your benefit. Christ models this concept in Philippians 2:4–7: "Do not merely look out for your own personal interests, but also for the interests of others. Have this attitude in yourselves which was also in Christ Jesus, who, although He existed in the form of God, did not regard equality with God a thing to be grasped [hung on to], but emptied Himself, taking the form of a bond-servant and being made in the likeness of men."

Paul commands this same attitude of husbands toward their wives, in Ephesians 5:28: "So husbands ought also to love their own wives as their own bodies. He who loves his own wife loves himself." Many of my clients love their spouses and children as much as they love themselves, which, unfortunately, is not very much. Their resource of love is minimal for themselves and therefore minimal for their family and friends. If we are to nourish and cherish others, we must increase our ability to nourish and cherish ourselves. The process for doing this is presented in the next chapters.

Sixth, *self-affirmation is not the same as self-conceit*. To say "I can" is affirmation. To say "I'm great" is conceit.

Recognizing my abilities and spiritual gifts is necessary if I am to participate in the body of Christ. To downplay or refuse to exercise my talents is to rob others of the benefits Christ has given them through me. Saying "I'm the greatest," even if you are boxer Muhammad Ali, expresses arrogance and lacks the humility of another truly great performer, such as football player Walter Payton. When persons are great at what they do, they have no need to proclaim greatness; they recognize their achievements without needing recognition from others.

Seventh, *self-worth is not the same as self-worship*. My value as a creation of God redeemed by God is a theme throughout this book. I have value because of Who created and redeemed me, not because of who I am and what I do. I affirm my significance as a child of God. I recognize my importance to the kingdom of God. I do not inflate my value; I do not exaggerate my significance. I hear, see, and feel myself in relation to God and his plan. I worship my Creator and Savior, valuing myself as a person made in the image of God. I reflect God's goodness and greatness through my obedience and service.

Eighth, *self-aware is not the same as self-absorbed*. I need to be aware of who I am and what I feel, believe, value, perceive, say, and act if I am to be responsible and constructive. This is called self-consciousness. To be aware of only myself is self-obsession, characteristic of immature personalities, like the narcissist. If I have not learned to be aware of me, I am probably not able to be aware of you in a way that enhances our relationship. My awareness of my spiritual and emotional immaturity and selfishness makes it possible for me to change. Without that awareness I have no chance to grow or to let you into my life. When I am self-absorbed, you can knock on my door, but you will get either no answer or rejection.

Marvin is this kind of person. His wife asks him to be involved in her life, and he accuses her of being selfish. His message to her is: "Leave me alone until I want something." Recently, several of Marvin's church friends confronted him with his self-absorption. He was surprised to learn that his friends experience him much the same way as his family does—aloof and locked up with his own feelings and needs. He was willing to hear their knock on his door. He will continue to let in others' awareness of him only if he is willing to see himself the way his family and friends see him. To see ourselves as others see us may be difficult, but it is crucial to self-awareness and satisfying relationships. Self-awareness is essential to healthy self-esteem because we cannot esteem ourselves without awareness of who we are.

A Counseling Illustration

Mary's call illustrates the confusion between self-interest and selfishness. She telephoned out of desperation, depressed and scared. Hours earlier, the staff in a psychiatric hospital had recommended that she be admitted because of immobilizing anxiety and depression. Although Mary was in counseling, outpatient treatment had not been effective. Mary asked me, "What can you say to me, from a Christian point of view, that can help me get out of this depression?" What she was asking for was an immediate solution so she would not have to be admitted.

We live in a world that can provide immediate answers and solutions to many problems. And we have come to expect, if not demand, quick results in our emotional and spiritual lives. Unfortunately, the answer is seldom the solution. The ability to implement what we are told or what we know does not develop immediately. Most of us are slow learners, slow in the sense of needing to experiment and practice over and over until we develop mastery. Understanding this dynamic of learning helps the pastor leave sermonizing in the sanctuary. What the minister brings to counseling is a listening ear, empathic responses, purposeful questions, and patience to coach and train slow-learning disciples.

Giving Mary the answer to her question was my temptation because an answer is the easiest of all possible responses as well as the least time-consuming. Yet Mary, like most of our clients and parishioners, was not ready to hear or implement my answer to her question. If she were to receive my help in the next twenty or thirty minutes, Mary needed to experience her anxiety and depression in a way that would make sense to her. In order to help her deal with her desperation, I would need to understand her anxiety and depression. So I wondered to myself, *Why is she depressed? What is she trying to push away from her consciousness? What about herself is so painful that she cannot face it?*

I translated these reflections into a question. "Mary, can you tell me when and where you first experienced this anxiety and depression?" She answered that although this experience had been part of her entire adult life, it most recently had occurred during the Easter holiday. "So what happened over your spring break?" Mary had planned to be helpful to other people, but her own exhaustion from being both mother and career woman had limited her. She was feeling guilty over her failure to achieve her goals.

She panicked over going to the hospital because she feared that secular counselors would encourage her to take care of herself. That message was intolerable to her, filtering through her evangelical ears as selfishness. Now she was calling me to find another answer to her desperation. She wanted an answer that would be more consistent with her Christian beliefs and assumptions.

To her surprise, I asked her, "Is it possible that taking care of yourself is a first step in helping you achieve the goal of being helpful to others?"

As we talked, I learned that Mary had been raised in a family and church that taught her to put herself last, not first. So, being told to take care of herself was a negative message. I tried another way of presenting the message: "Mary, if you are empty, exhausted, and without energy, how are you going to give to your child, your husband, and to others?" I observed that she must be feeling a great responsibility for others and could only pay attention to her needs when everyone else was satisfied. She agreed that this was her experience.

I then asked her to look at her hands. This request puzzled her. "I'm asking you to look at your hands to see if you have nail prints. Is it your job to save the world?"

"No," she answered, "but helping others is the only way I feel good about myself. I have no value unless I'm helping others."

I reflected, "So, because you have not helped people during your vacation, you feel guilty. Then you criticize and condemn yourself as a way of atoning for your sin?" These feelings and beliefs were, of course, at the center of her struggle with anxiety and depression. How could she free herself from the turmoil she was now going through? She would first have to challenge her belief that she was a bad person for taking care of herself physically and emotionally. She would also have to change the picture of herself as selfish when she found her energy level depleted. From Mary's perspective, it was not acceptable to be limited in her ability to give, to be a shepherd rather than a savior. It was not okay for Mary to be human. "Are you willing to hear God say it is okay to take care of yourself?" As I received a commitment from Mary, I asked, "Are you willing to see yourself as a human who needs rest in order to be helpful to others?" She agreed. So I asked, "Are you willing to feel happy and content with the sufficient but limited energy available to you?" She wasn't sure, but she would try.

Knowing that verbal commitment is not enough to achieve lasting change, I asked Mary, while we were on the phone, to look at her hands and remind herself that she was a shepherd, to tell herself that God expects her to do the work of only one human being. Although reserved, Mary was willing to begin talking to and picturing herself differently. So I guided her in her beginning attempts to talk positively to herself, to picture herself as a person whom God loved and valued, to feel God's permission to relax and take care of herself, and to act on these thoughts and feelings.

Mary did not go to the hospital that day because her anxiety and depression began to lift as we talked. I told her I would feel more comfortable knowing she was in contact with her therapist. I cautioned her not to expect that this brief conversation was all she needed. Continuing in therapy was essential to offset her pattern of trying to handle problems all by herself. Counseling was also crucial because of the history and intensity of struggles that would probably not disappear as a result of this brief conversation. She would need to practice what we had started and to anticipate mixed success. Because she is a teacher, I reminded her how long students take to learn what seems easy and natural to her, and cautioned her to be as patient and kind to herself as she is with her students. I remind you, the reader, of the same learning process. As you read each chapter, please remember that practicing what you read is essential in learning how to be an effective counselor. Once is not enough. If you are not sure you understand the above process, that is okay. Intended only as an illustration at this point, it is clearly developed in the following chapters.

Discovering Healthy Esteem: An Exercise

To determine your level of healthy esteem, answer the questions in the following list, identifying the situation, people, and circumstances in which the confusion occurs. Is confusion the result of what I have been taught, what I believe, what I feel toward myself? (These questions could be duplicated for in-session practice and homework with your counselees.)

1. How much do I confuse humiliation with humility?
2. How much do I confuse putting myself down with putting off my sinful self?
3. How much do I confuse self-degradation with self-denial?
4. How much do I confuse worthless with unworthy?
5. How much do I confuse selfishness with self-love?
6. How much do I confuse self-conceit with self-affirmation?
7. How much do I confuse self-worship with self-worth?
8. How much do I confuse self-absorbed with self-aware?

HEALTHY SELF-ESTEEM AND IDENTITY[7]

Healthy self-esteem can be determined by how I evaluate myself in comparison to others. It can also be assessed by exploring the eight previous questions. A third criterion of healthy self-esteem focuses on my identity in relationship: that is, who am I in relation to you? It goes beyond the first criterion of appraising myself realistically to considering how well I interact with you.

1. *How well am I willing to risk involvement with you?* Do I feel secure enough in myself to let you into my world? How threatened am I by your knowing me? Can I risk the possibility of your disliking me? Or, maybe even more threatening, can I risk the possibility of your liking me? Can I manage our needs for intimacy and space, dependence and independence, closeness and distance? Can I deal with your requests for my time, energy, attention, and affection, without experiencing you as an intruder?

2. *How well am I able to express my feelings to you?* Do I dare tell you what is going on in my heart? How much do I deny, suppress, or rationalize my feelings? Do I feel safe enough to share my hurts and fears, my anger and sadness, my happiness and excitement and tenderness? Can I appropriately put my feelings into words and actions? When I express feelings, do they appropriately involve you; or are they really feelings that I have toward others (displacement)? How well am I able to say what I think with courage and confidence in myself, and respect for you?

3. *How well am I able to know when my thoughts and feelings are mine and not yours?* Can I own my feeling experiences as mine without projecting them on you? That is, am I nondefensive to the point where I can let myself know what I am feeling without confusing my feelings of fright, anger, and sadness as yours? Can I admit when my fear or anger or sadness is experienced as coming from you?

4. *How well am I able to be aware that my childhood reactions are triggered in my relationship with you?* Can I distinguish between my response to you as immediate or historical? Is the way we interact, recalling feelings, memories, or behaviors,

similar to my childhood responses? Am I overreacting to you? Is the intensity of my response to you exaggerated in a given situation? Am I able to relate to you as you really are, or am I responding to you as a significant person from my past?

5. *How well am I able to accept feedback (compliments/ criticism/challenges) from you?* Can I learn from you? Can I see your feedback as a resource for me? Do I trust our relationship enough to know you compliment, criticize, and challenge me because you care for me and want to see me grow?

6. *How well am I able to ask for what I need/want?* How well am I able to meet my needs? Do I meet my needs without burdening you? Can I ask you to meet my needs when I really can't meet them myself?

7. *How well am I able to accept my limitations in light of your strengths?* Can I appreciate your abilities and talents without putting myself down? Can I affirm you without envy and jealousy? Can I use your strengths as a resource?

8. *How well am I able to be myself with you?* Do I feel safe enough to act, feel, or say what I am experiencing at the moment without monitoring myself? Can I trust our relationship to the point of knowing that I can act spontaneously without fear of rejection or ridicule? How much energy do I spend filtering my words, my emotions, and my behavior? How much energy do I exert defending myself? Can I live my values with integrity, or do I behave with you differently than I believe?

9. *How well am I able to let you be yourself with me?* Do I feel safe when you are yourself with me? Am I threatened when you are yourself? Do I become scared or angry or sad when I learn you are imperfect and inconsistent? Am I able to let you be who you are more than demand that you be who I want you to be? Do I respect you as much as I respect myself?

10. *How well am I able to celebrate your successes and mourn your losses?* Can I truly be happy for you without envy and jealousy? Can I encourage and compliment you genuinely? Can I tell others of your achievements with pride?

11. *How well am I able to differentiate no from rejection?* When you tell me no, can I distinguish a "not now" from "not

ever with you"? Can I hear no as a time- and energy-limited response more than a commentary on your love and value of me? Can I respect your needs and feelings without feeling discounted by you?

12. *How well am I able to let go of our negative past?* Can I recognize that the past cannot be changed, undone, or made up for; it can only be forgiven? Can I accept that you and I did our best, given our circumstances and information at that moment?

13. *How well am I able to compromise during conflict without losing myself (my integrity, values, and principles) or asking you to lose yourself?* When we problem-solve, can I do so without giving up what I really need? Am I able to tell you what I need and feel and hold my ground without depreciating you? When we come to an agreement, is it really an agreement; or have I given in or given away what is really important to me?

14. *How well am I able to care for you without rescuing you?* Can I help you only as much as you ask for and need? When I am helping you, how frequently do I feel like a victim? Can I help you without blaming you or feeling blamed?

15. *How well am I able to maintain confidentiality between us?* Do I keep your secrets and let you tell others your secrets? Do I treasure your confessions without using them to make me look good at your expense? Do I share myself with you in ways that I do not share with others? Do we have a special friendship in which we can share ourselves without fear of rejection, ridicule, or condemnation?

When I Was a Little Girl: A Counseling Illustration

Brenda is a multi-abused woman. As a child barely able to walk or talk, she was sent off to her grandparents when her parents were overwhelmed by the birth of a second girl. She would return home for visits, but would be sent back kicking and screaming to the grandparents. Because she was unable to tell her parents that her grandparents were physically and sexually abusing her, her parents assumed she was just a spoiled child.

During school, Brenda would live with her parents, but return to her grandparents in the summer. Still too frightened to tell her parents, she continued to be abused by her grand-parents until adolescence. The grandparents' minister also sex-ually abused her at their invitation.

As a teenager, Brenda was again sent to her grandparents' home because she had been molested by a teacher. After grad-uation from high school, she married a seemingly kind, caring man her father's age. He turned out to be abusive, also. A gam-bler, he paid his debts by selling Brenda's sexual favors against her will. She was raped repeatedly by as many as ten men. Her attempts to escape this abusive situation failed until the birth of their daughter.

When she was in labor, she pled to be taken to the hospital. Her husband swore at her and repeatedly kicked her in the stomach. He finally took her to the hospital, but dropped her off at the entrance. Her baby died thirty-six hours after birth. Her husband never visited Brenda, and she never returned home. After futile attempts to get her home, he eventually committed suicide. Now Brenda was free—except for haunting memories and self-hatred.

Ten years later, she entered therapy with me, overwhelmed by fear, guilt, and the belief that she was crazy and would never be well. After several years of weekly counseling, Brenda is coming to believe that she is a worthwhile human being who has a right to life, safety, security, love, and self-esteem. She is separating abuse from love, and the church from feelings of terror, seeing herself as God's creation who is lovable, valuable, and capable.

Brenda volunteers to be near children in a toddler-age Sun-day school class because she will never have another child of her own. A giving person, she derives satisfaction from caring for others. But she is finally coming to the place where she can be given to. She is slowly beginning to believe that she is worth care from others. This change has largely come through a loving, nonjudgmental counseling relationship.

When she began counseling, God was not a reality to her. He was not a caring, protecting God. Now, however, Brenda has come to believe God's love for her. She was recently bap-tized, as a sign she had accepted God's love and forgiveness; but she was baptized in my office inasmuch as a church bap-

tistry and pulpit still represent places where she was abused
by her grandparents' minister.

But let her tell you her own story. As you read her poem,
consider the importance of self-esteem in a person's spiritual
and emotional life. See the dimensions and criteria of self-
esteem illustrated through her own words.

When I was just a little girl,
I wasn't allowed to be
the little girl I really was
who felt and thought like me.

The hurt and scare remained inside;
I dared not let them out.
I heard them say so many things
and I began to doubt.

To know in my heart that they were wrong
to silence me, ignore me,
and continue to do those terrible things
that were so scary to me.

They called it love and also their right
"for God"—a thing to share,
with a man of the cloth in a long black robe
and still I remained in their care.

I began to think I must be bad
to be treated this way—but then—
they said it was love and I waited and waited
and it happened all over again.

They distorted my views and my own self-worth
with their lies and their lives and their acts;
I felt very confused and afraid to be me
and accepted their reasons as facts.

As I grew up, things stayed the same
and I searched for some love and care,

but I didn't know how and began to give out
much more than I should ever have dared.

I was hurt once again by a man that I knew
that I should have been able to trust;
I was blamed, sent away to a place that I feared
and dealt with in ways that weren't just.
I continued to search and need love from someone,
to be held in a way that was safe.
But I gave and gave without getting much back
till I felt there was no way to escape.

Again came the hurt, but much fiercer this time
when I married a man that was ill,
who beat me and forced me to do many things
completely against my will.

I wanted to die, but he kept me alive
to be used, hurt, discarded and shamed.
I suffered, I cried, I fought him, gave in—
still I was the one that was blamed.

Again I thought this was what love was about,
that the giver I always must be,
but it hurt me so much—I don't easily trust;
I want to be loved for just me.

By then the need to be held was so strong
that I didn't care who it might be.
I gave when they wanted, whatever their need,
not seeing how much it hurt me.

There were times I was scared and confused and sad,
yet the need to be loved, held, and caressed
continued in me till I thought I would die.
I really was doing my best.

Now I know I was wrong then and am glad I am safe,
that these things won't happen again.

I am grown now and know that I'm much better now
than ever before I have been.

I'm beginning to trust and have faith in myself,
to share secrets I've had for so long,
and I'm doing it with the friends I have made
who have made me feel that I belong.
The wounds are so deep and the hurt so real
that it scares me sometimes to think back,
but I've found I am strong and able to go
and remember those things from my past.

It just wasn't fair—those things in my past—
yet life needn't be like that, I guess,
so I continue to look back and share where I've been
in a way that I feel is the best
    because
when I was just a little girl,
I wasn't allowed to be
the little girl I really was
who felt and thought like me.

I am crying as I finish typing this poem. I am crying because
I feel sad for this little girl, now a grown woman, who is processing the pain she experienced as a child. I am crying because I am excited that she allows me into her inner world and
hears my words of comfort and affirmation, hears God's words
of love and nurture, and has become a Christian. What are
you feeling as you read this poem? Can you identify with her
struggle to be herself? What would you write to the title,
"When I was a little child?"

Summary

This chapter distinguished between biblical and nonbiblical
concepts of self-esteem, offering a biblically accurate and psychologically sound definition of self-esteem. It also introduced
questions to help explore and measure healthy self-esteem.

CHAPTER TWO

SELF-ESTEEM
A PSYCHO-THEOLOGICAL PROCESS

"WHO CARES FOR ME ANYWAY?" Carl yelled. "My father left my mom before I was born. She's an alcoholic who thinks she wants me; but when she goes on another binge, she sends me back here." Carl was responding angrily to my suggestion that God was a loving heavenly Father.

Three years later, when I was leaving the children's home, Carl came to say good-bye.

"Do you remember how angry I got at you when we first met?" he asked. How could I forget? At the time, I had felt embarrassed and sad. The incident was indelibly imprinted on my memory as a lesson in insensitive evangelism.

Carl continued, "You were telling me that God is a loving

heavenly Father. I got mad at you because I didn't even know what a loving father was. Well, I have come to know that God loves me the same way you do." Three years of weekly contact, of building models together, of my taking him to visit his mother and helping him process his sense of abandonment and rejection with its resulting anger and depression, were paying off. Carl was now seeing himself as a worthwhile human being who was truly loved.

Carl is one of many clients who have shown me that people rarely come to Christ if they haven't had loving human relationships to affirm their sense of worth and dignity. Furthermore, without some degree of self-caring or self-esteem, people can almost never respond to God's love, mercy, and grace. People with low self-esteem also have difficulty responding to a pastoral or therapeutic relationship.

But no one comes into the world with this self-love. Self-centeredness and narcissism, yes—but not self-esteem. That is acquired through nurturing relationships. When nurturing has not been adequate, children usually develop a variety of emotional and behavioral problems. In extreme instances, they may even die.[1] Those of us who survive develop positive or negative personality characteristics that invite others' attention. Usually, we develop behaviors that encourage more rejection. In defense of ourselves, we create pseudo forms of self-love (narcissism, arrogance, exaggerated self-confidence, bragging, or false humility) to substitute for the void left by the lack of others' love. As parents, we often produce children with self-esteem problems similar to our own (see chapter 6). The negative cycle continues until it is interrupted through a loving relationship—pastor, therapist, friend, God (treated in chapters 5–7).

Good parenting alone is no guarantee of positive self-esteem. Other significant relationships influence our views of ourselves. Critical and rejecting siblings, peers, teachers, or other important adults frequently contribute to our feelings of self-doubt. Beyond these human influences, most of us question our goodness or "okayness" because we instinctively are aware, at some level, of our sinful tendencies. When we are honest, we know that we do not measure up to God's standards. Furthermore, we do not even measure up to our own standards. So what is our hope? Our hope is to hear, see, and feel that we are loved, valued, and affirmed by God even though we are imperfect and sinful.

Like Carl, we need someone to tell us about and show us God's love. Unfortunately, this is not always our life experience, because other people sometimes doubt, question, and reject us. (Practical strategies for learning how to overcome low self-esteem that originates from rejection are taught in the following chapters.) Sometimes we even participate in the creation of our own feelings of insecurity, inadequacy, and inferiority. Since some rejection is self-induced, this book will help us identify how we create our own self-rejection through four negative sensory experiences. These are as follows:

1. negative self-talk,
2. negative self-picturing,
3. negative self-feelings (being scared, angry, sad),
4. negative self-behavior.

We will then learn how to change this negative pattern into positive and spiritually healthy self-acceptance, self-affirmation, self-esteem, and self-image.

In contrast to those with low self-esteem, people with high self-esteem utilize the four sensory experiences positively. That is, their *self-talk* is encouraging, their *self-picturing* is accurate and positive, their *self-feelings* are acceptable and appropriately expressed, and their *self-behavior* is constructive.

High self-esteem people use this sensory-grounded process (what they say, see, feel, and do) to face who they are. With God's help, they grow into beautiful people who know, accept, love, and share themselves. In addition, these four sense modalities (what we say/hear, see/look, feel/sense, and act/do), when translated into positive form, make up the central focus of an integrated counseling approach. Learning how to use these sensory resources helps build self-esteem in ourselves, our families, our congregations, and our clients. The following pages are addressed to learning this multimodal process of counseling and developing self-esteem.

A PRACTICAL METHODOLOGY

Practical methodologies for building self-esteem in ourselves, our families, and our clients are the core of this chapter. The focus in this section concerns *process* in counseling—the sequence of thoughts, feelings, and behaviors that leads to healthy self-esteem.

The story of Mary in chapter 1 introduced you to the concept of process. To further illustrate the process of building healthy, biblically accurate self-esteem, consider the story of Adam and Eve and discover how they could have thought and acted differently. A place for us to begin is to ask, "How did Eve forget who she was?" First of all, she *listened* to the crafty serpent deny God's warning that she would die if she ate from the tree. She didn't question or argue with Satan, nor did she consult with Adam or God on this matter. Her willingness to believe the serpent suggests that Eve already had some doubts about God's directions. This doubt was intensified when she looked at the tree and felt delight. So she rationalized: "This food will make me wise." This self-talk led to self-behavior, that is, picking the fruit, eating it, and sharing it with Adam.

Notice the sequence of Eve's yielding to temptation. It illustrates the *process* needed to bring about positive changes in our lives and those of our counselees.

She listened → looked → felt → talked to herself → acted.

Whether we are exploring the process of yielding to temptation or of reaching a desired goal, these four sense modalities are foundational. They may occur in a different sequence; but usually listening to others and/or talking to oneself, or looking/seeking/imagining are the first steps. Being careful to avoid the *sequence* of steps that Eve used (not the content of what she said, saw, felt, did) can help us avoid our temptations to be more, or less, than God intends us to be. Accepting who I am, a creature not the Creator, helps me avoid the temptation to play God. When I am aware of my unfulfilled desires, wishes, needs, feelings, and values, then I can avoid disobeying God by:

- listening to and evaluating what I say to myself about the desires, etc.;

- focusing on what I think about or imagine as ways of fulfilling them;
- attending to how I am choosing to act to satisfy them;
- recognizing and monitoring my emotional satisfaction level;

then I have learned to use what I say, see, feel, and do for my spiritual growth.

For example, had Adam and Eve reflected on the serpent's statement, "You will not die if you eat from the tree," she would have asked herself, *What makes his statement so attractive to me? What need, desire, or value am I trying to fulfill? What real or imagined deprivation am I wanting to overcome?* Then she could have stopped the temptation process. Eve could also have reflected on her feelings of not liking God's restrictions or her belief that God was trying to deprive her of something good. But, as you know, she did not talk to God. If she had, my fantasy is, we would not be concerned about self-esteem because they would have trusted God's judgment; and we would still be in the Garden of Eden, innocent and sinless. They would have said to themselves, *You know, Satan is right. I really want to be like God. I had better talk this over with God.*

As Eve looked at the fruit and desired it, she missed an opportunity to tell herself something very important about herself: "I want to be wise like God." Rather than accept herself as God's supreme creation, Eve yielded to the temptation to be equal with God. She grasped for what she saw as a solution to her discontent as a finite human being. Her experience teaches us that at the root of temptation is a belief that I can get what I feel I need by taking what God says I am forbidden to have.

Legitimate Needs and Illegitimate Means

Notice that Adam and Eve's desire to be like God was not an entirely illegitimate need or goal. They were already made in God's image, but failed to hear or see that reality. They desired to change something that was not changeable: they were not nor would they ever become God. Often our temptations involve similar desires, to be what we cannot be.

On the other hand, our temptations frequently involve needs

or goals that are acceptable. In such a situation, we yield to temptation in the mistaken belief that we can meet legitimate needs through sinful practices. For example, a legitimate need for affection may be illegitimately met through an illicit affair. A need for recognition may be met through showing off. Of course, to think we can meet our legitimate needs in illegitimate ways results in pain and dissatisfaction, either now or in the future. Remember Jesus' temptation. As a human being, he was legitimately hungry, needing protection and recognition for who he was, the Son of God. However, he did not meet these legitimate needs by yielding to Satan's provocations. Because Jesus already knew who he was, he did not choose to prove his identity by yielding to Satan's challenges. *When we know, accept, love, and share who we are, we do not need to prove who we are to anyone; therefore, we increase our chances of being able to avoid succumbing to temptation.*

So how do we help people behave differently? We help by assisting them to consider who they are and what they want through exploring what they are *listening to, looking at, feeling for,* or *acting out.*

These four dimensions help to organize explorations into ourselves or our clients. Remember Jesus' words: deal first with the log in your own eye before you tackle the speck in your neighbor's eye (Matthew 7:5). This means that, as helpers, we need to take the time to inventory and confess our sins, to know who we are, and to understand how our self-talk, self-perceptions, imaginations, feelings, desires, and behaviors are used to yield to temptation. When we deal with our own depravity, we develop the humility and right to confront others in their depravity.

Discovering and Accepting Who I Am

Chapter 1 presented exercises to help us discover what we would like to change about ourselves, what we like or dislike about ourselves, our level of self-esteem, the dimensions to our self-esteem, and our identity. To guide us in knowing and accepting who we are, the following two exercises utilize the sense modalities.

Instructions for Exercise 1: The purpose of this exercise is to become aware of ourselves in the four sense modalities primarily used in counseling—(1) listen, (2) look, (3) feel, (4) act. A chart is provided for you to record your observations. Begin by asking yourself, "What am I experiencing at this moment?" *Experiencing* means becoming aware of the four sense modalities, *e.g.*, "What am I saying/hearing, seeing/imagining, feeling/sensing, doing/behaving?"

I HEAR/SAY	I SEE/IMAGINE	I FEEL/SENSE	I DO/ACT
1. birds singing	2. birds eating at feeder	3. excited	4. stop, look, listen to birds
		5. happy	

Instructions for Exercise 2: Now that you have practiced becoming aware of what you say and see and how you feel and act in a given moment, choose a temptation, life experience, or specific issue that is puzzling you and chart the sequence of the outcome. You can begin anywhere in the four modalities listed below. If you have difficulty beginning with what you are saying to yourself, work backward from your actions or feelings. For example, "What was I feeling when I did ____?" or "What was I saying to myself or seeing when I felt or did ____?" Remember, the purpose of this exercise is to help you understand yourself in a new way, by becoming specifically aware of your thinking, feeling, and acting, noting how these modalities influence each other as they interconnect. Below is an example of one of my summer experiences. I begin with hearing the wind blow, then I see the sunshine, then I feel the cool breeze. Next I tell myself, "I'm going sailing." I see that the breeze velocity is good for sailing, feel the wind in my face, and then go sailing. There is more to the experience of sailing than I first realized as I developed this example. What is missing in this illustration is the process of preparing the boat for sailing. But now that I am remembering this step, I can reconstruct what I say, see, and feel as I rig the sails, put in the center board, fasten the rudder, and put on a life preserver.

Now it is your turn to practice. You may find it less threatening and easier to learn your sensory sequencing if you begin your practice by exploring a positive experience. When you understand this exercise, then investigate the four-step modality of one of your problem experiences.

I HEAR/SAY	I SEE/IMAGINE	I FEEL/SENSE	I DO/ACT
1. wind blowing,	2. sun shining,	3. gentle, cool breeze	
4. I'm going sailing	5. breeze	6. feel wind in my face	7. go sailing

Discovering and Accepting Who My Clients Are

Healthy relationships are characterized by love, that is, by accepting other people with all their spots and wrinkles without trying to change them because change is impossible until we become aware of and experience God's love toward us (1 John 4). To discover and accept ourselves is a necessary prelude to accepting others. Without loving and valuing ourselves, we love and value our clients pathologically.[2] Unfortunately, to love your neighbor as you love yourself can be negative as well as positive. Ministers and counselors, therefore, need to develop self-esteem before they can esteem clients. Make sure that you are building your self-esteem in healthy ways. Then you will be authentic in the counseling process of building self-esteem in the counselees. The following exercise is designed to develop positive regard for others as you discover and understand their sensory-processing sequence.

Instructions for Exercise 3: The purpose of this exercise is to become aware of your client in the four sense modalities, using the chart introduced above. If you have more than one person in a family as your client, do this exercise for each of them. Begin by asking yourself, "What is my client specifically experiencing in this situation? What is this client (CL) hearing, seeing, feeling, and doing?" I have used Mary (chapter 1) as an example for you to follow. The numbers indicate the steps in her process.

CL HEARS/SAYS	CL SEES/IMAGINES	CL FEELS/SENSES	CL DOES/ACTS
1. "take care of self" as selfish	2. self as bad	3. scared, guilty	4. refuses hospitalization
5. calls Dave	6. looks for positive Christian answer	7. feels depressed, panicked	8. practices sense modalities
		9. safe, excited	

A Counseling Illustration of the Sensory Cycle

This strategy can be used therapeutically as illustrated by LuAnn, a Christian, referred to me by her pastor. He was concerned about her lack of progress following psychiatric hospitalization. Having been diagnosed as paranoid schizophrenic, she was being treated exclusively through the medications Haldol and Elavil. The psychiatrist had attempted, but subsequently terminated, counseling because LuAnn was making little progress. Medication seemed to be a more effective and efficient treatment in masking symptoms of depression, suicidal thinking or ideas, auditory hallucinations, and guilt. But when she refused to take her medication, the symptoms would reappear. Her ability to work and survive independently had deteriorated to the point that she was able to live only with family supervision.

Because LuAnn was fearful and suspicious as she anticipated her first session with me, a supportive relative accompanied her. I began the interview by recognizing that she had seen many doctors and counselors. I wondered how she was feeling about coming that day. In my mind was this question: *Is she here because she wants to be here or because her pastor and relative want her to come for counseling?* Reservedly, she spoke of her desire to go back to work and to return to her own apartment. I asked what was stopping her from doing what she desired. LuAnn answered that she was tired all day, had little interest in getting out of bed, felt overwhelmed with the simplest of household chores, and experienced paralyzing guilt.

49

The Negative Cycle

I considered using the say, see, feel, act strategy to help her deal with her lethargy and lack of motivation. So I asked her, "What do you think about when you first awaken?" This question was my way of discovering her specific way of processing that led to depression and withdrawal from life.

LuAnn responded, "Oh, the birds and stray dogs and cats."

I could have asked any question using the four sense modalities; but since the auditory modality is commonly the first step in the negative process, I chose self-talk as the place to intervene. Had LuAnn's negative process begun with one of the other sensory experiences, I could have asked her the same question using that modality. For example, other possible explorations could be, "What do you *see* as you think about the animals? What do you *feel* when you think about the animals? What would you like to *do* when you think about the animals?" If you don't get the information you need to help change the negative process, merely ask the same question using a different modality.

Notice that she did not specifically tell me what she was thinking about the animals, so I needed to ask her another question to get those specifics. "Tell me what you are saying to yourself about the birds and stray dogs and cats."

Her response was, "Oh, how people are mistreating them. You know, I had fourteen stray cats before I went into the hospital." I learned that LuAnn had taken in stray animals to protect them from cruel people, beginning this practice after her mother had committed suicide. (I wondered privately, because I needed more information before I could present this insight, if this could possibly be her way of projecting and dealing with her guilt over her mother's death. LuAnn later confirmed that she held herself responsible for her mother's death.)

"Okay, now tell me how you see these animals being mistreated" was my next sense-modality exploration. LuAnn's response told me that she was making an assumption, known as mind reading, ". . . any animal running around loose is abandoned and mistreated."

"So when you *tell* yourself that animals are being mistreated and you *imagine* hungry, cold, stray animals, how do you *feel?*" At this point, I was testing my understanding of the way she got depressed. I wanted to know if I had grasped the say, see, feel sequence correctly.

"I feel sad and want to help them."

"When you bring them home, how does that affect your sadness?" Notice that I have asked her a question about how her behavior influences her feelings. This question helps me complete my understanding of the vicious sensory cycle that keeps LuAnn from functioning as a normal, healthy human being.

"Oh, I feel fine until the next morning."

"And then?"

"And then I am sad all over again because other dogs and cats are abandoned with no one to take care of them."

"And when you feel sad, what do you say or see?" Here I was trying to make a connection between her feelings, her self-talk, and her imagination.

"Oh, I tell myself I might as well stay in bed. What is the use of getting up? I feel tired."

If we track this lady's thinking, feeling, behaving process, we can chart it this way. "I wake up → I *say* to myself, animals are being mistreated → I don't want to *see* any stray dogs and cats because it makes me *feel* sad → so I'll just *stay* in bed."

The Positive Cycle

Notice the say, see, feel, behave sequence. Now that I have comprehended the content and process of her negative cycle, I can create a positive cycle, using the order and sequence of her negative sensory process. I asked her, "Do you know the chorus, 'This is the day the Lord has made'?" When she answered that she did, I asked her to sing this song when she woke up in the morning. She agreed to sing the chorus even though she thought the request was strange, a not uncommon response to homework assignments. I asked what might stop her from singing in the morning, also an important consideration because people usually resist change even though they are requesting help.

"Oh, I won't sing if I'm tired and depressed."

I asked whether she ever could do anything when she was tired and depressed. To reinforce her positive but weak response, I said, "Then you believe you could sing this song even if you are not feeling like it?"

"Yes, I think I can."

"LuAnn, this is what you can expect when you sing, 'This is the day the Lord has made.' You will find yourself thinking about and feeling good things, and they will help you get started in the morning. You know, if I thought about cruelty to animals and all the housework I had to do but hated, I would have a hard time getting up, too."

LuAnn laughed and said, "You really do understand what I go through each day."

My next intervention was to ask her to *sing* the chorus in the session in order to have LuAnn practice with me what I was asking her to do alone. I find a greater degree of success with homework when I help the client practice it in the session, providing an opportunity to work through unclear instructions, fearful inhibitions, and unspoken resistance. Of course, homework assignments are only as good as the capacity and motivation of the client to implement them.

I then asked her to *picture* the birds, dogs, and cats as God's handiwork, to see the sun, trees, grass, and sky as God's creation. She thought she could do that. So I asked her to *see* in her mind's eye, the birds, dogs, and cats. She closed her eyes and nodded her head. When I asked her to tell me what she was seeing, she answered, "I see the birds, dogs, and cats playing and eating."

Then I asked her to tell me what she was *feeling* at this moment as she saw the animals. This was a way of leading her to the *feeling* experience, which is a way of checking out the effectiveness and accuracy of the positive cycle. She smiled and said, "Good."

"And when you feel good, what will you do?"

"Oh, get out of bed and work around the house, probably."

Notice the "probably" in her response. She is not sure this strategy will work for her, yet she is willing to try it. As helpers, we need to remind ourselves that the first time we try something new, we are usually not 100 percent successful.

People often fear failure. "What if I can't do this on my own?" Assure them that their attempts are okay and that you will help them learn what gets in the way of positive thinking, feeling, acting. The desire to be successful in living is, of course, the motivation that brings people to us for counseling. They have had enough failure. They desire to achieve their goals, yet they fear growth is not possible. Creating hope by providing successful experiences in the counseling session is fundamental to engaging people in treatment. Our task is to encourage them to live, love, learn, and cope, using their own resources. Practiced homework is an affirmation that they can eventually become the adequate, independent persons they want to be.

Remember, healing takes time, energy, and experimentation. We will walk with our clients over the same terrain repeatedly until they begin to master the skills of living. Sharing our patience and hope with them, affirming that we will stay with them in their journey, and believing in their motivation and capacity to grow are essential for successful treatment. Our patience tells them that we love and value them as God's creation.

Was this lady healed of her schizophrenia by applying this exercise of singing, visualizing, feeling, and acting? I wish counseling were that easy! Because I have had enough experience in working with people to know that immediate change is rare, the most I hoped for was some beginning change in her depression and immobilization.

I also know that success comes from practice (sometimes called experimenting, or trial and error). One attempt is seldom enough. I can report that after six months in counseling, LuAnn has experienced a positive shift in her moods and behavior. She has almost no trouble getting out of bed when she practices the positive sensory cycle, beginning with singing to herself, "This is the day the Lord has made" or telling herself something like, "I am innocent of causing my mother's death." Her moods are increasingly consistent and pleasant. Her relatives report that she is easier to live with. Even though she refuses, at times, to share in the household chores, she is rising early enough to help with the children. After a period of unsuccessful interviewing, she got a job and continued in therapy for the first four months of successful employment, quite an accomplishment for someone who had been frequently hospitalized in a psychiatric ward and dysfunctional for four years.

The Spiritual Cycle: Sin, Atonement, Restitution

But LuAnn needed to challenge something else in counseling: a deep-seated belief that she was bad and deserved to be punished. Yes, she was a Christian. Yet she talked, looked, felt, and acted self-destructively.

At the root of these destructive beliefs, feelings, and actions was the conviction that she was responsible for her mother's death. She is attempting to atone for her "sin." What was her sin? As a single woman living with a sick mother, she always left her bedroom door open so she could hear Mother's calls for help. On the night that her mother died, LuAnn was so angry with Mother that she closed her bedroom door. What further complicated her mother's death was this: LuAnn, in response to her request, had given her mother a bottle of prescription pills. Her mother apparently took too many of the pills, deliberately or unintentionally, and died. LuAnn now believes she killed her mother. She says, "If only I had left my door open, then Mother could have called me. I'm sure she thought that I was shutting her out."

Is LuAnn really responsible for her mother's death? Could she have prevented her mother from killing herself? In talking with the relatives, I learned that her mother had a long history of attempted suicides. No, LuAnn is not responsible for her mother's suicide. No, LuAnn's actions did not cause her mother's death. But this is a rational approach to her dilemma, and rational approaches seldom work with distraught people.

What will work with people when their feelings and beliefs are irrational? In this case, LuAnn will need to face her anger and the guilt that resulted because she did not resolve that anger before mother died. Going to bed with unresolved resentments and bitterness and waking up to find a suicide left LuAnn with self-accusations and self-condemnations that dominate her thoughts and feelings and motivate her to self-punitive behavior.

A word of caution. One event is seldom powerful enough to create the amount of turmoil that existed in LuAnn's life. Counselors need to explore what else has been going on. Therapists frequently find a long history of unsatisfying relationships that precede the crisis even though one event is often primarily in the client's memory. This was true in LuAnn's life.

So why doesn't she accept Christ's forgiveness and payment for her sins? If you asked her, she would tell you that she has. What, then, is the problem? LuAnn is holding herself responsible for what she believes to be irresponsible and hostile behavior. She has separated the spiritual and psychological. Her "sin" of not being available to Mother twenty-four hours a day and giving her pills that she eventually used to kill herself have nothing to do with Christ's atonement, in LuAnn's mind. This lack of integration between the spiritual and emotional dimensions is fairly common in counselees, Christian and non-Christian alike, who believe they also must make restitution for their sins. While restitution may not be necessary for salvation, it is often necessary for growth and freedom from guilt. Scripture illustrates this profound psycho-spiritual truth. Many people in the Bible made restitution after their conversion. Zaccheus, the tax collector, restored four times what he had illegally charged for taxes. Mary, the prostitute, saved expensive perfume to pour on Jesus' feet. Peter, tradition tells us, asked to be hanged upside down because he did not deserve to be crucified the way Christ had been.

LuAnn experiences what many depressed and guilty people believe and feel, that she needs to make restitution. And what restitution is she attempting? Taking care of stray animals is a way of atoning for not taking care of Mother. The problem is that she cannot save all the stray dogs, cats, and birds. Therefore, in LuAnn's mind, her attempts do not free her from her own self-condemnation because they do not count. She also uses her depression and resulting social paralysis to punish herself because she does not deserve a happy and fulfilled life after what she did to Mother.

At one level this is a theological problem, but at another level it is a psychological one. Both need to be addressed. When you talk with people like LuAnn, you will discover that they believe Christ has forgiven them, yet they have not forgiven themselves. No matter how many times people go back to the altar or recommit their lives to Christ, they are haunted by their guilt and need for restitution until they can forgive themselves. The challenge of helping people take themselves off their own crosses is complicated by their inability or unwillingness to tell, see, feel, and act as lovable, valuable, and capable creations of the God who has called them to forgiveness, redemption, and service.

So how do you help people who have compartmentalized the spiritual and emotional aspects of their problem? The first step is to take the person's struggle in its totality, not treating it exclusively as a spiritual or emotional problem. The second step is to assist him or her to discover, accept, love, and share who he or she is as God's creation. The third step is to uncover the thinking, feeling, behaving patterns that keep him or her in a self-destructive, vicious cycle.

You can implement the successful accomplishment of these steps through the exploratory and experimental processes of counseling, illustrated in the stories of Mary (chapter 1) and Carl and LuAnn (chapter 2). The following, which summarize questions used in the exploratory process, can be used in any order. Give yourself permission to experiment with them so that you can discover how they can be best utilized in your counseling. They are adaptable to any counseling theory or system since they are only a means of gathering the information counselors need to be helpful.

PURPOSEFUL EXPLORATION QUESTIONS

1. *Determining the goal. What do you want?*[3] Counseling often ends in frustration for both the counselor and client because the problem has been explored to the exclusion of the goal or desired outcome. While it is important to know what the person's problem is, I have found it more productive to spend most of the counseling time inquiring into the person's

hopes, dreams, wants, needs, and desires. That is, what does this person want in life that is missing?

a. *Being specific.* If a counselee can tell you what he or she wants, you usually are given a generalization: "I want to be happy." "I want to feel good." "I wish we were getting along better." These are fuzzy, undefined goals. Unless they are developed specifically, you will find the counseling session going nowhere or ending rapidly without much being accomplished.

The following questions will help the counselee define specifically what he or she wants. You can also get specific by asking what, specifically, being happy means. "Can you tell me what you would experience if you felt good?" Or, "What would your family be doing if they got along better?" Or, "In what ways would you like to get along?"

b. *Being positive.* Another reason counseling sessions often go nowhere or end without much accomplished is because the individual fails to define the desired goal in positive terms. Counselees commonly state the goal in negative terms: "I want to stop worrying." Or, "I want to stop getting so angry." Or, "We have fallen out of love."

Translating a negative goal into a positive goal is achieved by the following kinds of responses: "What would you rather do than worry?" "Instead of getting angry how would you like to respond?" "What would you like to fall into?"

c. *Setting an achievable goal.* Attempting to help a person solve an insoluble problem or achieve an impossible goal is a common frustration for all of us in ministry. To avoid this pitfall in counseling, we need to ask ourselves whether we have helped this person define a goal that is *self-initiated and maintained;* that is, can this person get what he or she wants through his or her own efforts without changing others?

Frequently, clients will ask us to help them change their spouses, children, parents, and friends. Because we as helpers suffer from the desire to save the world, we fall into the trap of trying to help people change each other. Usually these attempts are painful and frustrating for everyone involved, and they seldom are successful. We as ministers and counselors need to recognize that we can change no one except ourselves.

Helping our counselees accept this reality is a significant goal of counseling, which we can achieve by asking such questions as, "How is your spouse's, child's, or friend's behavior a problem to you?" Or, "What is it that you need in order to live with this painful situation?" Or, "If we cannot get your spouse, child, or friend to change, what will you need?" A well-determined goal, then, is a desired state or outcome that is *specific, positive,* and *self-initiated.* It also may be worth asking, "Is the desired goal worth having?"

Pause for a moment and reflect on a counseling situation in which you are currently involved. "What is the person's goal as I understand it? How specific is it? Is the goal stated positively? Can the person I am working with initiate and achieve this goal without anyone else changing?"

2. *Documenting the evidence. How will you know when you reach your goal?* To know what you want is a necessary step for counseling to become productive. To know how to be sure you have reached your goal is equally important. People who consult us frequently want something they would not be able to recognize even if they got it. Thus, we should explore evidence to help people know when they have accomplished the desired change.

For example, when a man says, "I want to be happy," but cannot describe how he will know he is happy, you will then need to ask, "Have you ever been happy?" Or, "Describe a happy feeling you have had." You can also use the sensory modalities to frame questions: "Tell me what you were thinking, seeing, imagining, feeling, when you were happy." You will know that you have helped the client find evidence when his statements are sensory-grounded. He will then use variations of the sensory predicates say/hear, see/imagine, feel emotionally/feel physically, act/do.

3. *Discovering the ecology. How will your life be different when you reach your goal?* This question is often used to help develop a more specific, positive, and self-initiated goal. What you are listening to and looking for here is the hoped-for quality of life. Asking this question will frequently enable the client to tell you specifically, in sensory-identified terms, what his desired goal is, what he wishes he could say, see, feel, and do.

4. *Detecting the context. When, where, and with whom do you want this desired goal?* The context is the life situation(s), relationship(s), and time(s) through which the person wants to experience the desired goal. The context question is important to you as counselor because it helps you determine, with the counselee, how feasible and appropriate the goal is for the desired time, place, and person. For example, a person may want to learn how to be more assertive. But experimenting with assertiveness in the context of a marriage could be dangerous if the spouse is hostile and easily threatened. A parishioner may want to hold an important position in the church, but not have the personality, talent, or resources to carry the responsibility of that particular job. He or she may be able to be a leader in junior church, but not on the church board.

5. *Developing the resources. What do you need in order to reach your goal?* I stated earlier that much counseling ends in frustration for both the counselor and individual because the identified goal is not specific, positive, or self-initiated. The second most frequent reason for unsuccessful counseling is an oversight, not discovering what resources a person needs to achieve his or her goal. It is possible to have established a specific, positive, and self-initiated goal and yet discover that a person cannot achieve that goal for lack of resources.

Resources can be personal (internal), relational, or financial (external). That is, they can be qualities, characteristics, perspectives, or skills that come from within a person. As a therapist, I look for a person's strengths, such as the ability to express feelings, identify needs, empathize. Or when the strengths are underdeveloped or missing, I identify the inabilities and inhibitions that need to be addressed if the client is to reach the desired goal.

Resources can also be means that come from outside the person: friends, professionals, agencies, institutions, money, contacts, or opportunities. In addition to counseling, addictive clients like alcoholics or drug users or incest victims often need support groups. When people are in financial difficulty, they may need a lawyer or financial advisor. They may even need a job. A new Christian may need a discipler. Pastors frequently want a confidant and friend to help them go through the difficult and lonely times of being a minister.

As a minister or counselor, you are, for example, a resource for the person seeking your assistance. A church member who wants to hold an important church position may lack personal resources to fulfill the responsibilities. A counseling goal may be to help that person find ways to develop those needed skills. On the other hand, if this person could not develop the necessary skills and characteristics, then the goal of counseling would be to help the person accept his or her limitations and manage the resultant feelings of frustration, anger, hopelessness, and lowered self-esteem.

6. *Disclosing the blockages/hindrances. What stops you from reaching your goal?* Identifying the blockages and hurdles is often necessary to help a client move toward a desired goal. This question also aids in the process of determining how achievable the goal is. Some blockages and hurdles are immovable. For example, health, intelligence, finances, or other resources may just not be available. This lack may preclude reaching the desired outcome. A person may desire to be a doctor, but finds that entrance to medical school is impossible. A member of your congregation may want to be a missionary, but discovers no mission board will accept him or her. Repeated attempts to solve a problem by using the same unworkable strategies may also be blocking the person from reaching a goal. When he or she gives up the old and familiar ways, the individual opens a door to new and more effective means. Yet trying harder, rather than trying differently, is a common client behavior that the counselor needs to challenge if the client is to reach a desired goal. Trying differently requires counselees to identify what is stopping them from reaching their goal. It also requires a focus on identifying and developing the resources that are needed if the person is to change. Learning to counsel effectively takes practice and reflection. Can you take time to practice what you have just read?

Instructions for Exercise 4. Using the counselee(s) you chose in exercise 3, explore their answers to the six outcome questions. You may want to review the counseling interviews with Mary and LuAnn for help in understanding how to explore these dimensions.

1. *Determine the goal.* What do you want, need, desire?
   a. specific
   b. positive
   c. self-initiated and maintained
   d. worth working for
2. *Document the evidence.* How will you know when you reach your goal?
3. *Discover the ecology.* How will your life be different when you reach your goal?
4. *Detect the context.* When, where, and with whom do you want this desired goal?
5. *Develop the resources.* What do you need to reach your goal?
6. *Disclose the blockages.* What stops you from reaching your goal?

A word of encouragement: Now that you have completed exercises 1 through 4, you have probably discovered that you have not been able to fill in the requested answers as completely as you had hoped. This shows you what you need to learn about your counselee(s) and what to explore in your next session. Therefore, I encourage you to think of incomplete answers as *feedback*, not as *failure*. Remembering that no one learns without trial and error, give yourself permission to learn from the missing pieces. These missing pieces, labeled feedback, give us direction and help us find our way through the maze of counseling. *As you are patient with your own learning process, you will be patient with the learning processes of your clients.*

Summary

Discovering who I am as a helper and who my clients are can be achieved through charting the four-sensory modality sequence—what I hear/say, what I see/imagine, what I feel/sense, and what I do/act. You have been encouraged to begin with where you are before you explore where your clients are. Healthy esteem in helpers is fundamental to helping others build esteem in themselves. You were introduced to the negative and positive sensory sequence in LuAnn's struggle with guilt and depression.

This chapter addresses the importance of the counselor recognizing the difference between psychological and theological processing and demonstrates their relationship through a case example. You have been introduced to six questions that assist the helpee: be specific about what the person needs; learn how the person knows that he or she has gotten what is wanted; identify the place, people, and situation in which it is wanted; recognize how his or her life will be different when the goal is reached; discover the hindrances that prevent him or her from reaching the goal; develop the resources necessary to reach the goal.

CHAPTER THREE

TEACHING PEOPLE TO BUILD SELF-ESTEEM
A TWELVE-STEP PROCESS

TED AND DEE VOLUNTEERED TO BE INTERVIEWED in front of my seminary class. Concerned about her husband's low esteem, Dee thought I could help him when she heard me talk about developing self-esteem. Ted had been suffering from periodic depression since returning from a short-term mission project. Although he had anticipated being discipled and hired by the campus ministry leader for whom he had worked previously, Ted was ignored instead. Disappointed and angry, Ted harbored resentment toward this leader and turned much of the anger toward himself. He became depressed and unmotivated, questioning his worth as a human being and as a Christian worker.

Marriage to Dee, an affirming woman who believed in him, temporarily pulled him out of depression. But she was beginning to get exhausted from her cheerleading attempts to keep her husband in good spirits. They decided to consult me after Dee reported to Ted the twelve-step process of building self-esteem she was learning in class. Ted knew that he needed to improve his self-esteem because he was unable to derive satisfaction from his work, his Bible study, and prayer. He was ambivalent about his future as a missionary, and was paralyzed by his procrastinations, most notably, his failure to apply to the mission board for candidate status. He was berating himself because he thought that as a Christian he should be able to get on top of the depression, but failure and self-criticism only deepened his depression.

As I empathized with him over his disappointments, frustrations, and failures, Ted began to relax. I explored his feelings and his view of himself and wondered when he had begun to question his worth as a person and his value as a husband and child of God. Together we learned that Ted had come to adulthood with serious questions about his lovableness, value, and competence as a person. The immediate context of rejection, not being hired by the campus ministry, camouflaged years of feeling rejected and humiliated by his family. Current unfair treatment by his employer triggered feelings so intense that the emotions defied Ted's ability to accept them as legitimate. These rageful overreactions convinced him that something was radically wrong. Yet he had no sense of hope that he could learn to respond in more Christlike ways. His attempts to be loving and forgiving were short-lived, and repeated failure made him question the genuineness of his conversion. He also feared that his wife would become so disgusted with him and intolerant of his procrastination and depression that she would ultimately leave him.

Since I was interviewing Ted and Dee in the presence of my seminary class, I chose to stay with the current frustrations and failures rather than explore the past, because one session is not long enough to search out, understand, and process what has gone before. In addition, my counseling style is to begin with the present and deal with the past only as it is needed. Because reactions to the present are commonly repetitive patterns established over long periods of time, knowing the past is often not immediately necessary to the counselor's task. As I explored Ted's internal experience, I learned that he saw himself as fat and incapable; that he talked negatively to himself, anticipating what others might say to him, and that he acted in ways which reinforced his own self-hate, overeating, and procrastinating. His lack of hope that he was or could become a lovable, valuable, and capable person concerned me.

My first intervention was to create hope by seeking the basis of his despair. "What makes you think you are hopeless?" I asked.

I began by establishing an achievable goal through exploring what was blocking him and what resources he needed to develop self-esteem. Notice my use of the outcome questions outlined at the end of chapter 2.

My second intervention was to assert my belief that he could learn to get out of his depression as he discovered what he was saying, how he was looking, and how he was behaving toward himself (identifying his sensory cycle). I clearly identified his depression as a way to deal with the rage he was unable to accept or express. Most of our conversation focused on the beliefs he had adopted from the teachings of the campus ministry. He heard them demand a perfection, victory, and consistency in the Christian life that was not Ted's experience, leading him to conclude that something was wrong with him. They proclaimed *shoulds, musts,* and *have tos* that sounded more like the law than the gospel of grace.

My third intervention was to proclaim the gospel of grace from Romans 8: "What shall separate me from the love of God?" Nothing! Nothing! Nothing! "There is now no condemnation. . . ."

My fourth intervention was to send Ted home with the encouragement that building self-esteem in himself is a process.

What follow in this chapter are five stages in the change process that Ted will grow through as he begins to implement the twelve steps needed to build self-esteem. I ended the interview by reminding him that this one interview and reading the twelve steps are not enough to guarantee change, inviting him and his wife back for another session.

CHANGE: A FIVE-STAGE PROCESS

People can change their self-esteem! If we don't believe people can change, we are wasting our time in ministry. Yet people usually change slowly. True, some change radically, seemingly overnight, but this immediate change is not common. The more usual pattern is gradual. In Scripture, few people changed as immediately and radically as did the apostle Paul. The three-year trial-and-error, belief-and-doubt experience of the twelve disciples is the norm. The amount of our patience with people we try to help depends on this perspective.

Change is the product of process. That is, people change as they learn new ways of thinking, perceiving, expressing, and behaving. Change also is the result of time to learn, to practice, and to consolidate these new ways into people's personalities. People change by taking one step at a time. Just as people do not climb a mountain in a single step, neither do they change by taking only the first step. Rather, the change process includes five stages that people must walk through if they are to develop self-esteem: suffering → understanding → choosing → acting → maintaining.[1]

Stage One: Suffering

Change begins with people's *awareness* of discomfort or dissatisfaction with their lives and their way of coping with themselves and/or their relationships.[2] Dee was aware of Ted's suffering and helped him find a counselor.

Frequently, counselors must generate *hope* for clients that change is possible, as we saw in Ted's situation, because their repeated failure to change discourages their further trying. Awareness of pain with no hope leads to depression and despair. When resources to accomplish the change accompany the realization of a need to change, then hope and anticipation result.

Awareness of the need for change is illustrated by the question the Pharisees asked Jesus' disciples: "'Why is your Teacher eating with the tax-gatherers and sinners?'" Overhearing the question, Jesus answered, "'It is not those who are healthy who need a physician, but those who are sick'" (Matt. 9:11, 12). No one changes spiritually, emotionally, socially, or physically without recognizing a need for help. The Pharisees found recognizing their need for help to be intolerable and threatening to their self-esteem. Humility, therefore, is a necessary resource before we can ask for help. Acknowledging that someone is sick, dependent, or helpless does not, in Jesus' eyes, cause that person to lose his or her worth. Neither does Jesus require individuals to depreciate themselves. Just as Jesus' acceptance of sinners made it possible for them to welcome him at their parties, so does the helper's unconditional positive regard and nonjudgmental attitude enable the person who needs help to ask for it. Those who have to hang on to the pretense that they have their act together, that they can do it themselves, that they can earn their way into God's favor, will find it difficult to ask for or accept help. Remembering this common resistance will enable helpers to lovingly assure those in need that no one has to experience humiliation in order to receive help.

Stage Two: Understanding

Change continues as a person develops understanding and acceptance of dissatisfaction and discomfort. A person moves from the first step of "I am hurting" to the next step of "I am beginning to see." Some therapies label this the development of insight.[3]

This change stage is characterized by a willingness to learn new ways of looking at oneself, relationships, circumstances, problems, and possibilities. It is the experience of John 8:32: "'You shall know the truth, and the truth shall make you free.'" Discovering the truth about oneself, unfortunately, is usually frightening and painful. The story of the woman at the well, however, demonstrates that Jesus told the woman the truth about herself in a way she could accept. My prayer is that I will develop my ability to talk to people the way Jesus did, telling them the truth about themselves so that they can accept it, begin to change, and run into town to say, "'Come, see a man who told me all the things that I have done'" (John 4:29) without feeling horrible about themselves.

By acknowledging my own need for help, facing my own pretensions, and groaning over my own disobedience, I can identify with my clients as people who grieve God daily. Seeing myself as a person who takes offense at the cross and needs Christ's forgiveness, I develop an attitude that makes it possible for my clients to hear both the bad news and the good news, to feel my esteem for them. Knowing that they are loved, valued, and competent, they begin to feel esteem for themselves without hiding behind fabrications and defenses. They can then acknowledge, "I am lovable, capable, and valuable even though I am a sinner."

Stage Three: Choosing

The third stage in the process of change is "I will try differently." It involves recognizing that the old patterns must be surrendered, because trying harder does not lead to change. This stage of the change process identifies new choices, affirms new potentials, and adopts new lifestyles. The words of Jesus to the adulterous woman illustrate this change stage: "'Neither do I condemn you; go your way. From now on sin no more'" (John 8:11).

For Ted, this meant learning to face his anger rather than running from it, exploring its origin and legitimacy rather than merely confessing it, learning how to express his anger rather than suppressing it through overeating and depression. It meant terminating self-condemnation and replacing it with an honest appraisal of his feelings and behavior. Ted walked through the first two stages rapidly. Most of his counseling sessions have focused on developing this third stage, learning new ways to deal with his accumulated rage and immediate hurts.

Stage Four: Acting

Taking action is the fourth stage in the change process—"I am doing differently." The effort expended is not necessarily more, but it is different. This stage in the change process is characterized by experimenting with new views, ideas, ways of thinking, ways of relating, ways of expressing and behaving. It involves developing the skills, strengths, and resources needed for change to take place.

Ted practices saying, "I am hurt and angry, when you _____ (whatever the specific behavior or statement of the other person is) because I feel discounted, ignored, unloved." During counseling we reclaim the specifics of hurtful circumstances and relationships and practice saying what he wished he could have said in a given situation. Frequently, it is possible to assign Ted the homework assignment of going to people who have hurt him, to express what he needs to say to them. This homework is assigned by mutual agreement between Ted and me when we both have the sense that he has the strength and resources to confront a person constructively and redemptively. Ted has successfully confronted his wife and boss and is now working on dealing with his parents.

Stage Five: Maintaining

All change requires maintenance. Walking through the first four stages of the change process lasts when persons dedicate themselves to maintaining the growth they have achieved. Paul's New Testament letters, for example, admonish Christians to remember who they are and to be faithful to their commitment to Christ.

Ted is well on his way to maintaining his self-esteem without help from me and the daily cheerleading of his wife. Following more than a year of weekly counseling sessions, Ted has accomplished the following:

- is less self-condemning
- deals with his hurts more immediately
- feels less depressed
- challenges his depression when it comes by looking for unexpressed hurt and anger
- grieves for the child he and Dee recently lost
- procrastinates less frequently and for shorter periods of time
- has applied to the mission board for candidacy.

The major test of his ability to maintain self-esteem came when the mission board challenged his readiness to become a candidate and requested nine months of successful coping with his depression before accepting him as a candidate. Rather than take this as rejection, Ted accepts this delay as time to prepare for his life in missions and to consolidate the gains he has made. Ted's good progress does not mean that he will never again have difficulties with depression, hurt, anger, or low self-esteem. It does mean that he has new ways to cope with these feelings and difficult relationships.

CHANGE COMES THROUGH RELATIONSHIP

People can change; but they seldom, if ever, change by themselves. This fact underscores the crucial supportive and challenging role counselors and ministers play in the change process. Although clients may want to do it all by themselves, change is the product of relationships with others. In recognition of a client's need for autonomy and initiative, the helping relationship involves a collaborative process that in no way violates the freedom and control of the individual to run his or her own life. This theme is captured in O. Hobart Mowrer's pithy statement, "You alone can do it, but you can't do it alone."[4] Salvation, eternal or temporal, is the result of communion and fellowship with others and/or God. That humans cannot save themselves is central to Christianity. This basic belief is the key to the process of helping people change. The church, Alcoholics Anonymous, Weight Watchers, educational institutions—they all affirm the need for people to help people begin and maintain change.

But while change comes through relationships, it always begins inside the person. We cannot help people change without being let into their lives. Like Jesus, we stand on the outside of someone's life and knock on the door. Revelation 3:20 is the model for redemptive relationships: "'Behold, I stand at the door and knock; if anyone hears My voice and opens the door, I will come in to him, and will dine with him, and he with Me." As helpers, we are always on the outside, with no key or doorknob to enter another's life without permission. Entry is always by invitation. Change does not occur with forced entry.

We can get inside a person rather than get under that person's skin by using the same tools Jesus uses—being a safe enough person to be allowed in. We become such people by developing these qualities: a loving, nonjudging attitude; respect for the person regardless of the problem; empathic understanding; permission for self-determination; confidentiality; and, above all, real, nondefensive openness.

USING THE FIVE STAGES OF CHANGE TO IMPLEMENT THE TWELVE-STEP PROCESS

The five stages of change, introduced at the beginning of this chapter, provide counselors with a map that shows us where to begin our intervention in helping the client build self-esteem. To facilitate the twelve-step process of building self-esteem (elaborated below), a counselee must realize his or her need for esteem. Therefore, the helper needs to assess how much counselees are aware that self-esteem is a missing and desirable ingredient in their lives before moving beyond the first stage of change. Because people with low self-esteem may find it hard to believe they are worthy of another's love and concern, building a relationship may be difficult and time consuming.

Discovering that persons are dissatisfied with their level of self-esteem and developing a trusting relationship with them will open the door for the next stage in the change process— helping them understand and accept their need for self-esteem. At this point in the change process, the counselee will need to make some new choices based on the insights exposed during counseling. These insights will include many of the considerations of chapter 1—a biblically correct definition of self-esteem and a theologically correct interpretation of biblical concepts of self-esteem.

At this point in the counseling process, the person becomes aware of how self-image is based on cultural sources of self-esteem. That is, in American culture we are subtly taught that we are okay only if we are beautiful, bright, talented, wealthy, popular, and successful. Learning how to challenge these culturally determined bases of self-esteem is woven throughout the twelve steps outlined below.

71

TWELVE STEPS IN THE PROCESS OF BUILDING SELF-ESTEEM

Step One: Acknowledge the Problems Low Self-Esteem Produces

The first step in building self-esteem is acknowledging the problems low self-esteem produces in a person's life.[5] Table 2 pictures negative influences on the four modalities introduced in chapter 2. The pattern of influence is cyclical, beginning with negative internal dialogue, reinforced by negative self-picturing, resulting in negative feelings, and finally producing negative behavior.

The origin and direction of the sensory cycle are common as diagramed, but may differ for different people. Low self-esteem develops in relation to others—what others say to us, how others look at us, what others feel toward us, and how others act toward us. These responses shape our own messages, views, feelings, and behavior toward ourselves. The counseling process, as introduced in chapter 2, discovers the negative cyclical pattern and uses it to develop a positive cycle to bring about desired change.

A common pattern in low self-esteem is for counselees to repeat to themselves the negative messages given them by significant people in their lives. Often, these messages will be outside the awareness of the person with low esteem. Similarly, persons with low self-esteem will view themselves, feel toward themselves, and act toward themselves the way important people in their lives have done. The common cyclical pattern (indicated by the sequence of numbers) that maintains low esteem usually begins with negative internal dialogue, then moves on to negative self-pictures, negative self-feelings, and negative self-behavior (see the LuAnn illustration in chapter 2). This pattern may also get started by what persons say to themselves about their performance or how others treat them. On occasion, the cyclical process will begin with feelings that seem to have no obvious precipitant. Notice that the chart is counterclockwise. The reason for this will be explained in the next chapter under the topic of eye scan.

72

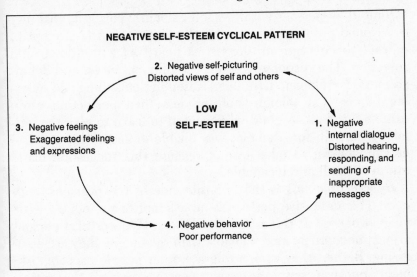

What are some of the common problems low self-esteem produces? The following list is not exhaustive, nor does a person with low self-esteem necessarily exhibit them all.

Guilt heads the list. The basis of this guilt is rooted more in a belief that the person is bad than that his or her behavior is bad. "I am evil" is a fundamental conviction characterizing this person.[6] It is frequently the expression of rape and incest victims or of people who have been severely and repeatedly humiliated in childhood. Seldom is this conviction of "badness" verifiable in real life. Frequently, abused people accept the abuser's opinion and feelings toward them. On occasion, missionaries and evangelistic counselors are confronted with people who believe they are too bad to be the recipients of God's grace. Frequently, this attitude was accepted from significant people in their lives. That is, they have come to believe about themselves what they have heard or imagined hearing about themselves from parents, siblings, or friends. LuAnn, whom you met in chapter 2, is an example of someone who believes she is guilty not only of what she has done, but also of what she is—an evil person who deserves punishment and for whom no atonement short of death will compensate.

Oversensitivity to criticism is another common problem

exhibited by persons with low self-esteem.[7] This is an inability to respond positively to constructive criticism. Any attempt to correct, encourage, or suggest is heard as a put-down and rejection. The response is often one of hurt, anger, and defensiveness. People who have been raised in demanding and exacting homes that tolerate nothing less than perfection often exhibit this trait. A child who wanted to learn to play the guitar by himself, for example, was unable to accept his parents' encouragement to take lessons because this suggestion made him feel small and incapable.

Hypercriticalness is the opposite side of the oversensitivity coin. This defensive posture is an attempt to protect a fragile view of oneself at the expense of others. Hypercritical persons are not necessarily more capable than the people they are criticizing. Rather, they cannot tolerate other people's accomplishments because those apparent successes diminish the critical person's self-worth. This is frequently an unconscious process; if a hypercritical person is confronted with this insight, the chances are he or she will deny it. Don was hypercritical. He drove his pastor to distraction with his criticisms of the sermon, church service, choir, Sunday school teachers, and church board. The pastor decided to confront Don with his critical spirit. Considering how he might approach him, the pastor decided to take him to lunch. During the meal, the pastor said, "Don, nothing in this church seems to make you happy. You find something wrong with everything and everybody. Can you tell me a time in your life when you were content?" Don was taken back by the pastor's nondefensive spirit and willingness to focus on his happiness. The pastor's next question, "Who criticized you as you were growing up?" betrayed a profound understanding of the roots of hypercriticalness. This was the start of Don's willingness to face the depreciation and frustration of not being able to please his parents as a child.

Embarrassment may also characterize the person of low esteem. This is a heightened sense of self-consciousness, accompanied by feelings of shame and guilt. "Excuse me, I'm sorry, I beg your pardon" are frequent inappropriate verbalizations. Fears of doing or saying the wrong thing predominate in such persons. They also cannot accept a compliment graciously.

Shyness relates to the feeling of embarrassment. The shy person is basically insecure and passive. Fear of rejection predominates. Somewhere in his or her life this person was taught that it is dangerous to ask for what one needs or to express what one feels.

Clowning is the opposite side of shyness. This person looks and sounds confident, but is not necessarily assured. Happy-go-lucky and assertive persons may feel as insecure as the shy person, but they act differently. Psychologically, clowning behavior may be a defense against low self-esteem.

Arrogance is often misnamed self-confidence. But usually underneath this facade of "I am better than others" is a fear of being common, ordinary, and average. These people expend a great deal of energy in showing the world how great they are. This lack of humility is typically found in people whose aloofness is a defense against low self-esteem.

Blaming others is a common human tendency. As such it is not limited to people with low self-esteem. A person's ability to take responsibility for his or her own actions, however, is a sign of maturity and self-esteem. Persons who are unable or unwilling to hold themselves responsible for what is happening in their lives may be persons of low self-esteem. "I am okay only if I am perfect" is a predominant belief for this person. A child who spilled milk while helping her father set the table for supper turned and yelled, "See what you made me do?" She dealt with her own self-criticism by yelling at her dad rather than yelling at herself.

Feeling blamed is closely related to blaming others. Projection, believing others feel toward you what you are unable to acknowledge as your feeling toward them, is the label for this defense mechanism. In its most extreme form, this attitude is known as paranoia. Low self-esteem persons perceive others as against them, which is a defense against their own anger and hostility toward others.

Self-negation is one of the more obvious ways that people with low self-esteem behave. Characteristically, this attitude makes individuals unable to acknowledge any of their strengths and abilities. They are continually discounting and diminishing their own accomplishments and person. Sometimes this behavior is an attempt to express humility and guard against pride, but frequently it actually represents the true negative beliefs of a person toward himself or herself.

For example, when I invited a woman to teach my Sunday school class, she declined, saying she wasn't capable of handling the responsibility. Using sarcasm, I said, "This is exactly the reason I'm asking you to teach. I want to see you fall on your face!" When she agreed to try, she was as successful as I had thought she would be. People's refusal to participate when we ask them to perform certain jobs in the church may actually reflect a poor appraisal of their own abilities. In chapter 1, we learned this to be characteristic of people with low self-esteem.

Insincerity is perhaps the saddest form of self-hatred because it is the most hidden expression of low self-esteem and destroys the possibility of a close, honest relationship. Insincerity is commonly an expression of fear that people will not like me if I am my true self. True, the more extreme expressions of insincerity can be detected. Most insincerity, however, is subtle. Take, for example, the hypocrisy of the scribes and Pharisees, or Judas's betrayal of Jesus. They knew they were hypocrites, but the religious leaders' followers and Judas's fellow disciples were unaware of their double-mindedness.

Addictions (alcohol, drugs, anorexia/bulimia) make up a large category of behaviors that at their core frequently evidence low self-esteem.

Homosexuality is also a behavior in which low self-esteem plays a significant role. Because homosexuality is an identity problem (Who am I?), self-appraisal of homosexual identity and orientation is frequently negative. In addition, "gay" people struggle with coming out of the closet to let family and friends know they are homosexuals because they fear severe reactions and rejections.

Marriage and family problems frequently have low self-esteem as a contributing factor.[8] How a person feels toward himself or herself influences how he or she feels toward a spouse, children, parents, and siblings. (For development of this theme see chapter 6, "Teaching Parents to Build Self-Esteem in Their Children").

As a rule of thumb, whatever problem a person brings to

counseling—inferiority, insecurity, inadequacy, impotence—self-esteem is probably a critical issue. Whether or not self-esteem is a negative force in a person's life, we who are counselors address the issue automatically when we relate to people with warmth, care, respect, confidentiality, and genuineness. That is, we reinforce positive esteem through the quality of our interactions with them.

Step Two: Believe That Loving Yourself Is Acceptable to God

The second step in building self-esteem in people is to assist them to believe that loving themselves is acceptable to God.[9] Central to helping counselees believe that loving themselves is permissible with God involves exploring their understanding of loving themselves. We will discover that they have confused many of the self-esteem concepts discussed in chapter 1. That is, they will not have adopted biblically accurate perceptions such as these: self-love is not selfishness, self-affirmation is not self-conceit, self-worth is not self-worship, self-awareness is not self-absorption, humility is not humiliation, putting off one's sinful self is not putting oneself down, self-denial is not self-degradation, and unworthiness is not worthlessness.

As counselors, we will need to affirm that self-love is the result of surrendering one's narcissism (I am the center of my world) and martyrdom (I will suffer needlessly) and accepting oneself as a reflection of God's image (I am his lovable, valuable, capable creation who is being redeemed). A biblical basis for believing that loving yourself is acceptable to God is found in Matthew 22:39: "'You shall love your neighbor as yourself.'" This theme is also carried out in Ephesians 5:28, where husbands are commanded to love their wives as they love their own bodies.

Christ and Paul assume that loving oneself is basic to how a person treats a neighbor or spouse. If I love myself, then I will treat you as well as I treat myself. Unfortunately, even though a person's love for himself is not always positive, the principle is still lived out. The principle is this: I will love you as much as I love myself. I may not love myself very much, and therefore I will not love you very much. Thus, my level of self-esteem affects my level of esteem for you. This being true, many of the problems we see in marriages and families can be traced to a parent's and spouse's low view of himself or herself. We cannot expect others to love another beyond their ability to love themselves.

A word of caution: Telling people to believe that loving themselves is acceptable to God does not usually result in their ability to do that. The process of believing is more complicated than merely hearing someone say "believe." To be told what to believe is a beginning point, yet that idea must be taken inside the person to form a belief. This process of "taking inside" what one is told begins with listening, then moves to comprehending and accepting, and, finally, it makes the belief one's personal possession. The believing process involves four dimensions:

- telling myself repeatedly, "God says it is acceptable for me to love myself";
- repeatedly picturing myself as God loving me;
- consistently acting in a loving way toward myself;
- feeling loving toward myself.

The next chapter will develop this process.

The goal of the second step in the process of building self-esteem is to accept myself as good, that is, as made in God's image. It is expressed in the following poem by an unknown author.

I'm a child playing hide-and-seek
    waiting for someone to find me
    and call my name
    and say, "you're it!"

And you did it, Lord!
You found me hiding
    in the silliest, saddest places,
    behind old grudges . . .
    under tones of disappointments . . .
    tangled up in guilt,

smothered with success,
choking on sobs that nobody hears.

You found me
and you whispered my name
and said, "you're it!"
And I believe you mean it . . .

And now maybe
the silent tears can roll out of my throat . . .
get wet on my cheeks . . .

And now maybe
I don't have to play hide-and-seek any more.

Step Three: Believe God Chooses to Need You

If believing is a process of hearing, seeing, feeling, and acting (internalizing what I hear, picturing what I see, experiencing what I feel, and acting on the belief that is inside of me), then the third step becomes a possibility. Do not stop, therefore, with telling counselees that God needs them to be part of his redemption plan. Rather, invite them, show them, recruit them, train them, assign them, and supervise them.

God needs people? On first reflection it sounds unbelievable, even heretical. God has no needs. He is self-sufficient, isn't he? True, but he has chosen to involve humans in the process of making himself known to the world. To be told in 1 Corinthians 3:16, 17 that we are the temple of God is exciting but awesome. The fact that God has chosen to dwell in human bodies suggests that we represent God wherever we are. We are the physical representations of God to the world. When they see us, they see the place where God dwells. This is a sobering thought: What I say and do reflects the God who lives in me. Yet this truth gives my life significance.

Paul argues in the passage cited above that as the temple of God, each of us is holy. He also warns that anyone who destroys the temple will be destroyed by God. When I recognize that I am the temple of God, I have a source of value that can build my self-esteem.

Another affirmation that God needs humans to do his redemptive work is found in the Sermon on the Mount. "'You are the salt of the earth. . . . You are the light of the world'" (Matt. 5:13, 14). Imagine sitting on the side of a mountain, listening to an itinerant preacher tell you that you are significant in God's plan for the world. Given our economic, political, and religious situation, most of us would have a hard time believing those words. "What do you mean I am the salt of the earth and the light of the world? Don't you know that I am sitting here listening to you because I am poor and unemployed? Don't you know that I am politically powerless? I am living in a country that is occupied by Romans. Don't you know that I am religiously insignificant? I am not a scribe, Pharisee, or rabbi."

Yet Jesus' affirmations are to such people. He says, "I need you to represent me to the world. I have empowered you with my Spirit." Accepting oneself as part of God's redemptive plan is a crucial step in the process of healthy self-esteem. Taking one's place in that process is facilitated by the next step.

Step Four: Discover Your Place in the Body of Christ

Believing that one is the salt and light of the earth becomes possible when a person not only hears, but also sees, that every Christian has a vital part to play in the body of Christ. This is the affirmation of Romans 12 and 1 Corinthians 12. Paul tells us that no one Christian is more important than any other Christian. We all have different assigned tasks and gifts that God wants us to exercise in the church. He encourages every person "not to think more highly of himself than he ought to think" (Rom. 12:3), but to exercise each gift for the benefit of others (v. 6). His message is, *think realistically about your person and your gifts.*[10]

While we are not to inflate our importance in the body of Christ, we are not to devalue our significance. We are not to think of ourselves as either superior or inferior. "If the foot should say, 'Because I am not a hand, I am not a part of the body,' it is not for this reason any less a part of the body. And if the ear should say, 'Because I am not an eye, I am not a part of the body,' it is not for this reason any the less a part of the body. If the whole body were an eye, where would the hearing be? If the whole were hearing, where would the sense of smell be? . . . And the eye cannot say to the hand, 'I have no need of you'; or again the head to the feet, 'I have no need of you'" (1 Cor. 12:15–18, 21).

Following my presentation on self-esteem in a local adult Sunday school class, Jerry approached me and asked, "Do you know what part of the body of Christ I am?"

Not knowing the man or his gifts, I replied, "No. What are you asking?" He told me in graphic, anatomical terms that he was the most despicable part of the body. Feeling sadness for this man, I expressed what I imagined to be his sense of shame and humiliation. I then asked, "How did you come to feel so dirty and insignificant?" Not uncommonly, this man was comparing his abilities and talents to those of others in the church and was not evaluating his "gifts" to be as important and significant as theirs. He was adopting the world's attitude of status and prestige, that is, people's significance and importance are based on the value that society places on their abilities and vocations. In addition, he was experiencing the church as not recognizing his gifts or asking him to participate in various activities.

I responded to him in four ways. First, I heard his pain and empathized with his negative self-picture and evaluation. "You see yourself negatively and feel dirty and despicable?"

Second, I explored the bases of his self-perception. "What has happened in your life that encourages you to see yourself as insignificant?"

Third, I encouraged him to listen to Paul: "'On the contrary, it is much truer that the members of the body which seem to be weaker are necessary; and those members of the body, which we deem less honorable, on these we bestow more abundant honor, and our unseemly members come to have more abundant seemliness, whereas our seemly members have no need of it. But God has so composed the body, giving more abundant honor to that member which lacked, that there should be no division in the body, but that the members should have the same care for one another . . .'" (1 Cor. 12:22–25). Hearing these words of edification and exhortation are seldom enough to change a person's perceptions, feelings, or behavior. But they are necessary to change as a person reminds himself or herself of the positive place a Christian holds in Christ's body.

Fourth, I asked this man what he thought his gifts were and how he could contribute to the church. I challenged him to check out his perception of his gifts with a couple of people who knew him. I then encouraged him to volunteer after discovering his gifts.

My responsibility in this encounter was not over. As part of the body of Christ, I asked one of the ministers where this man could be involved. I encouraged the pastor to see that he was invited to do some work in the church. I also talked to the membership deacon, encouraging him to help people find a place to serve as they are admitted to membership. Churches can be sensitive to the needs of the congregation in other ways as well. For example, in the church I attend, each year people are invited to respond to a questionnaire about their interests and abilities and where they would like to serve. More formally, people are given written invitations to run for various offices. Some churches hold training sessions for people who want to be involved in its ministries. Training is used as a way of both recruiting and preparing people to serve.

Step Five: Validate Yourself

Jerry's sense of insignificance came in some measure from his negative comparison of himself with other Christians. This is a sure way of becoming depressed and discouraged. When we compare ourselves to others, perhaps we will find others who are less talented than we are; but more likely we will find others who are better than we are. Paul addresses this issue in Galatians 6:4: "But let each one examine his own work, and then he will have reason for boasting in regard to himself alone, and not in regard to another." I like the Living Bible version of this verse, which says, "Let everyone be sure that he is doing his very best, for then he will have the personal satisfaction of work well done, and won't need to compare himself with someone else."

Validating myself is the process of endorsing my own life. It is like signing my name to a check. When I sign my check, it is now worth something because it has my signature. When I validate myself, I am worth something because I have signed my own life.

To do my best is to do what is possible. I measure my best with my potential, not with another's possible performance (2 Corinthians 10:12). Validating myself means that I do not need to outdo someone else; I do not need to beat someone in order to do my best. I examine the quality of my work in terms of what I know is within the sphere of my capabilities. The basis for the comparison is myself, not you. As a consequence, I can do my best and feel good about myself and my performance even if you can do better. I am not competing with you; I am competing against myself. If I validate myself, then I do not need to win over you to be acceptable in my own eyes. Nor do I have to be in control to be acceptable to myself. If I have leadership abilities and I exercise them appropriately, then I am doing my best. If I am a follower or disciple and exercise those abilities constructively, then I am doing my best.

Competition is a key dynamic in American economics and sports. To win over another person or team or product is a prime motivation for many of us. Many a person's self-esteem is based on achieving Number One status. Yet to be Number One is a goal most of us never achieve, and that failure often negatively affects our evaluation of ourselves. Most of us will never be valedictorian, president of the company, chairman of the church, or national or state athletic champion. Many of us will never be Number One at anything. We probably weren't even our spouse's first choice!

When I validate myself, I am okay even if I have no trophies, ribbons, or certificates that recognize me as a winner. I am a winner when I live up to my God-given gifts and abilities. I can affirm myself as an adequate person when I do my best, comparing my efforts to my abilities. I can affirm myself as I remember that no one is perfect. I can feel good about myself when I do not expect perfection as a human or as a sinner. I can affirm myself when I remember that God encourages me to do my best. He does not ask that I put myself down. God does not ask that I depreciate my efforts. He asks me to be humble, to recognize that he equips, empowers, and energizes me.

Paul, as well, encourages us to stop putting ourselves down because put-downs lead to self-righteousness, not to humility. "Let no one keep defrauding you of your prize by delighting in self-abasement . . . inflated without cause by his fleshly mind. . . . These are matters which have, to be sure, the appearance of wisdom in self-made religion and self-abasement and severe treatment of the body, but are of no value against fleshly indulgence" (Col. 2:18, 23).

Validate yourself is the theme of the following poem entitled "The Man in the Glass":

When you get what you want in your struggle for self,
and the world makes you king for a day,
just go to a mirror and look at yourself,
and see what that man has to say.
For it isn't your father or mother or wife,
whose judgment upon you must pass;
the fellow whose verdict counts most in your life
is the one staring back from the glass.
Some people might think you're a straight-shootin' chum,
and call you a wonderful guy,
but the man in the glass says you're only a bum,
if you can't look him straight in the eye.
He's the fellow to please, never mind all the rest,
for he's with you clear up to the end.
And you've passed your most dangerous, difficult test
if the guy in the glass is your friend.
You may fool the whole world down the pathway of years,
and get pats on the back as you pass.
But your final reward will be heartaches and tears
if you've cheated the man in the glass.

Anonymous

Step Six: Make Realistic Demands on Yourself

When I validate myself, I can then make realistic demands on myself. I can be who I really am without pretense, fear, or shame. I am freed from thinking more highly of myself than is realistic, and I am freed from thinking less of myself than my talents and abilities warrant. I do not have to deceive myself or others. "For if anyone thinks he is something when he is nothing, he deceives himself. But let each one examine his own work, and then he will have reason for boasting in regard to himself alone, and not in regard to another" (Gal. 6:3, 4).

Self-esteem is the product of making realistic demands on ourselves. People who love themselves do not have to boast beyond their abilities or overextend their efforts. They can be who they are and do what they can do. People who value themselves do not have to prove anything to themselves or to anyone else. On the other hand, they can commend themselves to the extent that they are commissioned by God (2 Corinthians 10:12–18). When people have realistically appraised themselves they can volunteer their abilities, gifts, and talents for God's service with the assurance they will be experienced as capable and humble.

Step Seven: Welcome the Truth about Yourself

To make realistic demands requires an inventory of a person's strengths and weaknesses. Welcoming the truth about oneself takes courage. In spite of Jesus' assurance that knowing the truth will set a person free (John 8:32), he offers no guarantees that the process will be comfortable. I have frequently thought the verse could be modified to read, "You shall know the truth and the truth shall set you free, but it will make you feel a little uncomfortable at first." For some, like the rich young ruler, the scribes, and Pharisees, knowing the truth was painful. Yet for others, like the woman at the well and Zaccheus, the truth relieved them of guilt and anxiety.

To welcome the truth about myself requires my willingness to become acquainted with who I am. This means that I am willing to take an inventory of my words, thoughts, imaginations, feelings, needs, defenses, behaviors, and relationships. Ask these questions: Was I willing to take this inventory as I read chapter 1? Am I willing to continue the inventory of myself as I work with people? Scripture encourages us to examine ourselves so that we do not fall into the same pit of temptations out of which we are helping others (Matthew 7:15).

Effective therapists review who they are—what they believe, think, feel, sense, and do. They are committed to becoming aware of their experience of themselves and their world. During a counseling session, they monitor their own internal experience. What am I feeling? What am I seeing? What am I hearing? How am I acting? This information aids you, the counselor, in understanding how you experience the people with whom you are working. It helps you understand what others may be experiencing in the counseling session with themselves, with each other, and with you, their counselor. It provides a basis for what and how you respond to your counselees. For example, if I am feeling tension at the beginning of a session, I ask whether it stems from my own internal experience or from what I am sensing in this individual, couple, or family. When I feel scared or angry, I wonder if this is just my private experience or if possibly my client(s) is feeling this emotion without expressing it.

Recently, a client complained that when she talked to me on the phone, I sounded cool, aloof, and rushed. This contrasted with how she experienced me face-to-face in a counseling session—warm, patient, caring. I listened with discomfort to her complaint. The person she was describing is not who I want to be on the telephone. Yet this was her experience. Was I willing to listen to her experience and check out whether others experienced me the same way? Was I feeling something negative toward this woman of which I was unaware? Did I have to defend myself or excuse my behavior? Was I going to blame her, pursuing her sense of rejection as her paranoia, or was I going to seriously consider that she was reacting to the sound, tone, and tempo of my voice that may in fact have sent an uncaring message? I cannot respond defensively if I am willing to welcome the truth about myself.

Step Eight: Live with God's Love and Forgiveness as a Way to Implement Change

I can welcome the truth about myself when I love and value myself. Yet my self-esteem dictates the degree of my willingness to hear the truth about myself. A foundation to self-esteem is my ability to love and forgive myself. The source of this ability is my relationship with God. As I experience God's love and forgiveness, I can then love and forgive myself. Living with God's love and forgiveness helps me change myself and my reactions to what I say, think, feel, and do as well as my reactions to people and circumstances.

God encourages me to remember that I was loved even while I was his enemy (Romans 5:8). He reminds me that his love is unconditional (Ephesians 2:4–8) and that he loved me before I loved him (1 John 4:10). God reminds me that while I was lost, I was still his creation. Being spiritually lost does not mean I am nothing. I am his creation, and he wants to redeem me. He is willing to forgive me. Will I accept his love and forgiveness? When I accept God's unconditional love, I am free to love God in return and to love and forgive my neighbor as God loves and forgives me.

We all desire to be loved unconditionally—just as we are, with no demands on us to change. We hope to receive this kind of love from our parents, spouses, children, and friends. Unfortunately, human ability to love unconditionally is limited, so we are often frustrated. Therefore, we need to change our expectations of who can love us unconditionally. As far as I have been able to determine, only three in the world can be expected to give you unconditional love—God, your counselor, and the family pet!

Step Nine: Parent Yourself

Because our parents failed us in that they didn't love us unconditionally and because no parent can give all the nurture, care, and love that we want and need, we will need to parent ourselves. Of course, some parents are more limited in their ability to give than others, which leaves some of us with more to do for ourselves than others will require. The fact that all human beings are insatiable is another reason we will need to parent ourselves. That there is someone who can give us all we need is a romantic ideal. Becoming mature depends on accepting the fact that no human relationship is adequate to meet all our needs. When we accept the fact that no relationship will be sufficient to meet all our needs, then we are free to enjoy our parents, our spouses, our children, our friends, and our churches without demanding that they be unconditionally loving. It also frees us to be limited in our ability to love others unconditionally.

The point of this encouragement to parent oneself is this: I must learn to support, care for, and love myself because I am not going to get all I want or need from the important people in my life. This may be a painful truth, but it certainly is a freeing truth. It frees us from unrealistic, suffocating dependency. Accepting this truth makes it possible to give up our attempts to control, manipulate, plead, placate, or demand that others meet our needs. It frees us to mature as independent, self-supporting adults. It frees us to ask for what we need in ways that do not overwhelm others. Accepting this truth allows us to receive thankfully what we get, knowing that gifts are given out of a person's available resources.

Step Ten: Give Yourself

Self-esteem builds when we give ourselves to the service of others. Jesus said, "'I tell you the truth, whatever you did for one of the least of these brothers of mine, you did for me'" (Matt. 25:40 NIV). This service to the poor, the hungry, the imprisoned, and the widows should make us feel good about ourselves. When we help others, feeling good about ourselves is promised in Scripture:

> "And if you give yourself to the hungry,
> And satisfy the desire of the afflicted,
> Then your light will rise in darkness,
> And your gloom will become like midday."
>
> Isa. 58:10

I read this as follows, "When you are helping others, your face will shine as brightly as the noonday sun." Helping others, therefore, can be part of a prescription for building self-esteem.

We can best give ourselves when we have a self to give. To be ourselves, we must recognize our feelings, our needs, our values, our perspectives, our beliefs—our overall identity.

Jesus, for example, gave of himself because he knew who he was. At age twelve, Jesus knew who he was at the temple. To his upset mother, he answered, "'Did you not know that I had to be in My Father's house?'" He knew who he was at the temptation. He did not have to respond when Satan said, "'If you are the Son of God, command that these stones become bread. . . . throw Yourself down [from the temple] . . . worship me.'" Jesus knew who he was at the trial. The high priest said to him, "'I adjure You by the living God, that You tell us whether You are the Christ, the Son of God.' Jesus said to him, 'You have said it yourself; nevertheless I tell you. . . .'" And Jesus knew who he was at the cross. The people mocked him, saying, "'If you are the Son of God, come down from the cross.' . . . 'He saved others; He cannot save Himself. He is the King of Israel; let Him now come down from the cross, and we shall believe in Him.'" But he resisted the temptation to respond to those mocking. Jesus knew another miracle would not prove to the crowd who he was.

Step Eleven: Meditate on Who You Are When Confronted by God

Self-esteem is an identity issue, and identity is dependent on relationships. The most important people in our lives define and influence our definition of ourselves. Who am I? Initially, I am who my parents, grandparents, siblings, friends, and teachers tell me I am. I do not know as a baby that I am being defined and influenced. The awareness of being who others think I am and want me to be develops slowly. It comes through hearing people say, "You're a good boy." Or, "My, what a lovely girl!" Or, "Naughty!"

Likewise, hearing what God has to say to us and reading how he sees us can define and influence our identities and develop positive self-esteem.

Carol is struggling with self-esteem. She has difficulty making decisions because she is fearful of making mistakes. She learned early in her life that she was expected to be perfect, without error. As an adult, she tells herself that to be perfect she needs to think and act just as her parents acted. Her tastes are different from Mom and Dad's, for example; yet this difference is not acceptable in her own eyes. Having been in counseling long enough to develop a more positive self-esteem, Carol expressed her struggle in a poem:

Value

Her mother blazed,
"Isn't she pretty!"
Her father snapped,
"Pretty is as pretty does."
God sighed.
"She is lovable,
redeemable,
and valuable
because
she's Mine."
But no one heard His words.

Fortunately, Carol is hearing God's words. She is learning to hear God's words through my encouragement to take God's words about herself seriously. I remind her what God says: I am his creation and redemption, I am his workmanship, I am part of his body, and he is preparing a place for me.

Requiring clients to read assigned Scripture passages as homework between sessions is also a way of exposing people to what God says about them. Here is a sample of the verses I frequently identify for my clients: 1 John 4:1–12, 3:17–22, Romans 5:6–11, Galatians 3:25–29, 1 Corinthians 12:4–30. A common practice in evangelism that can be used to build self-esteem is to substitute a person's name in John 3:16: "'For God so loved _____ (client's name), that He gave His only begotten Son, that [when] _____ (client's name) believes in Him . . .'"

Asking my clients to pray a written prayer also helps them to hear God's word, perspective, and feeling toward them. Below is a copy of the prayer by an unknown author that I frequently send home with my clients. I ask them to pray this prayer at least three times a day. When they tell me they don't believe what this prayer says about themselves, I tell them that they do not have to believe the prayer, just read it each day until the next session. At the next counseling session, I then use their feelings, thoughts and prayer experience as an agenda for the counseling process. I use this prayer with clients whether or not they have made a profession of faith. My experience is that repeating this prayer allows the people to see themselves through God's eyes, corrects their negative self-picture, and prepares them to accept Christ as their personal Savior.

I am God's child.
God created me and He loves me.
I was with God before I came into being.
He knew me then and He knows me now perfectly.
He knows me through and through.
God loves me just the way I am right now.
God accepts me just the way I am.
I am acceptable and lovable.
I am a beautiful child of God.
I have infinite worth.
All of creation is not complete without me.
I have been created individually.
I am unique in all ways.
God created me as that unique person and He loves me.
God chose me as His own.
God lives in me and I live in Him.
He abides in me and calls me His child.
He wants me to live fully and abundantly.
He frees me and gives me joy.
God gives me the gift of life through His grace alone.
I accept God's love this day and know He will love me
   forever.
I thank God for the real person I am.
I thank Him for creating me and giving me life.
I thank Him for truth and love and life.

Step Twelve: Be As Patient with the Process of Learning to Love Yourself As God Is

Patience with oneself is the product of realistic expectations. Is my hope of improved self-esteem based on real resources, time, and energy? Do I allow time to learn the process of loving myself?

George approached me following a seminar I led on self-esteem. "Dave, I heard you speak on self-esteem six years ago, and I am still struggling with loving myself. What am I doing wrong?"

"Tell me what you are doing and how you are doing it," I replied.

"Well, I'm going through the twelve steps, but my self-esteem does not seem to be improving that much."

George told me what he was doing (generalized form of desired state), but did not tell me *specifically* what he was doing or *how* he was going through the twelve steps. I had to choose what to explore: what he was doing, how he was doing it, or his unverbalized expectation that his self-esteem should have been achieved by then. Because other people were waiting to talk with me, I decided to bypass the *how* question and asked whether he was expecting his self-esteem to be fully developed with no self-doubts or struggles ever occurring again. Yes, he was. "Do you mean to tell me, Dave, that I will never totally master high self-esteem?"

"George, self-esteem, like any personal, emotional or spiritual development, takes time. It has been my experience that neither I nor my clients change immediately or totally. I am reminded of what Paul says in Philippians 1:6: 'For I am confident of this very thing, that He who began a good work in you will perfect it until the day of Christ Jesus.' Just as our spiritual life is a developmental process, so our self-esteem is an ongoing process. What would make it possible for you to expect your self-esteem to improve without expecting it to be totally achieved today?"

"I guess, if I'm not doing something wrong, then I can accept my self-esteem where I am today. But I thought something must be wrong with me if I'm not much better than I was when I first heard you speak." I responded by telling George that we could meet together later and take a more specific look at what he was doing to improve his self-esteem. And he agreed.

Patience with oneself depends on accepting the learning process. It also depends on knowing what the learning process is and how to implement it. In our high-tech society, fast and efficient answers set the stage for us to expect immediate and effective answers in other parts of our lives. This is an unrealistic expectation because personal growth is a lifetime process.

Summary

There is an answer to the problem of low self-esteem just as there is an answer to the problem of sin. We can and do give people answers to these problems. Yet telling the answer and helping people live the answer are very different. The answers are usually simple for the teacher, but the remedies are usually difficult for the student. Preaching and counseling, therefore, are two necessary but different sides to helping people change. Preaching is giving content; counseling is teaching process. This chapter has given content: twelve steps in helping people develop self-esteem. It has also outlined five stages in the process of change. How to teach the process of utilizing the twelve steps is the subject of the next chapter.

CHAPTER FOUR

TEACHING PEOPLE THEIR SENSORY PROCESS IN DEVELOPING SELF-ESTEEM

THE INSTRUCTIONS JON READ FOR ASSEMBLING his bicycle seemed simple enough. But as he attempted to attach the wheels and shifting and brake controls, he noticed how much easier it was to read the instructions than it was to execute them. He was glad when he finally got past the instructions and ended up with a finished bicycle.

Learning to counsel is similar to putting together a bicycle. Like Jon, some counselors are interested only in the end product. They assume that individuals will know how to put their lives together if only they have the right instructions. But strange as this may sound, effective counselors have learned that *the process is the product.* They understand that teaching content without teaching process is of little use to most clients. To help counselors become more effective, therefore, the focus in this chapter is on learning the process.[1]

If the reader is accustomed to teaching *content* without spending time teaching *process,* accepting the claim that the process is the product will be a radical shift in thinking and doing. Most students of counseling accept that knowing what to do or say does little good without knowing how to use the information to bring about change. However, as a teacher of the counseling process, I see students falling back into their old ways of teaching content and struggling with or forgetting the process. Hopefully, the reader will be able to avoid this tendency.

The previous chapter details what to say and teach to a low self-esteem person. Its content will help those counselees who have resources to understand and translate concepts into action. Yet people who consult counselors are in the office because they haven't learned how to build self-esteem. For them, therefore, the process is the product. They need to begin to say, see, feel, and act positively toward themselves. They also need to learn what is blocking them from implementing the twelve steps developed in chapter 3.

By the time a person consults a counselor, he or she will often be walking through the first three stages of the change process: 1) awareness and acceptance of pain or need, 2) understanding that a new way of looking at discomfort can facilitate the desired change, and 3) willingness to try new behaviors and thoughts. How to make use of this awareness, insight, and motivation to bring about change is what the person needs to learn in the fourth stage, which is thinking, acting, and feeling in new and more effective problem-solving ways.

Trying differently, then, is the process of 1) teaching the counselees their negative sensory cycle and 2) helping them transform their undesirable self-esteem into a positive sensory cycle: say/hear, see/look, feel/sense, and change/act. Identifying the negative sensory cycle is relatively simple once the counselor trains himself or herself to listen, look, and feel with the person. This chapter will help the counselor learn what to look for, listen to, and feel as a prelude to teaching this to others. Introducing two counseling methods will help counselors review and utilize the sensory sequence in their counseling: identifying the person's use of sensory predicates, and observing and recording his or her eye positions and movements while in the process of accessing and communicating information.

SENSORY PREDICATES

Two skills—being able to identify both the sensory predicates and the sensory modality sequence—are essential to the counseling process of helping people build self-esteem.

Listening to what clients say and understanding their intended and unintended meanings are basic to any counseling model. Looking at clients' nonverbal body language—their facial expressions, eye contact, rate and depth of breathing, what they do and when—is another skill. Hearing how they talk—volume, tone of voice, inflections, pauses, emphases, intensity, speed—is also a basic counseling skill. What is relatively new to counseling, however, is paying attention to the clients' verbal processes by listening to and understanding how they use sensory predicates.[2] (A sensory predicate is a descriptive word that matches the client's way of perceiving life experience.)

Humans have three primary sensory channels through which they take in and put out their experiences—*auditory* (what they hear/say), *visual* (what they see/look for), and *kinesthetic* (what they feel emotionally and sense physically). On occasion, a person may use olfactory predicates (taste and smell). Below is a list of common sensory words that humans use to describe their ways of receiving and representing life experiences. Counselors should familiarize themselves with these words, feeling free to add other sensory synonyms to the list.

Auditory	Visual	Kinesthetic	Smells, tastes
scream	picture	feel	bitter
hear	vague	warm	salty
screech	bright	touch	fragrant
shout	flash	handle	pungent
loud	blue	grasp	stale
amplify	see	soft	fresh
tune	focus	tight	taste
tone	perspective	smooth	sweet
harmonize	clear	rough	sour

Being aware of how clients use sensory predicates in phrases and sentences will help the counselor know how to respond in order to build rapport and facilitate communication.

Auditory

I *hear* her criticizing.
It doesn't *sound* right.
We're not *in tune*.
We're on different *wave lengths*.

Visual

The way it *looks* to me. . . .
I can't *imagine*. . . .
It's impossible to live up to the *picture* he has of me.
My own *image* is. . . .
That *looks* right.
I *see* myself focusing on. . . .
It *looks* impossible to me.

Kinesthetic

I don't *feel* saved.
I want to *grasp*. . . .
I want to be *close*.
I'm not *in touch* with. . . .

Now practice identifying sensory predicates by using the following exercises, designed to help you master the process of hearing and recording sensory predicates.

Exercise 1. Listen for sensory predicate cues. In the following list, underline the sensory words that identify a client's sensory representational custom.

Are you crying for help?
Look here; pay attention to me!
I want to tell you what I hear my parents saying.
What are you trying to show me?
Do you grasp what I'm feeling?
I can't describe it more clearly.
You're not in touch with what you are doing.
I don't know if what I'm saying sounds right to you.
Do you see what I mean?
I was ripped apart by the news of my best friend's death.
How do you see my situation?
Have you got time for me to bounce this off you?
You don't understand a word I'm saying.
I'm having a hard time grasping what you mean. Can you
    run it by me once more?

Check the accuracy of your responses (A = auditory, V = visual, K = kinesthetic): A,V,A,V,K,V,K,A,V,K,V,K,A,K.

Exercise 2. Record a conversation (social, business, or counseling). While listening to the tape, identify and record the sensory predicates used by yourself and others. Can you identify your most-used sensory modality or primary sensory channel?

SCRIPTURAL ILLUSTRATIONS OF THE SENSORY SEQUENCE

Inasmuch as the sensory cycle is based on human characteristics, the Bible illustrates its use. 1 John 1:1 is a clear example (In three of the verses that follow, I have italicized the sensory modalities for emphasis. They are presented in the New International Version, NIV):

That which was from the beginning, which we have *heard*,
which we have *seen* with our eyes, which we have *looked*
at and our hands have *touched*—this we *proclaim* concerning the Word of life.   (1 John 1:1)

We *proclaim* to you what we have *seen and heard,* so that you also may have *fellowship* with us.   (1 John 1:3)

When Jesus *landed* and *saw* a large crowd, he had *compassion* on them and *healed* their sick.   (Matt. 14:14)

Notice that this passage not only identifies Jesus' sensory experience, but specifies the sequence of sensory experience (the firing order). Jesus landed (k) and saw (v) the crowd; he then felt (k) compassion and he acted—he healed (k). The unspoken auditory in the passage can be assumed. That is, after he saw and felt, he talked to himself about alternatives before he decided to act/heal.

"Ask and it will be given to you; seek and you will find; knock and the door will be opened to you. For everyone who asks receives; he who seeks finds; and to him who knocks, the door will be opened."   (Matt. 7:7, 8)

Here, three sensory modalities are included with a suggested pattern or sequence for praying: ask—auditory, seek—visual, knock—kinesthetic.

"Go to this people and say,'You will be ever hearing but never understanding; you will be ever seeing but never perceiving.' For this people's heart has become calloused; they hardly hear with their ears, and they have closed their eyes. Otherwise they might see with their eyes, hear with their ears, understand with their hearts and turn and I would heal them."   (Acts 28:26, 27)

Paul uses a quotation from Isaiah 6:9, 10 to describe to the Jews why they were having a hard time accepting the good news of Jesus Christ.

When people hear but do not understand, they are using a filter (preconceived ideas, interpretations) that prevents them from being in tune with what is said. Older people, for example, often respond to what they think a person is saying because they cannot actually hear the message. Similarly, when persons look but do not see, their assumptions often prevent them from picturing what is there. (A husband may look for food in the refrigerator, but doesn't see the item until his wife comes and shows it to him!)

Exercise 3. Practice identifying the sensory predicates and sequence in the following passages:

"'Let your ear be attentive and your eyes open to hear the prayer your servant is praying before you day and night for your servants, the people of Israel. I confess the sins we Israelites, including myself and my father's house, have committed against you.'" (Neh. 1:6)

So the king asked me, "Why does your face look so sad when you are not ill? This can be nothing but sadness of heart." (Neh. 2:2)

Aware of their discussion, Jesus asked them: "Why are you talking about having no bread: Do you still not see or understand? Are your hearts hardened? Do you have eyes but fail to see, and ears but fail to hear? And don't you remember? When I broke the five loaves for the five thousand, how many basketfuls of pieces did you pick up?" (Mark 8:17–19)

The word of the Lord came to me: "Son of man, you are living among a rebellious people. They have eyes to see but do not see and ears to hear but do not hear, for they are a rebellious people. Therefore, son of man, pack your belongings for exile and in the daytime, as they watch, set out and go from where you are to another place. Perhaps they will understand, though they are a rebellious house. During the daytime, while they watch, bring out your belongings packed for exile. Then in the evening, while they are watching, go out like those who go into exile.

COUNSELING AND SELF-ESTEEM

While they watch, dig through the wall and take your belongings out through it. Put them on your shoulder as they are watching and carry them out at dusk. Cover your face so that you cannot see the land, for I have made you a sign to the house of Israel." So I did as I was commanded. During the day I brought out my things packed for exile. Then in the evening I dug through the wall with my hands. I took my belongings out at dusk, carrying them on my shoulders while they watched. In the morning the word of the Lord came to me: "Son of man, did not that rebellious house of Israel ask you, 'What are you doing?' Say to them, 'This is what the Sovereign Lord says: This oracle concerns the prince in Jerusalem and the whole house of Israel who are there.' Say to them, 'I am a sign to you.'"
(Ezek. 12:1–11)

They asked her, "Woman, why are you crying?" "They have taken my Lord away," she said, "and I don't know where they have put him."
(John 20:13)

"Therefore, my brothers, you whom I love and long for, my joy and crown, that is how you should stand firm in the Lord, dear friends! I plead with Euodia and I plead with Syntyche to agree with each other in the Lord. Yes, and I ask you, loyal yokefellow, help these women who have contended at my side in the cause of the gospel, along with Clement and the rest of my fellow workers, whose names are in the book of life. Rejoice in the Lord always. I will say it again: Rejoice! Let your gentleness be evident to all. The Lord is near. Do not be anxious about anything, but in everything, by prayer and petition, with thanksgiving, present your requests to God. And the peace of God, which transcends all understanding, will guard your hearts and your minds in Christ Jesus. Finally, brothers, whatever is true, whatever is noble, whatever is right, whatever is pure, whatever is lovely, whatever is admirable—if anything is excellent or praise-worthy—think about such things. Whatever you have learned or received or heard from me, or seen in me—put into practice. And the God of peace will be with you.

(Phil. 4:1–9)

Sensory Predicates and Eye Positions

The way humans process information can be observed not only by how they use sensory predicates, but also by their eye positions. The second way counselors can discover sensory modalities and sequences, therefore, is to observe a counselee's eye movements. When the eyes move (up, down, aside), he or she gives counselors an involuntary clue, allowing them to learn the person's way of accessing or processing information. They can then use the person's own sequence to teach effective coping strategies, to build rapport, and to facilitate exploration by matching this individual's use of predicates.

The illustration below, which indicates the relationship of eye positions to the specific sensory modalities, grew out of Bandler and Grinder's investigation of what good therapists do that makes them effective.[3] As they observed several well-known therapists who used different theoretical and therapeutic philosophies and styles, they discovered common ways counselors interact with counselees. Therapists were matching eye movements and sensory predicates. Bandler and Grinder conceptualized their observations into what they label the "representational system" (four sensory channels—auditory, visual, kinesthetic, olfactory) and the eye-scan chart.[4] (Note: When people's eyes focus straight ahead, i.e., do not move to one of the six eye positions, or are closed, they usually think visually. Some people use one sensory system almost exclusively. Many will have a primary system, yet will use the others moderately. Some individuals will be fairly balanced in the use of all three sensory systems. Occasionally, a person's eye movements do not fit these patterns. In such an event, listen for the sensory predicates.)

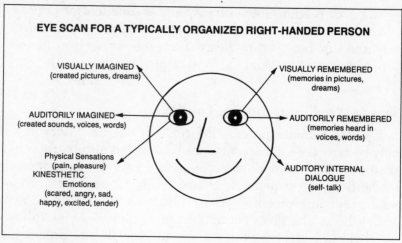

EYE SCAN FOR A TYPICALLY ORGANIZED RIGHT-HANDED PERSON

VISUALLY IMAGINED (created pictures, dreams)

VISUALLY REMEMBERED (memories in pictures, dreams)

AUDITORILY IMAGINED (created sounds, voices, words)

AUDITORILY REMEMBERED (memories heard in voices, words)

Physical Sensations (pain, pleasure) KINESTHETIC Emotions (scared, angry, sad, happy, excited, tender)

AUDITORY INTERNAL DIALOGUE (self- talk)

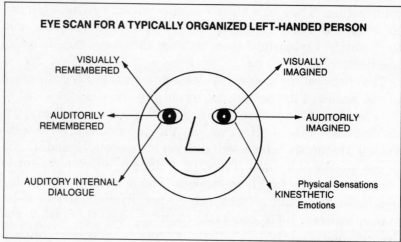

EYE SCAN FOR A TYPICALLY ORGANIZED LEFT-HANDED PERSON

VISUALLY REMEMBERED

VISUALLY IMAGINED

AUDITORILY REMEMBERED

AUDITORILY IMAGINED

AUDITORY INTERNAL DIALOGUE

Physical Sensations KINESTHETIC Emotions

The teaching point here: eye scan and sensory predicates are tools that help counselors enter the clients' experience—to hear when they hear, see when they see, feel when they feel.[5] Using their predicates is a powerful way to build rapport, talk their language, help them feel understood, and discover how they sequence their sensory process. In using the eye scan, no claim is made for knowing *what* clients see, hear, or feel. They will have to tell you what is going on inside themselves because helpers are not and cannot be mind readers. "For who among men knows the thoughts of a man except the spirit of the man, which is in him?" (1 Cor. 2:11). The eye scan will tell you only how they are processing, not what they are saying, seeing, and feeling.

Exercise 4: Become familiar with these charts by studying them and storing them in your memory. When you think you understand the eye scan, reproduce it on a separate sheet of paper. Then check the accuracy of your reproduction with the above charts. Make sure you note the differences between right- and left-handed people.

Exercise 5. Your next task is to learn the eye position for each of the sensory predicates. While hearing the person's use of sensory words, notice the position of his or her eyes.

When a person talks to himself, hears what he is saying, listens to what he has said or wants to say, his eyes are down left (his left, your right).

Auditory internal dialogue (self-talk)

When a person remembers what another has said, hears his tone of voice or actual words, plays a tune in his mind, his eyes will be to his left, your right.

Auditorily remembered

If the person says he sees, pictures, looks, focuses, perceives or thinks some thought, his eyes will generally be up left (his left, your right).

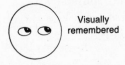

Visually remembered

When a person imagines, suspects, thinks, or guesses, his eyes will be up right (his right, your left).

When a person imagines, creates, tries to reconstruct what another may say, his eyes will be to his right, your left.

When a person feels, grasps, touches, handles, his eyes will be down right (his right, your left).

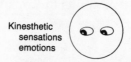

Exercise 6. Next, as people talk, practice watching their eyes. Identify the sensory predicates, and notice how the eye position and predicates match. You can tape an interview, watch the video, and practice noticing the eye movements of your counselees. An alternative to taping counselees is watching interviews or game shows like "The Newlywed Game" on television to become comfortable with your ability to see and match the eye movement to different sensory positions.

Exercise 7. Now take a moment to draw a circle and accompanying eye scan on another sheet of paper. This time, write the following labels in the appropriate places: self-talk (internal dialogue), other-talk, feelings, imagined pictures/thoughts, remembered pictures, remembered words and sounds, and imagined words and sounds.

How accurate are you? Use the chart at the top of p. 107 to confirm your answers.

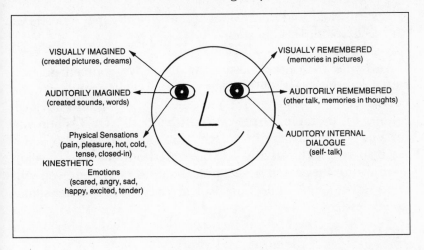

VISUALLY IMAGINED
(created pictures, dreams)

VISUALLY REMEMBERED
(memories in pictures)

AUDITORILY IMAGINED
(created sounds, words)

AUDITORILY REMEMBERED
(other talk, memories in thoughts)

Physical Sensations
(pain, pleasure, hot, cold,
tense, closed-in)
KINESTHETIC
Emotions
(scared, angry, sad,
happy, excited, tender)

AUDITORY INTERNAL
DIALOGUE
(self- talk)

Exercise 8. Draw and label the eye scan from memory, check the accuracy of your drawing, and write the appropriate sensory predicates in each eye position.

In the event you have difficulty identifying a person's sensory eye movements, the following questions can be useful. (Ask him or her to think of the answer, to nod when the answer is known, and to remain silent, keeping the answer to himself or herself):

- What is your name? (Does the person look, listen, or feel the answer?)
- Can you hear your mother calling your name? (Here you are being directive, asking the counselee to access by using the auditory channel.)
- Describe your favorite person. (This asks the counselee to access visually, to tell you what is seen.)
- Think about something you want very much. (You are trying to access feelings.)
- How many stoplights did you pass as you came here today? (This is another visual-accessing question.)
- What is your favorite song? (Watch the eyes to see if the person accesses visually, *seeing* the title, or auditorily, *hearing* the melody or singing the words.)
- Think about a time you were at the beach and felt the

warm sand and cool water. (You should get a kinesthetic access with this question.)

Add your own questions to this list. Give yourself permission to experiment with questions that help you learn the counselee's sensory system. You can be specific and obvious, asking, for example, "Are you right-handed?" Or, "When you dream, do you dream in color?" You can also ask the counselee to respond verbally to your questions. As you develop your ability to see and hear a person's sensory system, you will need fewer special questions to learn his primary representational system.

Time Out

I imagine you may be feeling overwhelmed by reading and practicing the exercises. You may be saying, "Counseling is more complicated than I thought." Can you remember what it was like when you learned to ride a bike? Balancing, steering, peddling, watching where you were going, braking, and getting on and off was an incredibly complicated process that took all your energy and concentration. But now you don't even have to consciously think about how to ride a bike. It comes naturally. So will counseling if you are willing to practice, take your falls, skin your knees and shins, but pick yourself up and try again and again and again. Are you willing to keep practicing?

Sensory Accessing and Observing Body Movements

Another aid to discovering your counselees' sensory sequences is to observe their hand/head or body movements. These movements will, in some clients, follow the eye scan. A feeling person, therefore, may use his or her right hand to gesture toward the waist or the head, or his or her body may lean right and down. A visual person will tend to gesture with his or her hands up toward the shoulders, and the body and head will tend to be kept erect. An auditory person may gesture horizontally above the waist, but below the shoulders.

Skilled counselors learn to use all three sensory modalities even though they would normally use one representational system. Instead, they have learned to be flexible and adaptable to their counselee's representational system. By taking time to discover your own sensory predicates, by listening to a tape of your counseling sessions and sermons, by asking a spouse or friend to give feedback, you can discover whether you are primarily auditory, visual, or kinesthetic. For example, do you tend to use feel, look, think, believe, hear, or listen?

Synchronizing the Person's Sensory Modalities

Another behavior characteristic of a skilled counselor is assisting counselees in the use of all three modalities to enhance life experiences. If a person sees herself, but cannot hear or feel herself, the counselor may ask her to picture herself and then listen to what she is saying. The counselor may then instruct her to get in touch with what she feels as she looks and listens to herself.

To bridge sensory modalities, the counselor begins with the person's primary representational system and then helps her move to the other two modalities. For example, at the beginning of this chapter, we left Jon trying to assemble a bicycle. As he reads the instructions, he has difficulty picturing how part A fits into part B. So he draws a picture, because he can see better than he can hear. When my friend Linda asks how to get someplace, I know she can't understand verbal directions; so I draw her a map. When she sees the map, she can find her way. Beverly has difficulty reading music; but if she hears the song, she can reproduce it through her singing or piano playing. As I was learning to sail, it was easier for me to have an experienced sailor show me how to get the feel of the boat than it was for me to read instructions on sailing.

Frank doesn't understand his wife's feelings. She wants him to talk to her, because talking feels like intimacy. Frank is kinesthetic, so intimacy is first physical sensations, and then emotional feelings. Frank needs to touch in order to feel close, and his wife needs to hear her husband share thoughts and feelings to feel close. To help Frank grasp his wife's experience, I ask him to remember what it feels like to have sexual intercourse with his wife. As he remembers that feeling, he blushes and looks away. I ask him what he is feeling. "Warm, tender, close, excited, happy," he responds. I tell him that this sensation is similar to the one his wife gets when he talks to her. Even though this explanation surprises him while he is still struggling to understand his wife cognitively, he now has a physical sensation that will be a bridge to auditory comprehension. He can now tell himself that what he feels during sex is what his wife feels when he talks to her.

Sensory Predicates and the Outcome Questions

Chapter 2 introduced six outcome questions:
1. What do you want?
2. How will you know when you get it?
3. How will your life be different when you get it?
4. When and where do you want it?
5. What do you need in order to get it?
6. What stops you from getting it?

Now, as you ask your clients these questions, remember to frame them in the client's primary representational system.

Determining the goal
Auditory: What do you hear yourself wanting?
Visual: What do you see/imagine you need?
Kinesthetic: What do you feel you need?

Documenting the evidence
Auditory: What will you hear when you reach your goal?
Visual: What will you see when you reach your goal?
Kinesthetic: What will you feel when you reach your goal?

Defining the context: Sensory predicates are not significant here.

Discerning the ecology
Auditory: When you reach your goal, how will your life sound? When you reach your goal, how will you tune in to your life?

Visual: As you get what you want, what will your life look like?

Kinesthetic: How will your life feel when you get what you want?

Determining the blockages

Auditory: What are you saying to yourself that stops you from getting what you want?

Visual: How are you looking at yourself that stops you from getting what you want?

Kinesthetic: In what way are your feelings preventing you from getting what you want?

Discovering the resources

Auditory: What do you need to hear in order to reach your goal? Think of what you need to tell yourself/spouse if you are to get what you want.

Visual: What do you need to see/look for in order to reach your goal? Look at what you need if you are to get what you want.

Kinesthetic: What do you need to feel in order to reach your goal? What feelings do you need to get in touch with that would help you get what you want?

Using Sensory Predicates in Therapeutic Interventions

As counselors see eye positions and hear sensory predicates, they can practice matching people's representational systems with therapeutic interventions. Below are some examples of therapeutic interventions framed with sensory predicates.

Empathy

Auditory empathy

I hear you saying. . . .
It sounds to me like. . . .
You're sounding. . . .
Am I hearing. . . ?

Visual empathy

   Your view of . . . is. . . .

   As I see what you're picturing, it looks like. . . .

   When you see . . . you feel. . . .

   What you're looking for, then, is. . . .

Kinesthetic empathy

   You feel . . . because. . . .

   So you're in touch with. . . .

   Your sense is . . . when. . . .

   That must feel. . . .

Probes

Auditory probes

   Can you tell me more about it?

   How does . . . sound to you?

   So as you listen to . . . what do you hear?

Visual probes

   What do you see, then, to be your major issue?

   Can you show me what you look for when . . . ?

   Would you be willing to draw a picture of how you see yourself?

Kinesthetic probes

   How do you feel when . . . ?

   When you feel scared, what is your body sensing?

   I noticed that you stop breathing when. . . .

   Can you let yourself feel that experience?

Prompts

Auditory prompts

   Which?

   Yes?

   Go on.

   For example?

Visual prompts

   I see.

Nod head.

Gesture with hand to go on.

Maintain comfortable eye contact.

Kinesthetic prompts

That feels?

Stay with that feeling.

Let yourself feel. . . .

Confrontation

Confrontation invites the counselee to consider discrepancies, incongruities, and distortions in his or her thinking, feeling, and doing. It is not an attack or punishment. Confrontation should help the person achieve the desired goals, especially when he or she is unconsciously being inconsistent.

Auditory confrontation

You say that you're dumb, yet you tell me that you're on the dean's list each quarter.

So you've gotten into the habit of telling yourself you're unattractive, yet you say people seek you out for friendships. How do you account for this contradiction?

I hear you say that you're glad to be with me, but your voice sounds unexcited and depressed.

Visual confrontation

I get the impression that you see yourself as entertaining and witty, but your friends see you as biting and hurtful.

I see you coming for help, yet I don't see you putting any of our ideas into practice. What's going on for you?

You look like you're about to cry, yet you seem unwilling to show your feelings.

Kinesthetic confrontation

You say you feel loving toward your wife, yet you hold on to feelings and don't express them in ways she can feel.

I get the feeling that you want to be in class, but you feel it is more than you can handle. You keep coming, but can't quite let yourself admit how overwhelmed you're feeling. Right?

So you're feeling as though you want to confront your boy-friend, but you're scared he'll reject you. I'm wondering what you feel you'll lose if you tell him what you feel.

Summary

Being able to identify both the sensory predicates and the sensory modality sequence is essential to the counseling process of helping people build self-esteem.

People with low self-esteem characteristically say, see, feel, and/or act in ways that reinforce their low self-esteem. The counselor's task is first to understand that negative sensory process and then to teach people how to use it positively. As we learn people's primary representational system and sensory sequence, we use these resources to teach them how to create and maintain a more desirable view, value, feeling of, and action toward themselves. Note that every human possesses the same sensory modalities—hearing, seeing, touching, feeling, tasting, smelling. However, the sensory sequence or pattern a person uses to gather or give out information will be unique to that individual.[6] This "firing order" is illustrated in the following counseling situation in the next chapter.[7]

CHAPTER FIVE

TEACHING COUNSELORS
THE SENSORY PROCESS
A COUNSELING SITUATION

ANDREW SOUGHT ME OUT in the dining hall after hearing me speak. When I invited him to join me, he sat down and began shifting in his seat, looking rapidly around the room. With his eyes focused down to his right, he asked, "Is it possible for a person with low self-esteem to build it up?" I debated within myself whether to deal with his question personally or factually as I noticed his discomfort. I chose to respond intellectually, given the public setting.[1]

Since I had introduced the sensory process in my speech, I decided to remind him of how it works. "Andrew, in my talk this morning, I outlined the twelve steps a person needs to take in building self-esteem. I also talked about how people could begin to implement those steps by what they say to themselves, how they look at themselves, and how they behave toward themselves. Our feelings. . . ."

Andrew interrupted me to confess, "I'm the one with low self-esteem." His confession opened the door for me to turn a purely factual and intellectual discussion into a personal and intimate conversation as I was given permission to be more than teacher to Andrew. So I shifted to a counseling response: "I can see that you are quite troubled. I imagine that things you have tried have left you still struggling with negative feelings about yourself."

Without looking at me, he said, "Yes, I've tried counseling, but I dropped out because I couldn't afford it."

"Oh? What were you and your counselor doing together to build self-esteem?" *My choice here was to go after what he had learned more than to go after his excuse.*

"Well, he told me to talk more positively to myself."

"Uh, huh; that sounds like a good place to start. What do you say to yourself?" *I picked up on the auditory instructions. I could have asked him what the counselor had told him; but since my time was limited, I asked him the more important question. I wanted to know whether he could hear. Generally, I start with self-talk because most low self-esteem people have rich negative put-downs that need to be challenged.*

"I can say all kinds of things, but I don't believe them in my heart."

"Okay. For example, what things do you say that you do believe?" *Notice that he didn't answer my question specifically, but focused on his disbelief. I had two choices—to ask about his difficulty in believing or to repeat the question. I chose to ask him to tell me what he said to himself that he did believe.*

"Nothing, really."

"There's *really nothing positive* you say to yourself that you believe?" *I emphasized the negative as a way of checking out and challenging Andrew to consider whether he really never ever said anything positive to himself.*

"Yes."

"You believe the negative self-talk?" *I did not ask him to tell* me his negative self-depreciations because my focus was on getting to the positives. He told me he was unable to say anything positive to himself that he did believe.

"Oh, yes."

"How come?" *I chose to go after the source of his negative self-talk because it would tell me how deeply rooted his low self-esteem is.*

"Well, it's closer to what my dad says to me."

"Go on!" *A minimal auditory prompt.*

"He called me a homosexual when I was younger, and I still hear it in my mind." *Notice the trigger to negative self-esteem was an auditory external message that he continued to repeat to himself. Listen for this pattern of self-destructive internal dialogue in your counselees since it is a common phenomenon.*

"Ouch! (Pause) Are you a homosexual?" *My verbal "ouch" was intended to convey empathy before I probed. I wanted to know whether Andrew believes and acts like a homosexual.*

"I like to cook and clean, and Dad thinks that's women's work."

"And how do you see yourself?" *He hadn't really answered my question, so I pursued the question of homosexuality by asking him to describe his view of himself. Dad thinks he's a girl, but what does he think?*

"I'm attracted more to men than to women." *Notice that Andrew told me what he felt more than how he sees himself.*

"Attracted how?" *A probe.*

"Emotionally and sexually."

"So how do you live out this attraction?" *I wanted to know whether he merely fantasized and felt or whether he acted out this attraction.*

"I buy pornography, fantasize, and masturbate a lot."

"Fantasize what?" *This question was intended to discover his unmet needs, not to uncover his specific sexual behavior.*

"Men liking me and wanting me." *This answer told me he needs male approval.*

"And how does that help your self-esteem?"

"Oh, it doesn't." *His answer surprised me. I didn't expect it.*

"Then here is one answer to your question on how to build self-esteem." *I could have explored my question about self-esteem, but chose to get to his first question since this was a one-time conversation.*

"What's that?"

"To stop buying pornography, fantasizing, and masturbating." *If this interview were the first of several rather than a one and only, I would have pushed my self-esteem question. I wanted to teach him process in the hope that he would be encouraged to continue processing by returning to his counselor.*

"Yeah, I know!" *It is common for clients to know what to do to solve their problems. Frequently they don't know how to stop, are unable to stop, or gain pleasure from their conflicting behavior that outweighs the pain of continuing.*

"So are you willing to take the step of not buying, fantasizing, and masturbating?" *Here I was checking out his motivation. I did not know at this point whether he had the internal resources to carry out the plan.*

"I guess so."

"You sound hesitant." *My guess was right. He lacks the motivation. Does he lack hope?*

"Well, I tried that but it doesn't help." *He has motivation, but he is feeling discouraged.*

"Help what?" *I wanted to know what his goal or desired state was before I helped him develop hope. I needed to know whether his goal was positive, specific, and self-initiated.*

"My desire to be accepted and affirmed by a man."

"Would any man's acceptance and affirmation be enough to make you feel good about yourself?" *Now I was asking about resources. My thinking was that an experience of acceptance with me could be a resource that would motivate him to seek out other healthy relationships with men rather than to use fantasy and masturbation.*

"It would help. It has helped. When I was a short-term missionary in _____, Mr. _____ kind of discipled me and spent a lot of time with me. He told me I wasn't gay, but was just confused as to who I am and should stop believing that I was gay. I stopped fantasizing and masturbating almost immediately; but since coming back to seminary, I've started all over again."

"Yes, what does that tell you?" *Rather than tell him the meaning of his behavior, I asked him to do the interpreting. If he can, I have another resource to help him reach his goal.*

"That I'm lonely and need to be close to people."

"Okay, what stops you from being close here?" *So he has had a healthy male relationship, but something is getting in the way of establishing it now.*

"I'm scared they'll reject me. I've gained the one hundred pounds that I lost when I was discipled by my missionary friend."

"So your fear of rejection stops you from reaching out?" *Empathic.*

"Uh, huh."

"Can you see the consequences of acting on your fear?" *My question here was an attempt to help him see that the consequences of withdrawing are more negative than those of reaching out.*

"Yes, I'm lonely and I fall into sin."

"What does that tell you?" *Pushing him gently.*

"I'd better reach out."

"Is there anything you need besides this recognition in order to reach out?" *I was exploring what other resources he needs to move forward.*

"Not that I can think of now." *I didn't really believe this, so in my next question I gently confronted his unrecognized courage to reach out.*

"I'm puzzled by something. You say you're scared to reach out, yet you came to me. What made that possible?"

"Well, I heard you were a counselor; so I knew you wouldn't reject me. And you're not going to be here long, so I had nothing to lose."

"Are you telling me that it is easy for you to reach out to me because I'm not going to be on campus more than a few days?

How different does it feel if I reject you when I'm leaving or reject you as a more permanent resident?" *I wanted to build on his question* "What do I have to lose?" *and motivate him to seek out other men on campus.*

"Well, when you put it that way, it doesn't sound so different."

"Andrew, we are not really done talking; but I am scheduled to teach in a few minutes. Let me take you back to your question about how you can build self-esteem. I want to show you the steps you can take based on what you have told me so far. Since I am on campus tomorrow, can I see you before your first class to follow up on what I am going to tell you now?" When he agreed, I outlined the following steps in building self-esteem, writing them on a napkin for Andrew to take with him.

1. Stop buying pornography, fantasizing, and masturbating.
2. Go home and throw out all pornographic material.
3. Reach out to other males by telling yourself what positives occurred in your relationship with the missionary and me and what the negative consequences are if you don't reach out.
4. Remember what your spiritual missionary friend said: you are not gay! Tell yourself, "I am not gay," at least three times a day.
5. Put that message positively. "I am a lovable, valuable, capable creation of God. He made me a male. I am a male."
6. Get back into counseling with a male counselor for support and further processing of your identity.
7. Since you are living at home, you will need to find a way to deal with the negative messages you hear from Dad. With counseling you will begin to learn how to tell Dad what you need from him. Even if he is able to give you love and acceptance, you will need to learn how to get affirmation from other males and how to be your own nurturing father.

Take a moment to identify Andrew's sensory cycle in this counseling session. In his sensory sequence, what sensory modality came first, second, third, and fourth: auditory → visual → kinesthetic → behavioral?

In less than thirty minutes Andrew and I identified the positive sensory strategy he needs if he is to become the person he wants to be—a whole, righteous, living servant of God. Andrew's sensory cycle begins with remembering what his father said to him (auditory remembered) and repeating to himself this negative message (auditory internal dialogue). This message results in feelings of rejection (kinesthetic), which he compensates for by homosexual fantasies (visual imagination) that lead to masturbating and overeating (behavior). What is missing at this point in Andrew's life is a supporting, challenging, therapeutic relationship to help facilitate his growing and changing.

In a follow-up conversation, Andrew told me he wanted to change himself. "Of course," I said, "and only *you* can do it. But you can't grow alone. Spiritual and emotional growth take place in relationship with others. This is why Jesus created the family and the church."

"Oh, I never thought of it that way."

"So if you can think of growing as naturally and normally occurring in a relationship, will you call your therapist to continue treatment?"

"Yes, but I have trouble getting to his office."

"So what do you need, to be able to get to his office?" *Is this a real problem or is it resistance? I decided to check it out by asking a resource question.* "Oh, I guess I can find a way. Maybe I'm not convinced it will work." *He told me it is resistance.*

"Are you telling me that you're afraid you'll put time, effort, and money into counseling, but you'll still be feeling negative toward yourself and won't change your behavior?" *My statement went beyond empathy. I suggested what he was not able to put into words.*

"Sort of. Maybe I don't want to change."

"Are you saying there are some benefits to fatness, loneliness, and masturbating that you don't want to lose?" *I again put into words what I assumed he was feeling. I could have asked him, "What do you mean when you say maybe you don't want to change?"*

"Well, when you put it that way, no." *As I reflected on his unspoken words and feelings, he had a chance to respond differently.*

"How would you put it so changing is positive?"

"Do you really believe I can be acceptable?" *His question suggested that he needed my belief as a resource to believe he can change.*

"What is your experience with me?" *I was asking whether he had evidence other than what I had said to him.*

"You accept me."

"And your experience of your missionary friend?" *On reflection, it would have been helpful for me to ask, "How do you know I accept you?" Andrew needed to discover how he knows what he knows.*

"He accepts me." *"How do you know?" is also a helpful therapeutic question here.*

"And your therapist?"

"He accepts me."

"And God?" *My intent was to take Andrew through all possible positive relationships in order to build an acceptance foundation for him to change his self-esteem.*

"I'm not so sure! Well, I know in my head God accepts me, but I'm not so sure in my heart."

"So your struggle is to move what you know in your head to knowing it in your heart."

"Oh, yeah! How do I do that?"

"Okay, let me draw you a picture." At this point I drew the eye-scan chart printed in the previous chapter and wrote in the self-behavior and self-talk and self-pictures that Andrew needs if he is to change his self-image and immoral fantasies and behavior. Pretend you are Andrew's counselor. Draw the eye scan and write in the appropriate positions, what he needs to say to himself, how he needs to look at himself, and how he needs to act toward himself in order to change. To aid you, see the previous pages for a description of his sensory cycle. Check your drawing and affirmations with the following discussion and description of his sensory process. Also see footnote 2 for Andrew's "correct" eye scan.

Andrew, like all clients, could begin the change process anywhere in his sensory cycle. I have, however, encouraged you to begin with the modality that triggers the person's negative cycle. In Andrew's experience, it was remembering his father say he was a homosexual. He repeated this to himself. So I have three choices as a counselor: (1) Have Andrew auditorially imagine his father saying, "You are my son; I am pleased with you." Watch his eyes and make sure they are in the auditory-imagined position. That is his wish, but it is probably unrealistic to expect that his dad is willing to ever give him this message. I ask people to imagine what can realistically be achieved because an unachievable fantasy can lead to increased frustration. (2) Have him remember what his missionary friend said to him, "You are not gay, only confused about who you are." If his eyes are not in the auditory-remembered position, direct him to move his eyes. (3) Have him send the message to himself (of the three, I prefer auditory internal dialogue). Look for his eyes to be in the self-talk position. "I am a man who needs male affirmation." Or, "I am lovable, valuable and capable, even though my dad doesn't think so." Or, "I can believe in myself, because my missionary friend and counselors believe in me." Can you think of another positive, internal dialogue message?

In actual counseling sessions, you would now check out how Andrew is feeling because his self-talk messages directly influence his feelings, then fantasies, and then behavior. If he was feeling accepted (safe, happy, excited and not scared, angry, or sad) then you would know the auditory intervention works for him. Positive change usually requires counselee responses in all four sensory modalities. In Andrew's situation then, I would experiment by leading him next to remember positive times with other males. I could have him tell himself stories about these positive experiences (self-talk). It is also possible to instruct Andrew to positively fantasize or make up in his mind what he would like to do with males. This last direction needs to be monitored so he doesn't fantasize lust experiences.

Next, I would have Andrew plan healthy activities with males. I would also ask him to think about what he would rather do than masturbate and overeat.

Then I would instruct Andrew to take himself through his sensory sequence so I can check his mastery of the process, observe how well it works for him, and help him fine-tune it so he can use this process to develop and maintain change. His eyes need to be in the right position for each message.

And lastly, I would ask Andrew to commit himself to seeing a male counselor on a weekly basis by having him use the phone in my office to call for an appointment.

When I sensed Andrew's resistance, I wondered, *What is keeping him stuck? Is it fright? Hopelessness? Unwillingness to repent? Have I, as his therapist, understood what the gains are of continuing sinful behavior and fantasies? Have I moved so fast that he's struggling with integrating these ideas in too short a time?* I had learned that he wasn't sure change was possible. Now he was shifting to the question, "How do I take what I know in my head and put it into my heart?"

In the time that remained, I gave him the formula for achieving heart change. Andrew, like us all, will practice to integrate his thoughts, emotions, and behaviors. In this model of therapy, believing is the result of three dynamics: saying is believing, seeing is believing, behaving is believing. Feeling is believing as well, but emotions are the product of what people say, see, and do. When people confuse their sense of disbelief with an emotional sensation, they often assume they need to feel different in order to establish the desired belief.

The above illustration gives the person specific behaviors, self-statements, and self-image visualizations that are unique to his own life struggle. The next paragraphs contain a discussion of generic approaches that are useful in any counseling situation. Suggested as illustrations, they should be selected by the counselor to match the individual's needs. (Ideally, counselors will use the information the person gives to frame a positive sensory strategy.)

My preference is to begin with auditory self-statements because this sensory modality is frequently the predominant modality. In Andrew's situation, however, I began with behavior and then moved to self-statements because of the addictive nature of pornography.

Counselors will similarly establish a behavioral contract with clients who are addicted to drugs and alcohol, or are involved in self-destructive behavior such as suicide or homicide. A contract to stop behavior is a starting place. Counselors will need to fill in and complete the sensory cycle for change to begin and to be maintained.

Remember, counseling is a process. Counselors may be able to lay out the positive, therapeutic sensory cycle; but it will take time and practice for the counselee to accept, implement, and experiment with the cycle before positive change occurs. The counselee will be inconsistent or reluctant and may even refuse to say, see, act, and feel. Obviously, therapy is a complicated process. Identifying the negative and positive sensory cycles is the easy part of counseling. The difficult part is working through the counselee's ambivalence, denial, rationalization, and resistance.

Summary

Chapter 4 introduced two counseling skills—identifying and using sensory predicates and identifying and using the eye scan. They developed out of a discovery that humans learn and communicate their understanding through three sensory channels: auditory, visual, kinesthetic. Chapter 5 then applied the sensory predicates and eye scan to basic counseling skills.

CHAPTER SIX

TEACHING PARENTS TO BUILD SELF-ESTEEM IN THEIR CHILDREN

JACK WAS RAISED IN AN EVIL FAMILY that abused him physically, sexually, and spiritually. Introduced into a satanic cult at age two by parents who were its high priest and priestess, he was repeatedly and ritualistically humiliated through verbal assault, physical torture, and rape. Often forced to drink animal and human blood laced with drugs, Jack participated in animal and human sacrifices until his late teens. After being in therapy for several years as an adult, he brought me a gift to express his appreciation for my sticking with him in spite of what I was learning about the horrible things he had done. A personalized cartoon plaque, it shows my office with signs claiming that I use a no-pain process of therapy and do head shrinking, I.Q. overhauling, and ego inflating.

Laughingly he said, "You do not use a no-pain process, you have not overhauled my I.Q., nor have you shrunk my head; but you have inflated my ego. I now believe that I am lovable, valuable, capable, and forgivable. You have taught me that I am not bad or evil even though I have done bad and evil deeds. You have taught me that I am not crazy even though I feel confused and crazy about my life. You have taught me that I am not stupid even though I feel stupid, that I am okay even though I was not able to escape from the cult sooner."

People with less dramatic histories also enter counseling convinced that they are silly, stupid, crazy, or evil. They express their beliefs by feeling inferior, insecure, inadequate, and insignificant. Many people camouflage these human feelings through overachievement, bravado, or arrogance. Others, unable to hide self-doubt and hatred, behave with shyness, self-depreciation, procrastination, and giving up. Not surprisingly, then, *most clients, regardless of the nature of the problem for which they seek counseling, struggle with self-esteem.*[1]

This struggle often has its roots in both current and historical relationships. A spouse, friend, employer, or pastor may, wittingly or unwittingly, contribute to a person's low self-esteem. Parents are usually the most significant source of self-esteem. Their attitudes, behavior, and words toward their children are as powerful today as when they were first expressed. Adult clients report that they still hear their parents' comments, actually repeat these comments to themselves, and look at themselves the way their parents looked at them. This behavior continues to reinforce the negative self-esteem and self-perception they learned in their childhood.

The greatest gift parents can give their children, therefore, is the repeated affirmation that they are lovable, valuable, capable, and forgivable persons by the way they treat them, talk to and about them, and feel toward them.

Children's self-esteem determines their response to life, whom they choose as friends and spouses, their performance in school and work. It points the way in their career choices, how they treat their own spouses and children, and how they respond to God's offer of love and forgiveness. Accepting this truth may cause parents to be frightened and overwhelmed by their truly difficult Christian task of bringing up their children in the "nurture and admonition of the Lord" (Eph. 6:4 KJV). On the other hand, parents do not have to be alone in this job.[2] This is where the church, Sunday school, Christian counseling and seminars, literature, and parent-support groups can help. This chapter describes the positive steps parents can take to build self-esteem in their children.

WORDS HURT AS MUCH AS STICKS AND STONES

Because I am both seminary professor and counselor, I am often invited to speak at Sunday school classes, retreats, and parent meetings. When I talk to parents on building self-esteem in their children, I begin with a balloon exercise to demonstrate the inflating and deflating power of what we say. As I stand alongside the lectern so that parents can see the deflated balloon in my hand, I say in a warm and caring voice, "I am glad you are here." I then blow into the balloon, slightly inflating it. Continuing, I say, "I like what you are wearing," and then pause to inflate the balloon more. I repeat this process with such affirmations as "I value your opinion. . . . I want to have lunch with you. . . . I need your help. . . . What do you think of my idea?" while inflating the balloon slightly each time. Then, changing the tone of my voice to cold and harsh, I make depreciating comments, such as, "You are sitting in my place. . . . That is the stupidest idea I have ever heard. . . . You should not feel that way. . . . I cannot believe you did that. . . . How many times do I have to tell you to pick up your clothes? When will you learn? You are just like your father . . . ," each time letting a little air out of the balloon until it is completely deflated.

Their laughter and elbow nudging during the demonstration communicate to me that they not only understand what I am saying and showing, but also identify with it because they have been both victims and victimizers in real life. I conclude the exercise by repeating, "The greatest gift we can give our children is the affirmation that they are lovable, valuable, capable, and forgivable."

CHILDREN MIRROR PARENTS' ESTEEM

"Our children's self-esteem is a reflection of our esteem toward ourselves, our spouses, and our children" is the next point I make to parents. On an overhead projector I put a chart which shows the relationship between our parents' esteem for us and our esteem of others. Notice in the following example that I have put peers, God, grandparents, and other significant people like uncles and aunts, brothers and sisters, and pastors on the same influence level as parents. In reality, although parents' esteem is the earliest and predominant influence, other significant people in children's lives can have an equally great impact on them. As children get older, they are apt to take their esteem from peers and teachers. Whatever parental esteem children receive provides a resource for them to accept esteem from others while protecting them from the negative assaults that children inevitably get from peers.

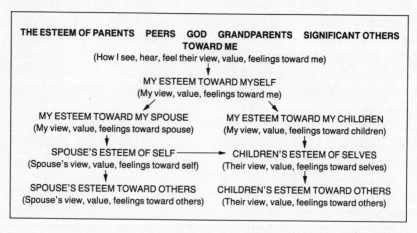

THE ESTEEM OF PARENTS   PEERS   GOD   GRANDPARENTS   SIGNIFICANT OTHERS
TOWARD ME
(How I see, hear, feel their view, value, feelings toward me)

MY ESTEEM TOWARD MYSELF
(My view, value, feelings toward me)

MY ESTEEM TOWARD MY SPOUSE   MY ESTEEM TOWARD MY CHILDREN
(My view, value, feelings toward spouse)   (My view, value, feelings toward children)

SPOUSE'S ESTEEM OF SELF ————▶ CHILDREN'S ESTEEM OF SELVES
(Spouse's view, value, feelings toward self)   (Their view, value, feelings toward selves)

SPOUSE'S ESTEEM TOWARD OTHERS   CHILDREN'S ESTEEM TOWARD OTHERS
(Spouse's view, value, feelings toward others)   (Their view, value, feelings toward others)

Be aware that parents must improve their own self-esteem before they can hope to build self-esteem in their children.[3] In other words, to help their children effectively, they must first give themselves the great gift of self-esteem. (Material in chapters 3, 4, 5, 7, and 8 facilitates this process.)

Parents of children with low self-esteem often need to be in therapy or counseling to learn how to challenge the negative messages they pass on from their own childhood. When parents bring children in for psychological treatment, therapists often explore the parents' esteem level and nurturing behaviors because parents are the most powerful and influential people in children's lives. Their feelings toward themselves affect their marital relationship, which, in turn, influences their treatment of their children. Helping parents build their own esteem will encourage a positive outcome in marriage, family, or child counseling.

A Counseling Illustration

How people's esteem toward themselves affects their esteem of their spouse and children is illustrated by Scott, a person in full-time parachurch ministry. All his energy and most of his time were being invested in ministry because his self-esteem came primarily from working spiritually with people. He condemned his wife as materialistic and selfish whenever she requested time with him or presented him with her "honey-do" list. When Laura felt angry with Scott, but could not express her feelings because "anger is not Christian," she became depressed or complained to Scott about the behavior of their adopted son. Scott, in turn, criticized her for not being loving and forgiving. His response resulted in more depression and repeated depreciations of the child. After tension in the home had become unbearable for both of them, they came to me for counseling for their child, whom they had identified as the problem. (Blaming a child for individual and marital problems is common. In this case, the blaming was partially legitimate because the son had an attention-deficit disorder and did provoke his sisters incessantly.) As I explored their experience, Scott and Laura told me that they had seen several other professionals, but had decided not to continue treatment either because the counselors were not Christians or because they disagreed with the professionals' suggestions.

After completing the diagnostic interviews, I told them I would like to share some observations that they might find both interesting and uncomfortable. Agreeing that their child did have problems with attention and impulse control, I advised them to treat his condition both medically and psychologically, referring them to a doctor who would evaluate medical treatment and to a school where their son could be tested for a learning disability. Then I focused on the nature of the tension in the home, repeating what I understood they were telling me.

I began with the husband, recognizing how important his ministry is to him and how frustrating it must be for him to come home and listen to his wife's complaints about his absence, their lack of money, or the behavior of their adopted son. I wondered if sometimes he might not even think it better to stay away, ministering to people, than to come home. Notice that I began with his experience, merely describing what he was probably feeling and needing without any evaluation of the rightness or wrongness of his perception, feeling, or response. This empathic expression is called "clarifying the person's side."

After Scott had acknowledged that I was understanding him correctly, I then expressed to Laura what I sensed was her experience. I wondered if being isolated all day without a car and realizing she did not have enough money to make the home look the way she wanted were contributing causes of her feeling lonely and hopeless. I also raised the question of whether her husband made her feel needed, or understood her frustrations and requests when he would sermonize to her that she should be more spiritual. She acknowledged that I had heard correctly what she was experiencing. I then drew a variation of the previous chart (page 130), noting how Scott and Laura were trying to build individual self-esteem—the husband through his ministry and sacrificial living, the wife through a relationship with her husband and making the house reflect her creativity and personality. The husband was asking the wife to be happy with the way things were and to stop acting "spiritually immature." The wife was asking the husband to respond positively to her feelings and needs, to take her seriously and not criticize her, to be in a relationship with her and not abandon her to a life that was making her feel lonely, uncared for, imprisoned, and hopeless.

I suggested that one aspect of the problem with their son was that his self-esteem was being attacked by two sisters who had picked up their mother's frustration and impatience. Maybe their children were feeling that neither parent had much left over to give them, I said. Scott and Laura seemed to find that an interesting and acceptable possibility.

I also wondered whether the daughters' attitudes toward their brother were a reflection of the mother's feelings toward the boy, which in turn reflected her feelings toward herself and her husband's treatment. Laura picked up on this observation by crying and saying, "Boy, are you hitting the nail on the head!"

Scott responded in bewilderment, "Are you saying that our son is acting out because I am putting his mother down?"

I answered, "Well, you have said it more bluntly than I would have; but you got the idea. When you feel that your ministry is threatened by your wife's demands for time and money, you get scared that your source of self-esteem will be lost; and you respond to your wife in a way that makes her feel uncared for and unloved. When she cannot get to you, she takes out her frustration on herself for not being more spiritual as well as on your son. You are the most important person in helping your wife and son be more Christlike. As you affirm her, she can affirm your son; and, in turn, your daughters will respond in kind. But you must find a way to keep your own esteem or you will not be able to affirm them."

Describing this process to counselees is not all there is to counseling. Helping each spouse deal with his or her own esteem issues takes time and positive practice. What happened in this session is merely the identification of the process of what is going wrong and what needs to be corrected. Knowing the process and seeing what needs to be done is the counselor's responsibility; and he or she cannot pass this information on to the counselees without becoming more aware of what the counselees are saying, thinking, feeling, and doing than they themselves are. Helping the counselees hear and accept the description without feeling condemned and judged is a refinable skill that makes it possible for them to continue therapy with minimal resistance.

SEVEN WAYS TO BUILD SELF-ESTEEM IN CHILDREN

Building self-esteem in families requires that parents understand how to speak to their children. Consider the following sentences:

If no one said, "I love you," we would doubt our lovableness!

If no one said, "I am glad you were born into our family," we would doubt our belonging!

If no one said, "I can see that you have done a good job," we would doubt our capability!

If no one said, "I need you," we would doubt our value!

If no one said, "It is okay to feel," we would doubt our humanness!

If no one said, "I forgive you," we would doubt our okayness!

If no one said, "Hello," we would doubt our existence!

If no one said, "It is okay to think," we would doubt our independence!

If no one said, "God loves you," we would doubt our eternal significance!

These dimensions to self-esteem can be developed by this formula: S.E. = E.I. − R.S. That is, Self-Esteem equals Ego Ideal minus Real Self. Our self-esteem is the result of comparing who we really are with who we wish ourselves to be. If we are growing toward our Ego Ideal without condemning ourselves for not being perfect or achieving the ideal, then we will have positive esteem. Our esteem, then, is a reflection of how well we accept the distance between our ideal selves and our real selves.

Most people find it helpful to distinguish between low self-esteem, pride, and healthy self-esteem. This is particularly true of Christians who hear divergent and negative teaching on the topic of self-esteem. The Types of Self-Esteem table on page 25 communicates this difference clearly. Notice that an accurate and realistic evaluation of oneself is the basis for evaluating the self as equal to others, not as superior or inferior. This is the message of both 1 Corinthians 12 and Romans 12, which discuss gifts from the Holy Spirit to believers. Those gifts may differ in kind, but are equally valuable to the church.

"I Love You"

The process of building self-esteem in a family begins with encouraging parents to tell and show all its members that they are loved. Children must hear and see that they are loved if they are to feel loved. Counselees frequently report that they cannot remember being told by their parents, "I love you." Families may be verbally unexpressive because Mom and Dad were raised in nonverbal families. The absence of verbal affirmation may be a sign of parental feelings toward children who are unplanned and unwanted; it may also be a sign of tension in the marriage or of a severe personal emotional pathology.

Whatever the reason, not being told "I love you" does not eliminate the need to be told. I have instructed nonverbal parents to tell their kids that, although they do not feel comfortable saying, "I love you," they will say it anyway, both because they mean it and because they want their children to hear that they are lovable. Children respond well as parents try to express love. They already know their parents are feeling and acting awkward. But when parents verbalize their feelings honestly, the message becomes congruent. How they talk, their tone of voice, facial expression, hand gestures, or body posture do make a difference in how children interpret the parents' message, "I love you." When parents feel loving, the words have positive meaning. If parents are not feeling love, children will not believe the message.

Furthermore, words without actions are shallow and hollow. Unless what parents say is accompanied by action, children will not believe the words. Parents must keep promises, show affection, and administer consistent discipline.

One way to express "I love you" is through nonsexual touch—a hand on the shoulder or elbow, a tap on the hand, or a hug. Families who are not physically expressive often feel uncomfortable when I suggest to parents that they hug their children daily. Virginia Satir, well-known family therapist, claims in her public seminars that humans need four hugs a day for survival, eight hugs a day for maintenance, and twelve hugs a day for growth. By verbally acknowledging their awkwardness in hugging, parents will interpret for the child their positive intent.

Parents also can show and tell their children that they love them through positive attitudes. Respect for their child's person, problems, perspectives, feelings, needs, beliefs, and privacy can be expressed through words and deeds. Allowing each child to be his or her unique self, not forcing him or her to be like brothers and sisters or other relatives or friends, sends an affirming message to the child.

Sometimes children accuse parents of being nonloving as a way of forcing them into making a decision the child wants, but which the parents consider to be dangerous or unacceptable. Parents may find this attempted manipulation difficult to handle because they want to be loved by their children. They fear saying no will rob them of their child's love. Little can hurt parents more than when a child says, "I hate you." Yet all parents experience their children's anger, whether parental restrictions are fair or not.

When parents hear their child say, "You don't love me," they may be tempted to either prove how much they love the child, or punish the child for being ungrateful. Thankfully, when the child becomes an adult and has children of his own, he then understands. Erma Bombeck expresses this parental sentiment in a series of statements beginning with "I loved you enough to . . . ." She writes, "I loved you enough to bug you about where you were going, with whom, and what time you would get home. I loved you enough to make you return a Milky Way with a bite out of it to a drug store and confess, 'I stole this.'"[4]

Most parents can supply their own list of "I loved you enough to . . ." statements. "I loved you enough to make you make your bed . . . clean up your room . . . brush your teeth . . . go to Sunday school . . . take out the garbage . . . save 10 percent of your allowance . . . admit I was wrong . . . ask you for forgiveness . . . allow you to be yourself more than what I wanted you to become."

"You Belong to This Family"

Telling and showing family members that they belong is the second of seven ways to build family self-esteem. Saying "I am glad you are a member of this family" makes the belonging point to children. Parents who share themselves with their children, and who share their ideas, feelings, hopes, wishes, frustrations, failures, and successes, communicate to children that they are a vital part of the parents' lives.

Because children ages five to nine commonly wonder whether they were adopted and whether Mom and Dad really are their parents, that is an important time for parental sensitivity. Birth certificates can be framed and hung on the children's bedroom walls, for example, showing that they really have their parents' name and are members of the family. In my family of origin, birth certificates were stored in the piano bench where we all could look at them. One day, when one of my brothers could not find his birth certificate, he decided it was missing because he had been adopted. He was relieved to learn that Mom had placed the certificate in the desk after using it for school registration.

Creating a family history and identity is another way to develop a sense of belonging. Pictures of grandparents, of parents as children, and of the parents' wedding and life before the children were born are wonderful ways to show that children have a history. Stories about relatives, how they came to America, where they came from in the old country, and family treasures and heirlooms testify to the reality of their history. While typing this chapter, I am listening to the ticking and chimes of my grandparents' clock, one of their wedding gifts. As a child visiting their home, I was intrigued with its character, charm, and chimes. In one of my bold childhood requests I asked my grandmother whether I could have that clock when she died. Several years later, when my grandparents' estate was being divided, the clock was delivered to me.

A genealogy of my family that my dad's cousin researched is

housed in my library. A quilt my wife's grandmother made is hanging in our bedroom on a wooden quilt rack made by her father. Children love to hear stories of what life was like while their parents and grandparents were growing up, when those stories are not used to rationalize why parents are making them do something. With video equipment readily available, tapes of family events are family historical treasures that future generations can see and hear. Instituting or creating family traditions is another way to create a family history. To my children I brought the tradition of waking them on their birthdays by singing to them, carrying a birthday cake with lighted candles, and serving a special breakfast.

Showing and telling children that they belong to their family is also accomplished by giving each child space, a place to call one's own. This need not be a separate bedroom; it can be a closet, or a drawer, or a box, or just time to themselves.

Ownership is another crucial dimension to belonging. To be able to call toys, clothes items, or books *theirs* demonstrates respect while affirming that something belongs to them. Privacy, secrets, and opinions are other aspects of belonging. "You belong" is the message sent when children sense they are wanted and cared for as much as the other family members.

Asking children to participate in the planning of vacations, in the purchasing of family items, and in giving opinions and telling their feelings on decisions that affect them also sends the "you belong" message. Making sure that each child has responsibilities to carry out for the family signals *belonging*. Parents need to send messages to their children that say, "You have lifetime membership in this family."

Robert Frost wrote, "'Home is the place where, when you have to go there, they have to take you in.'" Many of our counselees who do not have this *carte blanche* invitation to their families will need to create a place for themselves and their children if they are to develop a sense of belonging. This place is often the church or Bible-study group.

"You Are Capable"

Showing and telling each family member that he or she is capable is a third way to build self-esteem. Affirming this capability is positively powerful when parents believe what they are saying. I remind parents of the joyful encouragement they gave as their children were learning to smile, roll over, crawl, walk, and talk. Human need for encouragement continues throughout the life cycle. It is crucial in competitive American society for parents to affirm that it is okay for children to do their best even if they do not achieve Number One status.

Only one is president of an organization, only one receives a trophy for first place. Yet all human beings are capable. Parents demonstrate how to handle being average or finishing tenth or one thousandth by the way they live out their successes and failures. I tell my clients that the world belongs to the average person. For example, when my son entered college to study architecture, professors told him that A students would work for the B students, and B students would work for the C students. Most humans are C students, but that fact surprises parents. Being average needs to be defined as a reality, not as a disease. The student who wrote "The Average Child" expresses the discouragement of finding out he is average:

> I don't cause teachers trouble,
> my grades have been okay.
> I listen in my classes, and
> I'm in school every day.
>
> My teachers think I'm average;
> my parents think so too.
> I wish I didn't know that, 'cause
> there is lots I'd like to do.
>
> I'd like to build a rocket;
> I have a book that tells you how,
> or start a stamp collection;
> well, no use in trying now.
>
> 'Cause since I found I'm average
> I'm just smart enough, you see,
> to know there is nothing special
> that I should expect of me.

139

I'm part of that majority,
that hump part of the bell
who spends his life unnoticed
in an average kind of hell.

That children can be their best without being Number One is a truth parents need to affirm. I tell my children that I have never been Number One at anything. I was not even their mother's first choice!

One of my clients wears a belt buckle with this message: "The greatest accomplishment in life is not to not fall, but to pick yourself up after you fall and try again." Encouraging children to try again or to try differently is a parental gift of immeasurable worth. Helping children explore and experiment with their capabilities, to fail, to stop, to start something new, develops in children a sense that they are capable and do not have to be perfect at everything they attempt.

"I Believe in You"

This parental attitude which helps children believe in themselves, creating trust needed to become self-confident, is the fourth way parents build self-esteem in their children. Believing in their children's potential, saying, "I trust you, I believe in your ability to decide, I trust in your sense of what is right and good for you," fosters self-confidence. It is natural for parents to question their children's decisions or attempts. I tell those whom I counsel to express concern without shaming, humiliating, or hurting their children. That is a crucial relational skill that fosters parental influence and the children's own growth. Parents need to learn how to express their fear without becoming angry and depreciating. Counselors can teach parents to do this by helping them become aware of their feelings and assisting them in the practice of expressing their feelings constructively.

"I Take Your Feelings and Needs Seriously"

Children learn they are valuable, the fifth way to build self-esteem, when parents nurture, protect, and respond to their needs, take their feelings seriously, and discipline them with love and understanding rather than with rage and depreciation. Providing children with security as a way of protecting them, can be accomplished by teaching, among other things, the following:

- their home address
- how to use the telephone
- whom to contact when parents are not accessible
- how to call the police and fire department
- how to answer the phone and door when at home alone
- how to deal with strangers
- how to lock up the house after entering and leaving
- how to handle sexual approaches
- how to administer basic first aid
- how to use appliances.

When parents demonstrate protection by the way they drive, the way they cross the street, and how they use fire and dangerous tools, they convey to children the message, "You are valuable." Taking time to listen and respond to children empathically sends the message, "You are valuable."

Counselees often claim that their parents seldom took time to listen to them or took seriously what they said. But parents can learn the skill of listening to children's needs and feelings. Counselors may need to identify those needs and feelings for the parents. A short list I use is Maslow's hierarchy of needs: physical needs for food, water, shelter, rest, activity; security needs for physical safety and emotional security; needs for love and belonging; needs for self-esteem; and needs to self-actualize.[5] Parental willingness to take needs seriously is evidence that they esteem their children. The more children are valued, the more they will express their needs appropriately, constructively, and nonmanipulatively, and the more they will be able to respond to the needs of their parents.

Responding to children's feelings positively may require parents to learn first that feelings are legitimate, not wrong or immature. Feelings are merely the emotional experience of the person at a given moment in time. Parents who discount children's feelings by such statements as, "You shouldn't feel that way. Jesus doesn't like children who are angry!" teach children to depreciate themselves and to hide their feelings from themselves and others.

Unwittingly, they also teach the children to discount the parents' feelings. The more parents know and care about their children's feelings, the more children will respect, value, and respond positively to the parents' feelings. A child whose feelings are respected and encouraged is able to say, as did one of my clients' children, "Are you having a sad day, Mommy?" The mother was surprisingly comforted and encouraged by her young child's sensitivity.

Learning labels for feelings may also help parents respond effectively to their children. Six primary feeling words, represented by the acronym SASHET, should be sufficient for them to begin listening for feelings: scared, angry, sad, happy, excited, tender (see chapter 8 for the Feeling Recognition Exercise). Counselors and counselees can use their own words to express these six feelings as long as they are aware of them, accept them as important, and learn how to express them constructively.

Discipline and conflict management is another way parents can show children they are valuable. Teaching children how to act in various situations says, "You are valuable enough to me to teach you how to be respectful to others, how to respect yourself, how not to embarrass yourself, and how to deal with disagreements and problems." Parents tell children they are valuable when they let children know they are more important than whatever problem exists. When parents are unaware of what they are feeling or needing, frustration can build up to the point where they will say depreciating and hurtful things to their children. When I am shopping and hear parents yell something like, "Do that one more time and I'll kill you," or watch them beat a child who is obviously tired from being dragged around longer than he is able to tolerate, I feel sad and angry and think about offering my business card so these parents can call for an appointment.

"You Are Free to Be You"

Giving children independence by letting them make choices and take responsibility for themselves and for others, is the sixth way parents teach their children esteem. No child likes to be controlled all the time, although some parental decisions do provide a sense of safety and security. To develop into a person requires independence, freedom from having to choose what others choose or decide what others decide, freedom to have preferences and favorites. Independence results when parents give children more freedom as they mature. Choices available to a preschooler are qualitatively different from choices available to preteens and teenagers.

Including children in the decision-making process has cumulative benefits. Young children may be given a choice between eating carrots and peas, but eating a vegetable is not negotiable. As children mature, the choices may mature, from selecting the color of clothes to choosing their style—to shopping without parents. Some freedom to spend part of their allowances the way they wish is balanced by a previously agreed-upon amount that the child will save and give to church. This means that parents will need to allow children to make "foolish" purchases with the discretionary part of their allowances. Parents do not forfeit their right to discuss the child's decision with him or her, but they do forfeit their right to stop the purchase unless it conflicts with the family's values or is harmful to the child. Children need to learn that they are responsible for their decisions and will have to live with the consequences. If children spend all their allowance and then want to do something or buy something else, parents must gently but firmly say no to the children's request for advances on their allowance.

"Follow Me As I Follow God"

Telling and showing children that they have eternal significance is the seventh way parents build self-esteem in their children. Parents living out their spirituality as a relational lifestyle, not merely as a code of ethics or rules and regulations, models true, Christian spirituality for the child. Demonstrating a thankful attitude for God's daily provision of the material—food, clothing, shelter, health, safety—and of the spiritual—love, grace, mercy, forgiveness—shows a humble spirit that recognizes God, not the parents, as the source of all life's blessings. Reading Bible stories and inviting children to believe and trust in God are Christian-parent commitments.

Parents will need to be sensitive to their children's interest level in spiritual matters. Forcing Christianity on children is seldom effective. Participating in Sunday school and youth activities is not negotiable for children, but it may need to be negotiated with older teens in order to avoid rebellion. Any decision should result from discussion, focusing on the needs, feelings, values, and interests of both parents and children. Allowing children to make decisions about their clothes, toys, and recreation affirms their worth by accepting their need for independence. The risk for parents, however, is that they are not always pleased with their children's decisions. In response they may express anger rather than their fright when the decision is dangerous, expensive, unethical, or embarrassing. Learning to be in touch with their own feelings and needs enables parents to express their fears more than their anger and their needs more than depreciating comments. Parents who live well will show children by example and attitude that theirs is the kind of life worth emulating.

Serving others and God is part of a life of eternal significance. Children who experience their parents' servanthood will unconsciously catch the idea; hopefully they will live similar lives. While picnicking with my family when I was young, I saw my parents reach out to servicemen to share part of our Sunday lunch. One of these men was headed for the mission field after military discharge. My parents have served on his mission board from its inception to the present. The way my parents cared for their own parents, served in the church, tithed, and gave to religious groups had a positive impact on me. When asked why I wanted to go to seminary and graduate school as part of my preparation for social work, I wrote about these early-life memories that had encouraged me to be a helper.

Any instruction on building self-esteem in children should encourage parents to give their children affirmations and demonstrations that they are lovable, valuable, capable, and forgivable; that they belong to the family; that their parents believe in them and pray for them as children of God. "Children Learn What They Live," a plaque hanging in our home, reminds my wife and me how to influence the self-esteem of our children:

Children Learn What They Live

If a child lives with criticism,
   he learns to condemn.
If a child lives with hostility,
   he learns to fight.
If a child lives with ridicule,
   he learns to be shy.
If a child lives with shame,
   he learns to feel guilty.
If a child lives with tolerance,
   he learns to be patient.
If a child lives with encouragement,
   he learns confidence.
If a child lives with praise,
   he learns to appreciate.
If a child lives with fairness,
   he learns justice.
If a child lives with security,
   he learns to have faith.
If a child lives with approval,
   he learns to like himself.
If a child lives with acceptance and friendship,
   he learns to find love in the world.

           —Dorothy Law Nolte

Summary

The sensory process—telling, showing, and touching—teaches parents seven ways to build self-esteem in children. Parental self-esteem is foundational to children's learning self-esteem. Without parental affirmation, acceptance, and acknowledgment, however, the probability that children will respond to God's love is minimal.

CHAPTER SEVEN

TEACHING PEOPLE TO BE THEIR OWN NURTURING PARENTS

KAREN WAS BORN DURING THE TIME her mother and father were separated. Hurt and angry over her husband's leaving, her mother took out her feelings on Karen. To protect herself from her mother's criticism, Karen developed into a brat: a bright, articulate, sassy child. Underneath Karen's brazen facade was a lonely person who felt sad and scared. Although Father returned home, the emotional distance between her parents created little nurturing for Karen, and encouraged her to be provocative, resulting in more parental anger and rejection. Longing to be loved and valued, but frustrated in her attempts to get affirmation, Karen turned to food for comfort and isolated herself from her family to protect herself

147

from further hurt. Becoming an excellent student brought her some personal satisfaction as well as hope that her parents would now love her because of her achievements. When this strategy failed, Karen turned inward, became moody and was easily provoked.

Karen spurned marriage through fear of rejection and chose instead to sleep around. As a Christian, she knew her behavior was sinful; but the longing for love and affection overruled Christian values and commitments. By the time she entered counseling, she had begun to find one-night stands emotionally unfulfilling, was no longer able to tolerate guilt, and had become overweight and distraught. Although she wanted help, she feared criticism and rejection, wondering whether I would respond as her parents had. Instead, surprised by compassion and an understanding of her need for closeness and intimacy, Karen was disarmed.

My exploration of how she had gotten into her predicament revealed that she feared she was unlovable. To her, God was more punishing than loving, her relationship with fellow Christians was superficial, and her feelings toward herself were loathsome and hateful. As I got a clearer picture of her needs, I offered hope that she could be loved and affirmed even though her parents could not give her what she needed. First, her view of God needed to be corrected. She was expecting God to treat her as her parents had. Second, she was guarding herself so much that she wasn't giving her friends a chance to love her. Third, her treatment of herself needed to change because she was treating herself as badly as her parents had treated her.

I told her, "Your hope lies in hearing and seeing God as loving and valuing you, in learning to ask your friends for what you need, and in being your own nurturing parent." Encouraged, yet disbelieving she could be loved, Karen was willing to begin working with me to achieve those goals.

I gave her three homework assignments in the early stages of counseling: to read selected Scripture passages that affirmed the way God valued her (Psalm 139; Isaiah 49:15, 16; and 1 John 3:1–12), to ask her friends for at least four hugs a week, and to begin talking to herself the way she wished her parents had talked to her.

To help Karen understand the idea of nurturing herself as a parent, I drew the chart below, saying, "Our personalities have three parts: parent, adult and child. These are called ego states."[1]

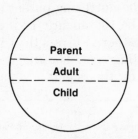

According to the theory of transactional analysis,[2] the child ego state has three parts: adapted—that part of personality which accommodates to the training, traumas, and experiences of childhood; little professor—the intuitive, creative, experimenter part of personality; natural child—the uncensored, impulsive, spontaneous part of personality that expresses both positive and negative feelings, thoughts, and behaviors.

The adult ego state is the monitoring and mediating part of personality that translates the messages of the parent and child to each other. Its values are fairness, justice, and conscientiousness. It is that part which analyzes facts and information and makes decisions. And it is the empathetic side of personality that "feels with" all the other ego states.

The parent ego state has both a critical and nurturing side.

Its positive and negative messages, recorded in the minds of receivers, play back involuntarily. The consequences of these messages are as real as if parental figures were actually talking. Creating positive parental messages, images, feelings, and actions from within the nurturing parent ego state is central to building clients' self-esteem. Likewise, to strengthen the adult ego state is to help the nurturing parent challenge the critical parent's messages. The therapeutic goal is not to destroy the critical parent, but rather to strengthen the nurturing parent and the adult mediating role. These ego states, then, become functional resources for the client.

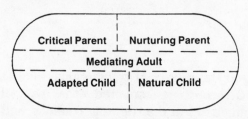

HOW TO BECOME OUR OWN NURTURING PARENTS

Where do counselors begin in the process of helping clients become their own nurturing parents? An effective intervention is to ask the question, "Have you ever taken care of other people, like child-sitting?" Most of the time I get an affirmative response. If my counselees haven't had this experience, I then develop as specifically as possible how they would treat a child, what they would say to the child, how they would look at the child, how they would feel toward the child, and what they would do with the child. (Sometimes I make a list as the client describes his or her child care, using it to develop a positive sensory sequence that can reveal how to treat himself or herself the same way.)

When counselees have completed their description of child caring, I ask a resource question: "What would make it possible for you to treat yourself the way you take care of this child?" They are often stunned by the question. It has not occurred to them that they could treat themselves as well as they treat someone else.

Part of this blindness is, of course, due to the belief that they are not worth nurturing. Clients with low self-esteem often believe, *before I can take good care of myself, I must take good care of others.* Some persons with low self-esteem are so narcissistic that they take the opposite position, *before I can take care of anyone else, I must take care of myself.* The first person is feeling like a martyr, a placater, a pleaser. The second person appears selfish. But the truth is that both are selfish. The servants only *look* altruistic; behind their good deeds is a desperate need for self-fulfillment.

When I write *selfish*, I'm reminded that people usually do whatever will bring them the greatest pleasure. The issue here is not selfishness so much as it is honesty about self-interest. From reading Scripture, Christians should know that people act out of self-interest. The fact that humans are selfish is a given—a reality of their old natures. It is the denial or rationalization of selfishness that prevents people from living unselfishly. Making one's self-interest open, honest, and conscious is a desirable choice that increases the possibility of treating others in a noncoercive, nonmanipulative, nonexploitive way. Consider the following observation:

> Selfishness is not the issue. You will always act selfishly (*i.e.*, out of self-interest) no matter how vehemently you resist or protest to the contrary, because such action is automatic. You have no choice in the matter. What you can choose is whether you will be rationally selfish or irrationally selfish. . . . If you're rationally selfish you chiefly regard your own interests, but not solely.[3]

Persons who are irrationally selfish not only focus on their own interests, but also deny or rationalize that self-interest. Counselor language labels this behavior *ingenuine, incongruent, not authentic* behavior. Christian language labels this hiding behavior *sin* or *self-righteousness*. God does not ask humans to deny their self-interest. He only asks people to admit it and to consider the interests of others. Paul writes in Philippians 2:4: "Do not merely look out for your own interests, but also for the interests of others." He then cites Jesus as an example of a person whose attitude allowed him to sacrifice himself for us. Jesus chose to become like human beings, yet did not lose his Godness. Jesus' incarnate example teaches that humans can love each other and give up privileged position without losing identity.

When people give, they remain who they really are— lovable, valuable, capable. To love means to give up the burden of selfishness. The power to give up selfishness is found in relationship with Christ. Becoming the giving, unselfish person God wants humans to be is the result of growing in God's grace; it is not simply a human possibility.

An honest expression of self-interest is a necessity if human relationships are to be trusting and growing. To encourage confession of self-interest is an invitation to enter into a mutual relationship of respecting each others' needs and feelings. And it is an invitation to help others get what they want and need without exploiting the relationship or sacrificing self, secretly hoping to get what is needed without the other person knowing or choosing to give it. As Hillel, the ancient Jewish philosopher, said, "If you are not for you, who will be? If you are only for you, what's the purpose?"

NURTURING AND SENSORY PROCESS

Persons become their own nurturing parents and counselors help them realize that goal by identifying and specifying the elements in the sensory process. The process looks like the chart below; it sounds like a compassionate, caring parent; and it feels like a parent lovingly holding the child.

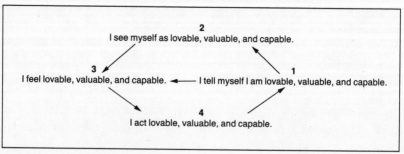

2
I see myself as lovable, valuable, and capable.

3
I feel lovable, valuable, and capable. ◄——— I tell myself I am lovable, valuable, and capable. **1**

4
I act lovable, valuable, and capable.

Nurturing the self involves changing negative self-talk to positive self-talk, creating or remembering positive pictures/images of self, acting positively toward self, and then experiencing positive feelings toward self. We could call this self-talk, self-picturing, self-behavior, and self-feeling.

Self-Talk

Scripture recognizes the power of what a person says to himself. "For as [a man] thinks within himself, so he is" (Prov. 23:7). A growing body of Christian literature also recognizes the power of positive self-talk.[4] Any statements that express self-doubt, self-hate, or self-negating must be challenged in order to develop self-esteem. These challenges will be made first by the counselor and then by the counselee. When a client says, "I am a klutz," the counselor can challenge this statement by questioning the over-generalization: "Are you saying you are always a klutz? That you never, ever act gracefully?"

"How could I be so stupid?" can be challenged by an empathic statement followed by questioning the assumption: "Now that you know what you could have done or said, you feel angry at yourself, maybe a little humiliated. Do you find it helpful to depreciate yourself?"

"How terrible of me to forget your birthday!" can be challenged by pointing out the person's need to be perfect: "You expect yourself never, ever to forget something; so when you do forget, you berate yourself. How does depreciating yourself help you deal with your guilt for not being perfect?"

Positive nurturing messages can be encouraged by asking the person to complete the following: "I wish my mom would have said to me. . . ." "I wish my dad would have told me. . . ," or any variation of the above (like granddad, grandma, uncle, aunt, brother, sister, spouse, or friends).

In addition, counselees can learn self-nurturing statements through modeling respectful affirmations. "I respect your courage in deciding to seek help. . . ." "You have shared very personal details of your life. . . ." "I appreciate your trust in our relationship."

When I visited Operation PUSH in Chicago several years

ago, I heard Jesse Jackson stir the crowd with, "I am some-body! I may be poor—but I am somebody. I may be in prison—but I am somebody! I may be uneducated—but I am somebody." I encourage clients to say, "I am somebody to God! . . . I am a sinner—but I am somebody to God! . . . I am a layman—but I am somebody to God. . . . I am a pastor of a small church—but I am somebody to God. . . . I am single—but I am somebody to God. . . . I am a blue-collar worker—but I am somebody to God. . . . I am a woman—but I am somebody to God. . . . I am adopted—but I am somebody to God. . . . I am retired—but I am somebody to God. . . . I have never been chairman of the church, a member of the church board, Sunday school superintendent, or a foreign missionary—but I am somebody to God."

Counselors can also prompt positive self-talk by suggesting positive alternatives to the people's own negative appraisals. Translate "I'm a klutz" to "While I'm sometimes awkward, on the whole I keep my balance very well." Reframe "How could I be so stupid?" to "I'm excited that I'm able to catch myself in mistakes and am willing to learn from them." Change "How terrible of me to forget your birthday" to "I care enough about my friend to feel sad when I forget something as important to him and me as his birthday."

Clients can also mimic, memorize, or read "I am . . . " self-talk statements, like the following:

I AM
    lovable, valuable, and capable.
    somebody.
    significant.
    God's child.
    adequate.
    entitled to my needs, feelings, and values.
    entitled to make mistakes.
    human.
    unique.
    like all others.
    like some others.
    like no others.
    glad I was born.

Other "I" statements include:

I matter in this world.

I make a difference in people's lives when I radiate hope, joy, and trust.

The world is a better place because I'm here.

Counselors can help people translate negative self-statements like *I should, I must, I have to, I can't* into *I want, I will, I choose, I'll give it my best try.* Destructive *shoulds* can be turned into a code of ethics, moving from guilt to responsibility, punishment to correction, and *ought* to *is.*[5]

Another approach to affirmation is from Pamela Levin, whose self-talk messages can be used as therapeutic interventions from counselor to client or as nurturing parent messages to the person's self-hating child.[6] These affirmations are in developmental order, beginning with what children need to hear at birth. The affirmations are reflections of developmental needs and are crucial for the development of self-esteem. Below is a sample of the affirmations that hurting people need to learn to give themselves, and that parents need to learn to give to their children.

In the early months of life, children need to know that they have a right to exist and that their parents are glad that they were born.

I am glad that you were born.

It is okay for you to be here.

You have a right to be fed, touched, and nurtured.

I am glad that you are you (a boy or a girl).

Welcome to our house.

I like you.

As children grow older, other messages become important to their self-esteem, such as:

You have the right to explore.

It is okay to be curious.

You can get attention without acting naughty.

It is okay for you to try things, to touch, smell, taste, listen, look.

And as children become more mobile they need to hear:

It is okay to have your own mind.
You can try things and have my support.
It is okay for you to feel what you feel and ask for what
   you need.
You can think and feel at the same time.
It is okay to imagine things; wishing does not make them
   come true.

School-age children need to sense from their parents:

You can have friends and family too.
It is okay to have your own ideas.
You can be healthy and still have needs to be taken care
   of.
Learning to do things your way is okay with me.
It is okay for you to disagree.

Teens need permission to grow into adults.

It is okay to sprout wings.
You can feel sexual without feeling guilty.
It is okay to be on your own.
You can be responsible for your own life (feelings, needs,
   values, behavior).
It is okay for you to grow and have a place among adults.
You can leave home and still have a place to come back to.
You are welcome home.

Counselors will think of other nurturing statements that directly relate to their counselees' issues. These may include support for persons who are making realistic requests and setting achievable expectations for themselves by separating their personal worth from their behavior, valuing themselves even when their behavior needs changing or correction, supporting their own power to control themselves and to make choices that determine their lives, affirming their ability to meet physical and emotional needs while being sensitive to the needs of others, and relinquishing their love of power (control, manipulation, competition) to their power of love (approving, accepting, nurturing).

Exercise 1. Take a moment to ask yourself the following: In the above list of permission messages, which ones do I wish my parents had said to me? As I read the above self-affirmations, which ones awaken feelings in me?

Exercise 2. Which messages am I giving to myself? Which messages do I need to begin giving to myself?

Exercise 3. Which messages am I giving to my spouse, children, clients, parishioners? Which ones do I need to begin giving the people I serve?

Self-Picturing

Self-image is a person's mental self-portrait. How people see themselves is a reflection of what the most "significant others" in their lives say to them and how they treat them. My parents act as a mirror to myself. What I see may be an accurate reflection of what my parents say to me—how they look, how they feel, and how they act toward me. On the other hand, this picture I have of myself may be distorted. Counselors want to take seriously the person's picture of himself or herself. Whether it is accurate or not is of little significance since the person is acting as if it were true. Self-concept, then, is an illusion. It is based on answers to three questions:

Who do I think I am?

Who do you think I am?

Who do I think you think I am?

From all of a person's life experiences, he has built an image of himself in his mind, fashioning and distorting that image to make it what he wants or fears it to be. The portrait he has painted of himself is as faithful as he can paint today. Tomorrow he may paint another image, which may be more or less beautiful than today's. The person's hope is that his mental image of himself is dynamic, living. Paul Tournier, in *The Healing of Persons*, claims that each look at the self gives the person an opportunity to create a fresh and desirable self-portrait.[7] Our self-image is learned. First, we develop a consciousness of self; then we learn a value to ourself.

What creates in me a consciousness of self is the consciousness I have of a not-self, of an external world from which firstly I distinguish myself, which next I enter in relationship. Psychologists have described this birth of self-consciousness in the infant. There is, then, a double movement, first of separation and then of relation, between self and things.[8]

Who am I? My parents show and tell me. I am male/female, I am wanted/not wanted, valued/devalued, nourished/neglected, attractive/ugly, okay/not okay. My memory of who I am in my parents' view influences me today either positively or negatively. If the influence is negative, I can challenge and create a more positive view because as an adult I have more resources than I had as a child to be my own nurturing parent.

Inasmuch as self-esteem is self-perpetuating, the therapeutic task is to help counselees form a positive mental picture. Self-esteem "has a circular effect, for it correlates already existing beliefs about self, and so tends to reinforce and maintain its own existence, i.e., each individual collects and organizes thousands of pieces of information about himself, that vary in clarity, precision and importance."[9] Counselors help persons collect and create new pieces of information that challenge or substitute the existing negative self-image. This new, positive set of images and beliefs and perspectives then reinforces and maintains a healthy and productive self-concept. Think you are or think you are not; either way you'll be right. What is true in a person's mind will be true in that person's behavior, feelings, and relationships.

A person begins to change his view of himself when his counselor views him positively, seeing the person's strengths, value, worth, abilities, and significance. This counselee can borrow the counselor's perspective and begin to see himself positively. This process is both subtle and obvious. Nonverbally, the counselor conveys respect to the helpee. He or she communicates positive regard through understanding, kind, nonjudgmental facial expressions. The counselor also expresses attitudes verbally: "It must have taken a lot of courage to call for help. . . . I'm impressed with how determined you are to put your life together. . . . I see you working hard at your marriage. . . . I get the impression I see you more positively than you see yourself. . . . I see strengths in you that you are apparently not seeing in yourself. For example, . . ."

Counselors can also help individuals change their mental pictures of themselves by exploring negative self-images and providing alternative metaphors. "I want you to describe yourself as an animal."

"I'm a turkey."

"Really? In what ways are you like a turkey?"

"I see myself as a klutz—awkward, unable to express myself very well, and not valued by others."

"I notice you haven't pointed out the beauty and pride of turkeys. When I think of turkeys I get a picture of a proud bird pictured on a Thanksgiving card. His plume is bright red and erect, his tail is fanned, and he is standing as though he were strutting his attractiveness. Would you be willing to think of yourself as a proud and beautiful bird?"

Another approach counselors can use to explore a person's self-image is to ask directly, "How do you see yourself?" If you get the impression the counselee is negative about his or her personality or physical appearance, you can ask, "What do you see when you look in a mirror?" Your response can be a challenge. "You describe yourself as having big/small ears, too long/short a nose; being fat/thin, ugly, over/underweight. Are you really saying that you would be more lovable and valuable if you were physically different?" Or, "I get the impression that the way you see yourself leaves you feeling hopeless because all the things wrong with you are not alterable. I would be depressed, too, if I believed that the way I looked determined my worth." One of my favorite ways of exploring self-image is to request: "Describe three qualities you see in yourself." Or, "Please finish this sentence positively: 'I see myself as. . . . What I like about myself is. . . .'" A further way to explore self-image is to ask, "Tell me how you would like to look." Or, "Think about and finish these sentences: 'I want to be. . . .'" Or, "My ideal self looks like. . . ."

The focus of exploring a person's self-image is to clarify the picture and develop possible positive alternative concepts. The treatment goals are to build a positive self-picture or belief, to change embarrassed or negative self-consciousness to positive self-awareness, to reinforce the individual's positive view of himself or herself, to change the person's excessive worrying about how he or she looks to others, to affirm a positive mental image so as to free the counselee to live without crippling preoccupation of self. Developing a positive self-image results in less worry about what others think; less shame, guilt, and fear; fewer negative comparisons to others; more honesty about what a person wants; and less pleasing of others at unwanted personal expense.

Self-Behavior

How we treat ourselves is a response to how we picture and talk to ourselves. Either our behavior matches our self-image and self-talk, or we are living lives of incongruity. Persons who appear to be taking good care of themselves may be accurately reflecting their positive pictures and thoughts. On the other hand, people can seem to be taking good care of themselves, but may be indulging themselves in order to feel and look positive. Either way, their behavior reflects the negative or positive self-view and self-talk and self-feelings.

One task of counselors is to affirm a person's positive behavior and at the same time reinforce that the person is more than his or her behavior.

> Being is more fundamental than doing, quality is more fundamental than activity, that the reality of what a man does is determined by what he is.[10]

By focusing on the person's inner qualities more than on behavior, the counselor de-emphasizes performance as the basis for building self-esteem. Integrity is a reflection of a person living out positive personal qualities while acknowledging and challenging negative qualities within oneself. Helping counselees accept a discrepancy between their behavior and their self-image is a goal of counseling. The counseling intervention may also take the form of challenging behavior or talk that reinforces the negative sensory cycle.

Exploring how a person behaves toward himself or herself can be accomplished by simply asking, "How do you treat yourself? . . . How do you take care of yourself? . . . What have you done for yourself this week? . . . Tell me how you treat yourself as well as you treat your spouse, family, children, friends, or neighbors?"

Consider this: "Well, how do you treat yourself? What is the transaction like? Does it resemble writing a letter, or is it more like sending a bill? It may be more like passing a law or, on occasion, sentencing a prisoner."[11] Low self-esteem clients, notorious for unfriendly treatment of themselves, wonder why they feel angry and depressed. If they learn to send themselves a letter rather than a bill, they will eventually begin to feel positive. If, instead of passing laws or sentencing themselves, they act graciously and forgiving, their esteem will increase.

Counselors can encourage individuals to treat themselves at least as well as they treat other people. This will be a new message to many of them. They have been taught, "Do to others what you would have them do to you" (Matt. 7:12 NIV).

They also need to be taught to do unto themselves as they do unto others. Of course, this assumes the person is acting positively toward others. The sad reality is that many people who talk and view themselves negatively will treat others the same way. So it is imperative that counselors get a complete, accurate picture of how clients relate, because people will do unto others as they do unto themselves.[12]

In healthy development, children learn to take care of themselves before they begin to think of other people. "It is our natural progression to think of ourselves and then to go past ourselves and think about others."[13] This natural progression depends on how totally our caretakers are "for us," how sensitive they are to our vulnerability and fragility, and how receptive we are to their influence. When we are loved and cared for, we develop both self-love and love for others. However, "When . . . these outside influences are antithetical to what and whom a growing person actually is . . . the very vulnerable, fragile and highly receptive child develops self-hate for himself" and frequently develops hatred for others as well.[14]

Persons with healthy self-esteem, therefore, find it relatively easy to treat themselves and others well. Low self-esteem persons, on the other hand, either treat others better than themselves, often at their own expense, or treat others worse than themselves.

Maybe a theological parenthesis is needed here. We are all born sinners and as such have a tendency to be selfish. But other influences (parents, grandparents, siblings, peers—in addition to human depravity) affect our treatment of ourselves and others. That is, how other people treat us influences how we treat ourselves. These psychological influences are relative and do not have the absolute impact that our sinfulness does. As a sinner I have no power to control or modify my being or behavior, but am totally dependent on God's grace for my salvation.

When it comes to how I respond to the way I was treated as an infant, however, I have more choices as well as more resources. I may respond to mistreatment and inadequate nurturing by becoming a delightful, loving, gentle child. But chances are greater that I will respond negatively, becoming stubborn, aggressive, anorexic, bullying, delinquent, disrespectful, criminal, alcoholic, drug-addicted, raping, spouse- or child-beating. Yet I may become a pastor, a missionary, a creative citizen, or a useful therapist as a way to mitigate my mistreatment. This is what I mean by the relative influence of neglectful or abusive parenting.

So as a therapist I find it helpful to ask, "If we are all sinners, what happened in this client's life to encourage him to cope with his pain by becoming this specific kind of sinner?" An answer then shows the counselor how to guide toward constructive self-behavior.

Clinical experience demonstrates that before people can take good care of anything or anyone, they must take good care of themselves, that is, be their own nurturing parents.[15] So what do they need in order to take care of themselves? How do they wish their parents had treated them? Are they willing to treat themselves as they wish the important people in their lives would have treated them?

Translated, these are questions counselors can ask counselees: "Tell me how you wish your mom/dad would have treated you." "Make a list of what you missed out on as you were growing up." When therapists discover what those specific wishful behaviors are, they can ask, "Are you willing to treat yourself to the affirmations and experiences you wish you had received from your parents?"

We want to affirm this truth to our counselees: The more I take good care of myself, the less resentment and anger I feel toward myself, my parents, my friends, and God, and the more loving I become toward myself and others.

Chapter 2 introduced six outcome questions which can be used with any of the sensory-sequence (say/hear, see/look, feel/sense, act/do) issues. For example, regarding behavior, I would ask my clients the blockage question: "How are you stopping yourself from getting what you want?" Or, "What are you doing that is robbing you of your desires?" Or, ask resource questions: "What do I need in order to treat myself better? What can I do to be good to myself? How can I be good to myself now? What am I not doing for myself? What would I be better off doing without or not doing? Is there a better way for me to take care of myself today?"

A note of caution: Self-esteem can be either encouraged or discouraged by ways in which people evaluate their actions. Psychologically, a sense of competence comes as the result of learning to act, to do, to master, and to control. Because I am capable, I can now see myself positively and feel good about myself. However, if I rely solely on my performance for self-esteem, I'm vulnerable to a lowered self-image, critical self-evaluation, and rejecting feelings when my performance does not match my ideal view or expectations of myself. Consequently, my self-esteem needs a more constant source than my behavior.

Today, I may teach, preach, counsel, and lead very well and, therefore, feel and see myself positively. But how do I see and feel toward myself when my performance is average or below? Am I still okay as a person? Those whose self-esteem is rooted in their relationship with their Creator and Redeemer take variable performance in stride. But those persons who believe that the level of their performance reflects their worth become depressed, sad, angry, scared, competitive, helpless, or hopeless when they evaluate their performance as unacceptable. It is crucial for self-esteem to have a sense of adequacy, to know we can do something well. It is devastating if we need to perform perfectly or better than others in order to have self-esteem.

Theologically, we reject the belief in salvation by works. Yet, psychologically, many of us and our counselees act as though salvation were humanly achieved. The spiritual struggle for adequacy, in addition to being a denial of the human need for God, may also be a reflection of the human need for a sense of adequacy (competency), which is fundamental to healthy self-esteem. The apostle Paul, struggling with his predisposition to sin, declares in Romans 7:15–25 that his adequacy is dependent on Christ. Having learned that Christ makes him adequate, he boldly declares in Philippians 4:13: "I can do all things through Him who strengthens me."

When Paul claimed that he was adequate, he recognized God as the source of his adequacy: "Not that we are adequate in ourselves to consider anything as coming from ourselves, but our adequacy is from God, who also made us adequate as servants of a new covenant, not of the letter, but of the Spirit; for the letter kills, but the Spirit gives life" (2 Cor. 3:5, 6). This sense of spiritual adequacy converted itself into a psychological sense of adequacy, as Paul goes on to say: "Having therefore such a hope, we use great boldness in our speech, and are not as Moses, who used to put a veil over his face that the sons of Israel might not look intently at the end of what was fading away" (vv. 12, 13). Paul could also have claimed, once God had called him to be a messenger to the Gentiles, that he was bold in his speech and not like Moses, who pleaded for God to let Aaron be the spokesman to Pharaoh.

Scripture asks us to recognize that our spiritual adequacy is from God. Low-esteem people, however, tend to confuse spiritual inadequacy with psychological inadequacy. And this confusion leads to severe problems, such as believing that they are not lovable, valuable, or capable enough to be God's redeemed child, or doubting their right to serve God. Ministering to low-esteem people is difficult because they believe they are not worth either the pastor's or God's time and attention. It is crucial that helpers make it clear that *nowhere in Scripture is man asked to consider himself psychologically inadequate or beyond God's redemptive love.*

Biblically, it is okay to be self-confident, but not to be confident in self. Timothy, for example, is given permission to be confident even though he is youthful (1 Tim. 4:12). Paul encourages the Corinthians to be confident: "Run in such a way that you may win" (1 Cor. 9:24). Of his own self-confidence he writes, ". . . I myself might have confidence even in the flesh. If anyone else has a mind to put confidence in the flesh, I far more . . ." (Phil. 3:4), and, "Not that I have already obtained it, or have already become perfect, but I press on in order that I may lay hold of that for which also I was laid hold of by Christ Jesus. . . . I press on toward the goal for the prize of the upward call of God in Christ Jesus" (vv. 12, 14). Elsewhere Paul says, "I am confident of this very thing, that He who began a good work in you will perfect it until the day of Christ Jesus" (Phil. 1:6).

Christians are encouraged to consider that their spiritual adequacy not only comes as a redemptive gift from God, but also comes from internalizing Scripture. "All Scripture is inspired by God and profitable for teaching, for reproof, for correction, for training in righteousness; that the man of God may be *adequate*, equipped for every good work" (2 Tim. 3:16, 17 italics added). Paul also instructed Timothy that adequacy comes from cleansing oneself: "If a man cleanses himself from these things, he will be a vessel for honor, sanctified, useful to the Master, *prepared* for every good work" (2 Tim. 2:21 italics added).

Christian counselors need to affirm:

We achieve our [spiritual] adequacy through [God's] unceasing love. We do not become sufficient, approved, or adequate; rather we are declared to be such! When we believe (hear, see, tell, act, feel) this, we become achievers and humanitarians as an effect, consequence, and byproduct of our new-found self. . . . When a person has accepted his adequacy as a gift, he immediately perceives a new standard for achievement.[16]

Summary

Thus far in this chapter we have discussed three actions that are vital to the nurturing of self: changing negative self-talk to positive self-talk, creating or remembering a positive image of self, and acting positively toward self. In the following chapter we will look closely at a fourth action and conclude this discussion with illustrations and observations from the counseling experience.

CHAPTER EIGHT

TEACHING COUNSELEES TO NURTURE THEMSELVES THROUGH RECOGNIZING AND ACCEPTING FEELINGS

PEOPLE OFTEN TALK ABOUT HOW THEY FEEL toward themselves without realizing that feelings result from what a person says, sees, and does. Feelings become the end product of the sensory sequence. They have no existence independent of self-talk, self-image, and self-behavior. Feelings may seem to come out of nowhere; but these emotions grow out of what a person unconsciously hears, sees, and does.

How people feel toward themselves, then, reflects their view of themselves, their internal dialogue, and their actions toward themselves. When these sensory modalities are positive, feelings will be positive (happy, excited, tender). Negative sensory modalities produce negative emotions (scared, angry, sad). People with low self-esteem must challenge what they say to themselves, how they picture themselves, and how they treat themselves if their self-feelings are to be positive. Self-hate originates not as a feeling, but as an auditory, visual experience which is reinforced by self-defeating behavior. (See chart below for sensory-sequence flow. The numbers indicate the direction of the sequence. They are counterclockwise because they match the eye-scan for a righthanded person.)

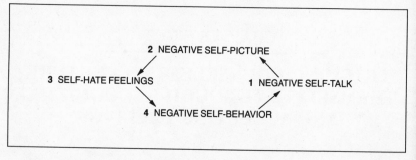

How people talk to themselves, what they say to themselves, frequently repeats the negative messages they have actually heard from significant people in their lives. These negative messages can also be their interpretations of how they were treated by these important figures. People do not usually come to feel negatively toward themselves without outside help.

A senior citizen who quit eighth grade to help his family financially seldom reads today because of the humiliation he felt when teachers and students laughed at his attempts to read. This was, of course, only one humiliating experience among many he received from a tyrannical and abusive father. But he continues to berate himself in much the same way his father, teacher, and fellow students laughed at him.

Not surprisingly, he is both critical of others and self-effacing. Either he does not consider his feelings and needs, or he discounts others' feelings and needs. Since he does not know how to play and enjoy life, he works. Relaxing is so difficult for him that even though he talks about wanting to fish and enjoy retirement, he chooses to find odd jobs instead.

Wanting to be accepted and to please others leads this man to shortchange himself by charging less than the going rate for his work. Teaching clients to identify the source of their self-feelings in what and how they talk to themselves, look at themselves, and act toward themselves, then, is a crucial step in their learning how to change negative feelings.

Because the negative cycle is self-perpetuating, the counselor can begin intervention at any of the four sensory modalities. A counselee's complaint will often indicate where the counselor should begin exploring. A person who reports feeling negative about himself or herself, for example, indicates that the exploration should begin with the feelings. "You feel lousy about yourself because. . . . " Or, "Tell me what you mean when you say you feel lousy about yourself."

The counseling starting point, then, is the client's sensory representation of the problem. When a person says, "I feel really terrible about myself," the counselor may encourage the individual to tell more, by prompting: "Go on. How terrible do you feel? What, specifically, are your terrible feelings? What does *terrible* feel like?"

Counselees may talk about their feelings without actually experiencing them in the present. To discover whether an individual is feeling terrible, counselors need to ask, "Are you feeling terrible now?" If they are not, ask, "What are you feeling now?"

Counselors need to anticipate the person's inability to describe feelings, since many people, especially males, seldom examine feelings or practice expressing them. When they have a sense of discomfort toward themselves or others, and when they describe their feelings as bad or horrible, I take time to teach them the six feeling words which chapter 6 asks parents to learn: scared, angry, sad, happy, excited, and tender— SASHET. (Although there are more feeling words than these six, most can be placed under one of the SASHET headings. The chart on pages 172–73 suggests several possible synonyms.) Your counselees often have their own words which represent cultural, geographical, and family environments. These can easily be added to the chart for their use. Becoming aware of feelings and identifying them with understandable labels is an important therapeutic goal. People may be able to recognize their physiological sensations more than their emotions.

IDENTIFYING THE EVIDENCE OF FEELINGS

"How do I recognize the feeling?" is the next question that helps clients identify body sensations. Remember that feelings are both emotional and physiological. Identifying the context in which they experience feelings is the third assignment in the feeling-recognition exercise.

In counseling sessions, I frequently ask my clients to become aware of what they are feeling at that time. I then ask them to remember what they were feeling as they came to the session. Finally, I ask them to anticipate what they will feel as they leave. People who have a hard time identifying what they feel often have difficulty knowing how they process their feelings. Do they express them appropriately (verbally, respectfully, kindly, lovingly)? Or do they implode (hold them in, repress, suppress, discount), resulting in headaches, backaches, stomachaches? Or do they explode (uncontrolled and inappropriate letting go, swearing, depreciating, hitting, leaving)?

Learning to accept feelings, especially those labeled "negative" (scared, angry, sad), is often necessary before clients can discover what they do with feelings. To help them accept feelings, I let clients know that feelings tell them something is going wrong. When we allow ourselves to pay attention to our feelings, they tell us what we need and what is missing in our lives. Accepting feelings enables us to become aware of what is going on inside us and frees us to ask for what we need.

I will self-disclose when I think disclosure clarifies my point for a client, sharing how my childhood negative feelings were squelched through various punishments. Learning as a child to implode my negative feelings has influenced my lack of spontaneity in expressing positive emotions (happiness, excitement, tenderness). As an adult I am learning how to feel and express fright, anger, and sadness without judging or criticizing myself. And this growing ability to express my feelings is benefiting relationships with my wife, my children, and others.

I further emphasize that, although clients may not like the

way they express feelings, it is okay for Christians to feel and then learn how to express their feelings in ways that are Christlike.[2] I cite Ephesians 4:26 as an example of feeling anger and as an encouragement to process the anger rather than store it where it leads to resentment and bitterness. Feelings, therefore, are not right or wrong. Humans cannot control the appearance of their feelings; they can only control their expression. Scaredness, anger, sadness, happiness, excitement, or tenderness are beyond conscious control, usually spontaneous, catching people by surprise.

Lastly, I ask clients, "Whom does this feeling involve?" This question puts the feelings into a relational context. I am interested in discovering who the people are in their lives that, from their perspective, seem to be causing pain. When I discover who these people are, I then ask, "What have you said to these people? How have you told them what you feel and need?" Notice that I do not ask them why they feel what they experience, because asking why before what, how, when, and whom leads more to frustration and bewilderment than to clarity and freedom. *Why* people feel what they do usually surfaces after answering the other questions in the chart.

Using the Feeling Recognition Exercise as a daily diary is an effective tool that helps people identify and express feelings. Counselors can also invite them to experience "terrible" feelings. Watch the counselees' eyes to learn how they access the source of their discomfort. Are their eyes down to their right, indicating *feeling* access? Listen also to their sensory predicates. Are they kinesthetic?

After the counselor gains a sense of the counselees' terrible feelings—scared, angry, sad, guilty, ashamed—he or she explores the sensory source of these feelings, locating their pictures, memories, thoughts, self-talk, and behavior. Humans may say they feel terrible after learning they hurt someone's feelings. How did they (the counselees) discover this? Did someone tell them—"You hurt my feelings"? Did they catch themselves in the process by seeing the person's hurt expression; did their conscience tell them they had violated a social norm? The purpose of these questions is to discover how they process information. Counselors are interested in the sensory

FEELING RECOGNITION EXERCISE

EMOTION	SENSATION	CONTEXT	EXPRESSION	RELATIONSHIP
What am I feeling?	How do I physically recognize what I am feeling?	When/where do I have this feeling?	What do I do with feeling? express/ implode/explode?	Whom does feeling involve, if anyone?
SCARED Panic-stricken Afraid Terrified Stress-filled Frightened Nervous Anxious Jittery Startled Tense	Tight down the back of the neck and in shoulders, tight across chest, constricted in breathing			
ANGRY Violent Upset Rage-filled Resentful Irate Disgusted Furious Frustrated Inflamed Irritated Mad Depressed	Tight jaw, clenched fists, pain in pit of stomach, tension in neck, arms want to hit			
SAD Grieved Dejected Mournful Distressed Melancholy Mopey Heartbroken Blue	Tightness in throat, behind the eyes, and down the center of the chest			

HAPPY

Joyous
Complete
Fulfilled
Optimistic
Satisfied

Content
Relaxed
Pleased
Peaceful
Glad

Relaxed muscles

EXCITED

Ecstatic
Energetic
Aroused
Effusive
Bouncy

Perky
Sexual
Antsy
Nervous
Jittery

Jumpy and shivery all
over, fast pulse

TENDER

Intimate
Loving
Warm-hearted
Gentle
Soft

"With you"
Touched
Kind
Empathic
Sympathetic

Soft tears around eyes,
"full" sensations
around heart, arms
want to hug

This exercise is designed to help you become aware of your feeling experience. **1.** Familiarize yourself with the six SASHET words (scared, angry, sad, happy, excited, tender). Feel free to add your feeling vocabulary to the chart. **2.** Begin with identifying a feeling. Do this at least three times per day. If you are not able to identify an emotion, then describe the physical sensations that accompany the feeling and match it to one of the SASHET experiences. **3.** Write the place, time, and circumstances of your feeling. **4.** Monitor what you do with your feeling. Do you put it into appropriate words and actions (express)? Or hold it in (implode)? Or put the feeling into destructive words and actions (explode)? **5.** Write in who this feeling is toward.

sequence that precedes the terrible feelings, because that identifies the process to be used in counseling.

Helpers assist people in processing their feelings by encouraging them to attempt the following:

- become aware of feelings (emotions and physical sensations),
- identify and label these feelings (SASHET, plus specific body responses, e.g., tightness, temperature, shaking, hair raising),
- accept their feelings as facts (indicators that something is wrong),
- accept their feelings as resources (indicators that something is needed),
- learn to express their feelings constructively and appropriately (challenging implosion and explosion of feelings),
- complete the feelings by connecting them to auditory and visual memories and thoughts, to behaviors of self and others, and to auditory and visual imaginations (learning their sensory sequence).

People often want to rid themselves of painful feelings without processing.[3] Ventilation of feelings, however, is seldom enough to complete the process even though it may provide temporary relief. Counseling helps people move beyond catharsis to connecting their feelings with all sensory modalities. Counselees must also accept their feelings without judging. They must discover their sensory sources (what am I saying to myself, remembering others saying to me, visualizing?), imagine what they think others might say or do, and identify the behavior involved in maintaining painful feelings. Such a completing of feelings does not mean that a person is numb or does not feel. It means he or she is freed to feel without imploding or exploding. Such persons can make sense out of their feelings, learn where they are coming from in their own sensory experiences and how they unconsciously maintain them (sensory sequence), and so discover the sensory steps they need to reduce or change painful feelings to those they desire.

Processing feelings is possible when people view their feelings as indicators that they need to pay attention to some deprivation in their lives. Christian counselees typically evaluate negative feelings as wrong, sinful, immoral, or a measure of their worthlessness. Self-condemnation prevents them from exploring the source and meaning of their feelings and frustrates their completing the process. Prejudging feelings inhibits processing and leads to self-hate (lowered esteem) and self-punishment (atonement) rather than to confession, repentance, and restoration.

My experience with evangelical pastors and seminarians teaches me that they tend to view feelings as sinful, focusing on the sin issue in people's problems more than on exploring the feeling process. Identifying and labeling sin may be important somewhere in the process, but it is seldom helpful early in counseling because people also tend to moralize their feelings and thus terminate help. Even if feelings are discovered to be sinful (a depraved response to a hurtful, threatening, depriving relationship), low self-esteem people still need the patient, compassionate, loving, and understanding response of the pastor and counselor to facilitate learning new ways to express feelings.

To identify their feelings as sin prematurely reinforces their own sense of badness and does not help them learn to respond maturely or to process their feelings constructively. I find it helpful to remind myself that as a sinner saved by God's grace, I cannot avoid turning fear into distrust and anxiety, anger into hatred, sadness into despair, happiness into addiction, excitement into lust, tenderness into selfishness. I may be able to not sin occasionally, but I am a sinner. I need forgiveness, not only for my specific sins, but also for my very person. I feel what I feel, accepting my feelings as me. I confess what I feel without condemning myself. I become aware of me, but I do not deny (implode) me. I accept me, not judge (reject) me. I experience me, not rationalize me. My feelings are me! I feel what I do not want to feel, and do not feel what I want to feel. Wretched man that I am! Who shall deliver me from what I feel? I cannot *not* feel. I cannot achieve moral perfection. "Thanks be to God through Jesus Christ. . . . There is therefore now no condemnation for those who are in Christ Jesus" (Rom. 7:25–8:1).

Working through feelings may also require the helpee to express emotions in all sensory modes: to express the painful feelings in deep breathing, to sound the pain with vocalizations (shouting, groans, crying—not necessarily with words), and to move the body (tears, thrashing arms or legs, stamping, hitting pillows, pacing). Teaching clients to breathe deeply from their diaphragms relaxes the chest muscles and makes it easier for the body to let go of the feeling both physiologically and emotionally. Vocalizing the pain reduces the tendency to implode feelings, and body movement encourages freedom to feel.

Counselors need to anticipate the discomfort or embarrassment their counselees may experience as they breathe deeply, sound loudly, and move freely. Discomfort will be minimized when the counselor encourages these expressions one at a time and gives the person time to experiment. Some explanation for deep breathing, loud sounding, and free body movement is also helpful in reducing inhibition. Keep in mind that people are seeking help because they do not know how to finish feelings or free themselves from inhibitions or control explosions. Learning feeling-expression skill is like learning any other skill; it takes time, patience, practice, and understanding. The feeling-process cycle can be summarized as follows: awareness (experiencing/labeling) → acceptance (non-judging/entitling) → expression (appropriate verbalizing/behaving) → completion (finishing).

Take a moment to practice these feeling-expression skills. Start by asking, "What am I emotionally feeling at this moment when Dave asks me to practice these skills (reluctant, hesitant, anxious, excited)? Am I accepting these feelings as a legitimate experience, or am I judging myself?" Then, "What physical sensations am I aware of? How am I breathing (high in chest, middle chest, lower chest)? Is my breathing shallow or deep? What sound can I put to this feeling?" Now vocalize a sound. Was the sound high or low, soft or loud? Next, what body movement did you put to this feeling? Are you completing your feelings, or do you need to process them again? A rule of thumb: Do not ask others to finish their feelings until you as a helper have learned how to process your feelings. Ministers learn that they cannot take their congregations spiritually any farther than they have traveled themselves. This is also true emotionally.

A Counseling Illustration

If terrible feelings are the product of what people say to themselves, how they look at themselves, and how they act toward themselves, then counselor explorations focus on uncovering what they are saying, seeing, and doing before these terrible feelings occur. I work back from the feeling by asking what persons are aware of before they feel terrible about themselves.

In this illustration, Bob sees himself as a turkey—clumsy, awkward, and tactless. He depreciates himself by labeling himself as a turkey. The behavior that precipitates these pictures and evaluations is his forgetting to pick up a friend for a concert. Bob has left himself no room to make a mistake, to forget, to be human, or to forgive himself. So he verbally punishes himself and pays for his "sin" by feeling terrible. This is how Bob's sensory sequence can be diagramed:

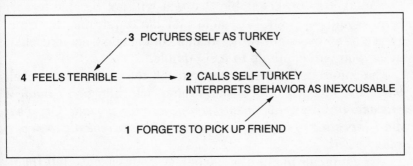

As I show Bob his sensory sequence, I ask for feedback: "Does this description of the process make sense to you?" His feedback gives me an opportunity to check my understanding of how he ends up feeling terrible. I also want to fine-tune and clarify these generalizations as specifically as possible. When both Bob and I agree that this diagram captures the process of how he feels terrible, we then have the firing order that tells us what sensory sequence to follow in order to incite positive feelings.

Bob's firing order can also be diagramed this way: behavior (forgets to pick up friend) → auditory internal dialogue (interprets behavior as unacceptable) → auditory internal dialogue continues (calls self a turkey) → visual remembered (sees self as turkey who has acted this way before) → kinesthetic experience (feels terrible).

To translate this negative sensory sequence into a positive therapeutic strategy, I ask, "Whenever you make a mistake, do you criticize yourself to the point of feeling bad about yourself?" I am looking for a pattern here. Is this an isolated incident, or is the client dealing with a general tendency to depreciate himself? Another way to determine whether someone is struggling with a patterned response is to measure the intensity of his discomfort. Usually one incident is not enough to cause severe discomfort. People will, however, come for help when a specific situation has precipitated discomfort.

Facilitating an ability to nurture oneself begins in this case with challenging the negative appraisal of his behavior. The challenge will first come from the counselor: "I hear you saying that forgetting to pick up your friend is unacceptable behavior. Is it so unacceptable that you will not be able to *ever* forgive yourself?" Or, "If you are unable to reframe this experience as an oversight rather than a commentary on your character, you will continue to feel terrible."

The counseling point here is to teach the client how to challenge the internal critical parent and help him say, *I made a mistake, but does this mean I am a horrible person?* Or, *what am I expecting of myself, perfection?* Or, *is it realistic to never, ever forget?*

The counselor might also encourage counselees to tell themselves, *my friend has forgiven me, so I can forgive myself. She still sees me as okay, so I can look at myself the same way. My behavior is only part of me. One mistake does not reflect who I really am; one mistake does not make me a bad person.*

Following the counselees' sensory sequence, the next therapeutic intervention is to direct them to picture themselves positively. The counselor might instruct Bob to picture himself when he did treat his friend well: "Can you remember when you treated a person well? It could be this friend you forgot or anyone. When you remember a situation, let me know by nodding your head. Okay, good. Now get a picture of yourself in this specific situation, particularly noticing how well you see yourself. As you see yourself, please describe what you see."

The description should include positive facial expressions and confident body posture. This exercise is repeated until the client can visualize himself positively. The counselor may need to take him back to what he is saying to himself or hearing others say to him in order to develop a positive self-image. When the client has difficulty seeing a positive picture, it is common for him to repeat negative self-statements or remember negative statements made to him by others.

When the client has successfully created positive self-talk and self-image, have him practice moving from auditory internal dialogue to visual-remembered experiences before adding the positive behavior or feelings.

Acting out positive behavior may be needed before the client is able to feel positive. Paying back what was stolen or asking forgiveness for violating an agreement are examples of behavior that may need to precede the experience of positive feelings.

The last step in the therapeutic intervention is to add feelings. While the client is talking positively to himself (looking down to his left), and picturing himself positively (looking up to his left), the counselor instructs him to look down to his right and get the feelings. Notice that the right-handed eye scan has been added to this last intervention. These instructions may seem strange to counselees. They may even feel silly or embarrassed when asked to try something new. This is not an uncommon response. Before I ask counselees to experiment, I explain what I am about to ask them to do, verbalizing that they may feel uncomfortable. When persons resist my instructions, I ask them what they heard me ask them and what makes my request uncomfortable. Taking time to prepare counselees for new behaviors usually results in cooperation. I may introduce the instructions for using the eye scan like this: "Please look down to your left and tell yourself out loud that you are a fine person who made a mistake that is forgivable by you and by your friend. Now look up to your left and focus on a positive picture of yourself, reporting what you see. When you have yourself in view, look down to your right and experience whatever feelings come. Please report what you are feeling."

The client's feelings should be positive. When the client is not experiencing positive feelings, he may sense that negative thoughts, pictures, or memories are invading the process, overwhelming positive self-talking and self-imaging. If the feelings are not positive, ask, "What else do you need to say to yourself or see in order to feel better?" Have the client add these new pieces of information to the sensory sequence as he repeats the process.

Be sure to help the client challenge the negative talk and pictures. Teaching the client to do this for himself will occupy much of the counseling session. Make sure the client understands his sensory sequence and how to challenge the negative internal dialogue and negative self-picturing before assigning this sequence as homework. Explain to the client that he will no doubt have mixed success with this new tool. Follow-up sessions will try to correct problems he experiences in using his sensory sequence and will help him apply the process to other uncomfortable life experiences.

A Second Counseling Illustration

Art asked to see me after hearing me speak on "Building Self-Esteem in Yourself." He reported that he cries frequently, particularly after disappointments. He has asked the Lord to help him stop; but because his prayers have not been answered, he wonders how he can get rid of crying and depression.

I responded, "Art, you seem to know why you cry. You get disappointed, but that doesn't help. You have tried praying; but when that does not bring you relief, you end up feeling frustrated."

"Yes, that is exactly it. Let me tell you what disappointed me this week." He went on to describe how he had studied all day Saturday for a seminary test, basing his reading on the teacher's recommendations and putting aside writing a paper for another class. Then on Wednesday, the day before the test, the professor announced that it would be on the Gospel of John only and not include the commentaries, which Art had been diligent to read. Although relieved that the test would cover less material than expected, Art irritably complained that he had wasted time studying unnecessarily. Trying to console Art, the professor argued that Art would be able to use this material in his sermons someday. Not convinced, Art went to his room and cried. He wanted to scream, but did not want anyone to hear him. He has cried every day since the announced test change, but wants to stop.

"Art, I hear you are feeling disappointed as well as angry, but do not have a way to express it." When Art agreed that he was angry, I asked, "How do you express your anger?" I was searching for other ways Art has to express anger in addition to crying.

In the process of telling me he had no other ways, Art described his childhood. His mother died during his birth. His father died when he was seven, and he was raised by an austere aunt who did not express affection verbally or physically. She demanded that Art be well-behaved, which meant he was to be seen and not heard. When he attempted to express his feelings or ask for affection, he was told to be quiet. Art traced the crying and depression to life with his aunt. Even now, he said, he is unable to be his true self when he goes home. I responded, "From what you say, I gather there is really no place you feel that you can be yourself."

Art looked down to his right and softly said, "True."

During most of our conversation I noticed that Art was accessing and representing himself in the kinesthetic modality. He occasionally looked up left, the visual-remembered modality. I asked him to remember this recent test disappointment and describe what he had thought about or said to himself before he cried and felt depressed. I was asking him to backtrack as a way of helping him discover the sensory process that led him to the crying behavior and depressed feelings. What we discovered was this: Art talks to himself the way his aunt did—*Be quiet. Shut up. Your feelings and needs do not count.* In other words, he bottles up his feelings until they are under pressure. When a disappointment comes, therefore, the bottle cap has to come off to release the pressure; then he cries. But even his crying is so controlled that he can put the cap back on his feelings and re-experience the depression.

This explanation made sense to him. "What can I do about this?" he asked.

"Have you ever said nurturing and kind things to another person?"

"Yes."

"Well, how about saying to yourself those kind things you say to others?"

"That sounds weird."

"Of course, you don't have much experience talking kindly to yourself. I have another idea. Could you think of what you wished your aunt were saying to you?"

Hesitantly he said, "Maybe."

"Okay, so share some of those thoughts with me now."

"You mean like, 'I love you.' 'Tell me how you feel.' 'I am listening to you.' 'What do you need?'"

"Exactly. You have started a good list. Would you be willing to begin telling yourself these nurturing affirmations?"

"Well, I have not done it before."

"True. That is why you are crying and depressed. Can you choose one of these positive statements and say it out loud to yourself now?"

"Okay, I love myself."

"What do you experience as you say that you love yourself?"

"It is weird, but it feels kind of good."

"Now when you say 'I love myself,' look up to your left and find a picture of yourself" (as his counselor, I watched to see if he looked up to the left as he did this).

"Uh, huh."

"What are you seeing?"

"I am smiling and jumping up and down."

"Good. Now look down to your right and let yourself feel that love."

"Oh, I feel happy and excited."

"Art, you can have this experience any time you want it. Start with a positive affirmation, something you wish your aunt were saying to you, then look for a positive picture of yourself. When you have yourself in focus, let yourself feel what you need to feel. Does this make sense to you?"

"Yes."

"Can you describe the steps that we have practiced?"

After Art had told me what he had heard me say, and I was

satisfied that he comprehended and could duplicate the sensory experience, I asked, "Would you be willing to pursue further counseling?" I told Art that although I was just visiting his seminary, I was concerned about how much hurt and anger he had to deal with all by himself. "What we have done today is a start. I would like you to see Mr. Davidson."

"Oh, I cannot afford him."

"He tells me he sees seminary students at a reduced fee."

"Really? Then I will be happy to see him."

"He is out of town until Monday. Will you call him then?"

"Yes."

Take a moment to diagram Art's sensory process. Compare your diagram to the one below. It is organized using the four sensory modalities and eye-scan. Follow the numbers. They show the beginning and sequencing of his sensory process.

1) Feels disappointment. → 2) Cries. → 3) Remembers aunt's words, "Be quiet!" → 4) Tells self, "I have got to stop this." → 5) Results in temporary relief, but angry feelings stifled. → 6) Prays to God for help. → 7) Believes he has no right to feelings. → 8) Feels depressed. → 9) Cuts self off from feeling. → 10) Stops crying until next disappointment.

Now diagram Art's new sensory strategy. This diagram is less complicated. Compare yours to the one below:

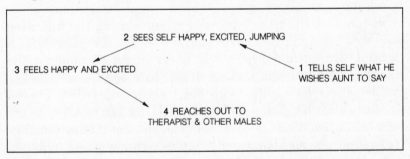

Nurturing Yourself: Sharon's Homework Assignment

Sharon came to me depressed, discouraged, and humiliated. Sexually active although single and a Christian, she felt torn between her Christian values and her intense needs and feelings for love. She was rationalizing what she knew was right with what made her feel good for a while. Failing to live with the conflict between her head and her heart, she now sought counseling despite the fact that she had little hope that a counselor could help a single Christian woman find affection and peace of mind.

Sharon came to counseling anticipating a critical, judgmental person who would throw her sin in her face and tell her to repent and live right. She was surprised that I was listening with compassion to her struggle. After hearing her story and learning what she wanted from counseling, I said, "You seem to be hurting very deeply, believing there is no way you can live your Christian life and still get your needs met for love and affection." As she agreed, I said, "Do you have any friends who hug and affirm you?"

"No," she replied. "I get hugged only when I am having sex." I wondered what stopped her from asking for or giving hugs in a nonsexual context. She answered that she was too embarrassed to ask.

"You've got to be kidding!" I said, surprised. "Are you telling me that having intercourse is less embarrassing than asking for a hug?"

Sharon agreed that was strange. I then suggested that on the following Sunday she ask four people in her church for a hug. Hesitatingly, Sharon said she finds it easier to hug people than to ask for hugs. So we agreed that she would start there.

Sharon took the risk of asking for hugs during the following weeks of counseling. As her courage to ask for affection increased, Sharon found herself in fewer sexual encounters. She was then able to begin looking at self-hate and its roots in her problematic relationships with her mother and father. Sharon was born after her father had separated from her mother. Angry over her husband's affair and abandonment, her mother took her frustration out on Sharon with verbal put-downs and minimal care. Attempts to please Mother and win her affection through achieving scholastically, being helpful with housework, and staying in her room out of Mother's way were not successful.

184

Sharon responded by becoming sarcastic, demanding, and argumentative. Father's return to the home brought little relief to her since her mother received Father coldly.

Leaving home provided Sharon some relief. At least she didn't have to deal with her parents' marital tension. Vowing never to call or go home, Sharon began her college and career experience. But she would become angry that her mother seldom called to inquire about her welfare. This gave Sharon some ambivalence about her separation; part of her wanted desperately for Mother to call and invite a relationship, but another part of her dreaded Mother's calls. Reluctantly, Sharon would occasionally go home, partly out of guilt and partly in hope that her mother would finally be affirming. Always disappointed at the reception her mother gave her, Sharon vowed never to go back to her parents' home. This vow lasted for a year or more.

As I helped her come to grips with the probability that she would never get what she needed from her parents, Sharon accepted a homework assignment that I had discussed with her several times. I instructed her to think of her experience with her parents and tell herself that, in spite of how she was treated, she is lovable, valuable, and capable. I asked her to write her affirmations on a sheet of paper and bring them to the next session. She was allowed to use my affirmations of her as a guide. I wanted her to tell herself what she had wanted to hear from her parents all these years. The main difference was that she was now her own nurturing parent.

Below are Sharon's affirmations. They remain taped to her refrigerator and bathroom mirror as daily reminders that she can be to herself what her parents were not to her.

I am somebody, even though I was born at the very worst time in my parents' marriage.

I am valuable, even though my mother couldn't process her anger and hate toward her mother and my father and took arguments out on me.

I am lovable, even though my parents were not capable of hugging me and telling me they loved me.

I am lovable, even though I was, and am at times, a brat.

I am valuable, even though my mother told me she did not like the person I was becoming.

I am worthwhile, even though I believed my mother when she told me if anyone knew me they would not like me.

I am capable, even though nothing I did was good enough to gain my mother's approval.

I am somebody, even though I hid everything about me from others so no one would know me.

I am lovable, even when I am angry and hateful.

I am valuable, even when I do not want to forgive and want others to hurt as much as they have hurt me.

I am capable, even though I do not perform up to my standards.

I am valuable, even though I am single.

I am somebody, valuable, lovable and capable even when I do not feel that way.

I am lovable, even though I am fat.

I am somebody, lovable, valuable, and capable because God created me and HE delights in His creation.

Teaching people to be their own nurturing parents takes patience and requires understanding of how they reinforce their critical parent. Learning to challenge the critical and accusing parent that lives inside is rewarding when counselors learn their counselees' sensory sequences and teach them how to translate negative messages, pictures, behaviors, and feelings into positive ones. A tool I created to help clients affirm themselves is an adaptation of the love chapter, 1 Corinthians 13:4–7. I instruct them to read this affirmation at least once daily.

When I am *patient* with myself,
Then I am tolerant of myself;
Then I put up with myself;
Then I do not easily become perturbed with myself;
Then I give myself time to accomplish tasks at my own speed and energy;
Then I act, using my best judgment without feeling excessively guilty or regretting my actions when my decisions turn out less than perfect.

When I am *kind* to myself,
Then I am considerate of my feelings and needs as legitimate without becoming preoccupied with them or feeling selfish;
Then I think well of myself, accepting my feelings as part of me, neither good nor bad;
Then I see the good (God) in myself, that is, recognizing my humanness without confusing it with my sinfulness;
Then I constructively criticize myself no more than I affirm or appreciate myself;
Then I am merciful, sympathetic, and generous to myself as much as I am to others.

When I am *sharing* with myself,
Then I see myself as a person of value and interest to myself;
Then I am not jealous or possessive of my abilities or gifts;
Then I am willing to risk getting to know myself;
Then I am willing to risk letting others get to know me;
Then I am desirous of investing myself in others;
Then I recognize and accept my talents, gifts, and abilities;
Then I affirm myself;
Then I give gifts to myself without feeling selfish or guilty.

When I am *modest* with myself,
Then I am humble without feeling humiliated;
Then I feel equal without feeling superior or inferior;
Then I do not set myself out for display;
Then I recognize that no man is an island or is sufficient alone;
Then I see myself as part of the body of Christ, no more or less important than others;
Then I make realistic assessments of my strengths and weaknesses;
Then I do not need to cherish inflated ideas of my importance.

When I am *moral* to myself,
Then I take no pleasure in injustice to other people;

Then I am happy with the truth;

Then I consider my personal needs and desires in relation to other people's needs and desires;

Then I balance my rights with my responsibilities;

Then I am cooperative rather than competitive to the point of causing others to lose face or respect;

Then I help myself by refusing to be my own worst enemy;

Then I stop others from unnecessarily walking all over me, refusing to be a martyr, but choosing servanthood.

When I am *forgiving* of myself,

Then I do not keep records of suffered wrongs;

Then I allow myself to make mistakes and to fail;

Then I see myself as a sinner saved by grace, not a sinner condemned to death;

Then I am forgetful of my wrongs and sins after confessions;

Then I accept God's forgiveness and do not try to atone for my sins;

Then I make restitution for my sins to people I have hurt;

Then I do not try to meet conditions of God's love but realize that God's love is free;

Then I do not allow humility to build up to self-hate and depression;

Then I see myself as loved by God, using this knowledge to love God, self, others in grateful response;

Then I am not fearful to know myself, refusing to hide from me;

Then I am willing to pray, "Search me, oh God, and know my thoughts";

Then I believe the truth does make me free; it takes the pressure off to be someone I am not.

When I am *hopeful* with myself,

Then I never give up on myself;

Then I believe the best about myself and others;

Then I expect the best of me;

Then I have a vision of what I am becoming in Christ;

Then I have confidence that God will help me recognize the good in difficult circumstances.

When I am *faithful* to myself,
Then I am trustful of God's love and salvation;
Then I am confident of God's ability to help me deal with my problems;
Then I trust myself;
Then I am loyal to my values and standards;
Then I do not spend time worrying about tomorrow;
Then I do not let the sun go down on today's upsetting experiences without processing them.

Summary

All of us have a critical and nurturing parent living inside us. The last two chapters have focused on strengthening the nurturing parent through positive self-talking, self-picturing, self-feeling, and self-behaving. Self-nurturing is necessary to maintaining healthy self-esteem. People with low esteem have not been practicing nurturing themselves because they fear selfishness. They will need as much counselor, family, and friend affirmation as possible. When the counselor is the only affirming source, creating a support group is often necessary. This can be a therapeutic group, a Bible study group, or a fellowship group. Using a person's relationship with God is also a powerful resource. The next chapter addresses the process of helping counselees receive God as their affirmer.

CHAPTER NINE

TEACHING COUNSELEES TO EXPERIENCE GOD AS THEIR NURTURING PARENT

NEAL CALLED ME FROM THE HOSPITAL emergency room after his son Donald had taken an overdose of sleeping pills. The psychiatrist wanted to admit Donald to the psychiatric ward for observation and treatment, but the father asked whether I thought hospitalization was really necessary. Whether Donald needed to be hospitalized depended on his willingness and ability to make a commitment to living, his level of depression and despair, and his medical condition. Not sure of the answers to these questions and knowing that this hospital admitted people only if they were acutely suicidal, I accepted the doctor's recommendation. Neal responded with several objections: Donald had already missed a lot of school; what would the kids at school think? wouldn't hospitalization label him as crazy? he wasn't serious about killing himself but only wanted attention.

Hearing the father's resistance to hospitalization, I said, "Neal, you sound scared that hospitalization is going to be more harmful than helpful. You also seem to believe that Donald's attempt was not serious. My experience with suicide attempts tells me that it is safer to err in the direction of hospitalization than to release a person prematurely."

"But Dave," the father said, "Can't you see him for out-patient counseling?" I assured Neal that I would be glad to see him and his son when it was safe for Donald to be released from the hospital. Reluctantly, he agreed.

Six weeks later, Donald's mother called to schedule a family counseling appointment inasmuch as he was being released from the hospital. Family counseling was recommended because of conflict between Donald and his older brother, and because Donald did not feel his parents listened to him or cared whether he existed. His despair seemed rooted in his perception that his father was busy with his work and showed little interest in talking with or listening to him. His mother, he complained, did not take him seriously and put him down by discounting his feelings.

Donald's feelings of family neglect are real to him. Regardless of how caring his parents think they are, they need to take Donald's view seriously, if they are to help him live. On the other hand, both the parents and Donald need to know that children inevitably feel their parents have failed them as nurturing people. No child ever gets enough love, care, or nurture, not because parents are necessarily inadequate, but because humans are insatiable in their need for affirmation and significance. This awareness does not excuse Donald's parents from correcting their neglect and insensitivity, nor does it excuse Donald from learning how to supplement what his parents give him by learning to care for himself, thus building his own self-esteem.

Donald is also wondering whether God cares for him. He claims that he does not see much proof of God's existence or care in the lives of either his parents or other Christians. Contributing to Donald's questions about God are disappointing experiences with God's representatives in his own life. When his youth minister visited Donald in the hospital, he promised to have breakfast with Donald regularly, but forgot the first appointment and has not called Donald to apologize or make another appointment. Already vulnerable to rejection and wondering whether anyone really cares for him, Donald uses this experience to question further his lovableness and to deepen his doubts about God.

Donald makes it very clear that he wants no "God talk" from his parents, the church, or me, but he does want relationships with people who show their love for him by listening to him and taking him seriously. I do not know whether Donald will let God into his life. I do know that experiencing me as a loving, understanding, caring therapist who affirms his worth and significance as a human being increases the possibility that he will be able to hear God say, "I love you and want you in my family."

NATURAL PARENTS—AND GOD AS NURTURING PARENT

Helping those whom they counsel experience God as their nurturing parent is one of the counselor's most important tasks. It is often difficult because people's negative relationships with their parents influence the quality of their relationships with God. Carl, the boy whose father abandoned him before he was born and whose alcoholic mother repeatedly ran him in and out of foster homes, and Brenda, whose parents, grandparents, minister, teacher, and husband sexually abused her, testify to our human tendency to see God in much the same way as we see our parents, especially our fathers.

Notice how the process of learning to receive God as nurturing parent is aided or hindered by the individual's human nurturing experience. Many people are not able to see God as nurturing parent until they experience the counselor, or their pastor, or their spouse or friend as nurturing.

Cognitively they may be able to comprehend what Christian counselors tell them, but emotionally the "good news" will feel like empty, nice-sounding phrases until they have human experiences of being understood, loved, and cared for unconditionally. While counselors in general can be surrogates in this nurturing experience, Christian counselors become God's representatives in their lives. The apostle James says, "Religion that God our Father accepts as pure and faultless is this: to look after orphans and widows in their distress. . . . Suppose a brother or sister is without clothes and daily food. If one of you says to him, 'Go, I wish you well; keep warm and well fed,' but does nothing about his physical needs, what good is it?" (James 1:27, 2:16 NIV). When counselees recognize God as the most significant other in their lives and accept him as their heavenly Father, he becomes a resource for nurture that supplements and substitutes for what was lacking in their human parenting.

> . . . the thought of our Maker becoming our perfect parent—faithful in love and care, generous and thoughtful, interested in all we do, respecting our individuality, skilful in training us, wise in guidance, always available, helping us to find ourselves in maturity, integrity, and uprightness—is a thought which can have meaning for everybody, whether we come to it by saying, "I had a wonderful father, and I see that God is like that, only more so," or by saying, "My father disappointed me here, and here, and here, but God, praise His name, will be very different," or even by saying, "I have never known what it is to have a father on earth, but thank God I now have one in heaven."[1]

Our task as Christian counselors is to be the healing link between persons' experiences of parents and God. The counselor's job is to enable people to hear God say, "'Can a mother forget the baby at her breast and have no compassion on the child she has borne? Though she may forget, I will not forget you! See, I have engraved you on the palms of my hands; your walls are ever before me'" (Isa. 49:15, 16 NIV). Hearing these words of affirmation is part of the process of helping people accept God as nurturing parent.

The processes and information that precede or follow this chapter are often preliminary to the step of letting God be nurturing parent. Although the counselor's inclination may be to begin with the "bad news" proclamation—"you are a sinner"—the "good news" proclamation—"God loves you and forgives you"—is a more productive starting place for the person who is in the process of building self-esteem. Persons with low self-esteem often hear "you are a sinner" as confirmation that they are bad or evil and therefore unlovable or unacceptable.

"Begin where the client is" is a guiding principle in counseling. Effective counseling results when the counselor resists the temptation to begin where he or she is and starts instead where counselees are in their self-talk, self-image, self-behavior, and self-feelings. This means that the counselor will go back to where the counselees are in their journey and walk with them rather than beckon them to come to where the counselor is or thinks they should be. Being with them in their struggle builds rapport and provides comfort and strength.

David, in Psalm 23, for example, describes this experience of God being where he is.

> Yea, though I walk through the valley of the shadow of death, I will fear no evil; for thou art with me; thy rod and thy staff they comfort me. Thou preparest a table before me in the presence of mine enemies; thou anointest my head with oil; my cup runneth over. Surely goodness and mercy shall follow me all the days of my life; and I will dwell in the house of the Lord forever. (KJV)

Janet, a former client who had become a missionary candidate and was visiting friends in the area, reminisced about how her counseling experience affected her relationship with God. "Dave, you will never know how much help you have been to me," she said. "Even though it has been years since I was in therapy with you, I still remember how you accepted me and let me be where I was without any judgment, criticism, or nagging.

"More than any insight you shared with me, more than any understanding you had of me, more than any intervention you made with me, your unconditional acceptance of where I was is an ongoing help. It opened the door to understanding God's unconditional love for me. Now when I struggle with my husband or kids, I remind myself of how you accepted me and how God accepts me and my family wherever we are in our growth." This is an example of the positive effect a Christian counselor may have when he or she is God's representative in a person's life and when the client is treated as a valuable person made in God's image.

Presenting God As a Nurturing Parent

There are several ways to present God as nurturing parent. Being a nurturing, nonjudgmental person is one way a counselor can prepare people to hear that God loves them unconditionally. Affirming that Jesus is their advocate (1 John 2:1), not their accuser, is another. The essence of anyone making God his or her nurturing parent is to hear that he is an accepter not an adversary (Isaiah 58:8, 9). For people to hear that God invites them to repentance, not to criticism, will require a positive therapeutic experience. If they are to hear that God is their Savior, not their Judge, then they will first need to experience therapists as understanding, not judging. God is their commender and commander, not their condemner (John 8:10, 11; Romans 8:1). Proclaiming that God is for them, not against them (Romans 8:31); that nothing can separate them from God's love (Romans 8:33, 38); that God is their comforter, not their criticizer (John 14), is meaningful in the context of a human relationship that provides this quality experience.

The principle of God's grace, lived out in people's relationships with a gracious counselor, teaches them that they are worthwhile because Christ purchased them. What God was willing to pay to redeem them establishes their worth factually; but without caring human relationships, many people will not be able to apply this truth emotionally or spiritually.

Counselors also proclaim that human worth is a product of God's creative activity. He determines and assigns value because he is the potter and humans are the clay (Isaiah 45:9). The fact that people do not create their own existence (being) is a humbling, yet affirming, reality. Because humans have nothing to do with their birth and because the source of their life is God, their worth is beyond human measure. Another way God affirms human worth is established through the reason he created life: we are God's gift to himself. By mirroring God's love and forgiveness, effective counselors live out God's message to clients that they are loved unconditionally—on the basis of God's act, not on the basis of their behavior or intentions. This truth is hard for many people to believe because it means their existence is God's doing, not theirs, and that they are lovable regardless of what they do with their humanness (Romans 5:8). *The gospel teaches that humans have worth and value independent of their sinfulness.* For Christian counselors, this truth is sometimes difficult to grasp, especially when working with people who are unrepentant.

The Sensory Process of God As Nurturer

The process of experiencing God as nurturing parent follows the same sensory sequence used throughout the counseling experience. Persons build their self-esteem through hearing God's message, seeing God's action, and feeling God's touch. Really believing God's love of and value for them results from hearing God's message. Paul claims, "Faith comes from hearing the message and the message is heard through the word of Christ" (Rom. 10:17 NIV).

The physical act of hearing is not enough. Jesus asks, "'Having ears, do you not hear?'" (Mark 8:18). Clients must comprehend and accept the message if they are to come to faith in God's love for them. As Jesus demonstrated, comprehension and acceptance often result from dialogue. Sometimes this dialogue is brief, as with Zaccheus (Luke 19), or the woman at the well (John 4). Frequently, comprehension and acceptance take place over a long period of time, as with the twelve disciples, and Nicodemus. Jesus was patient as long as the inquirer desired to learn and did not play self-righteous games.

People need to hear that God does not love us because we are valuable; we are valuable because God loves us (Martin Luther). The principle of God's grace teaches us that we are worthwhile because Christ redeemed us.

Our worth is also dependent on God's creative activity. God determines and assigns our value by creating us in his image and by paying the highest price for our salvation, the death of his Son. Humans, on the other hand, seem to have this predisposition: to establish their own worth through how well they do, how good they look, and how powerful they are. People tend to judge their value by their performance, appearance, and "importance." Not surprisingly, these are fleeting and unreliable bases for establishing or maintaining self-esteem. Yet, many resist the truth that performance, position, prestige, power, and appearance do not influence God's acceptance. Our value, from God's viewpoint, is not based on being perfect or on achieving some difficult feat. Our value is a birthday gift which comes with our existence because God created us. How we look, how we act, how we think, what we say and what we do—these are important to God *after* we have accepted his love and forgiveness. Before our conversion, they have no influence on God's grace. After our conversion, however, our behavior does matter to God. He asks for loving obedience to his will, not perfection. Many confuse obedience with perfection; and this confusion leads to shame, failure, and a lowered self-esteem. Having responded to appeals to rededicate their lives to Christ, but having failed repeatedly to live righteously, people often give up trying to please God because they realize they cannot be consistent.

Doris came to me in despair. As a young adult, no matter how hard she tries, she cannot live up to her own standards. She fears that she disappoints God to the point of being cast out of his loving mercy and forgiveness. Raised by loving Christian parents, but worshiping in a church that preaches the law of condemnation more than the gospel of grace, Doris is ready to give up being a Christian and let herself be possessed by the negative forces that seem so powerful in her life.

Doris does not realize that her experience of failing as a Christian is common. When asked whether she had read the apostle Paul's words about not being able to do what he wanted to do, and doing what he did not want to do, she said she remembers reading that somewhere, but those words did not comfort her. So, I read Romans 7:15–8:1 and 1 John 1:5–10 to her. I encouraged her to read these passages to herself during the week in the hope that she would hear that Paul's struggle and hers are similar; this realization would allow her to esteem herself despite her failures and would allow her to respond, as Paul did in Romans 7:22–25:

For I joyfully concur with the law of God in the inner man, but I see a different law in the members of my body, waging war against the law of my mind, and making me a prisoner of the law of sin which is in my members. Wretched man that I am! Who will set me free from the body of this death? Thanks be to God through Jesus Christ our Lord! So then, on the one hand I myself with my mind am serving the law of God, but on the other, with my flesh the law of sin.

A fellow counselor shared a quotation from J. I. Packer that I use as a handout to clients who are struggling with their sin nature:

God in redemption finds us all more or less disintegrated personalities. Disintegration and loss of rational control are aspects of our sinful and fallen state. Trying to play God to ourselves, we are largely out of control of ourselves and also out of touch with ourselves, or at least with a great deal of ourselves, including most of what is central to our real selves. But God's gracious purpose is to bring us into a reconciled relationship with himself, through Christ, and through the outworking of that relationship to reintegrate us and make us whole beings again.[2]

To see God's action, counselees will need to learn *how* to look at the world and themselves, and *what* to look for in their current and past history.

As the psalmist writes, "The heavens are telling the glory of God; and their expanse is declaring the work of His hands" (Ps. 19:1). In relation to self-esteem, people can be taught to look at themselves from God's point of view. "So from now on we regard no one from a worldly point of view. Though we once regarded Christ in this way, we do so no longer. Therefore, if anyone is in Christ, he is a new creation, the old has gone, the new has come!" (2 Cor. 5:16, 17).

When people look at themselves from God's point of view, they look clean, fresh, new, white as snow (Psalms 51:7; Isaiah

1:18). I have used Philippians 4:8 to help clients look at themselves the way God perceives them.

> Finally, brethren, whatever is true, whatever is honorable, whatever is right, whatever is pure, whatever is lovely, whatever is of good repute, if there is any excellence and if anything worthy of praise, let your mind dwell on these things.

I instruct them, "Let your mind dwell on these qualities and answer from each of these three viewpoints. You will need to use Scripture to answer the first statement, 'God sees me as . . .'; and then use your experiences with others and yourself to answer the other two statements. You have not been thinking like this, so expect that it will take some time and energy to generate positive responses. Bring this worksheet back to your next session so we can talk about what you are experiencing."

I write out the exercise as I explain it to them. Below is a sample of the diagram, and sample answers.

PHILIPPIANS 4:8			
	God sees me as	Others see me as	I see myself as
TRUE	When I repent of my sin	When I am honest with them	When I say what I think and feel
HONORABLE	When I submit to God's will	When I keep my promises	
RIGHT	When I accept his forgiveness. When I reflect on his laws.		When I express my feelings, ask for what I need, and live by God's values.
PURE			
LOVELY			
GOOD REPUTE			
EXCELLENT			
WORTHY OF PRAISE			

To feel God's touch, counselees will need to learn to feel tenderness, love, or compassion. Some of them need to learn that touch can be safe inasmuch as they previously have been abused. They need to learn the differences between green flag touch and red flag touch, safe touch and harmful touch, appropriate touch and inappropriate touch, affectionate touch and sexual touch, nurturing touch and taking touch.[3] God's touch is safe and nurturing. He wants to give out of the abundance of his resources. "'If you then, being evil, know how to give good gifts to your children, how much more shall your Father who is in heaven give what is good to those who ask Him!'" (Matt. 7:11).

Many long for an accepting, giving relationship with another human and with God. This longing for closeness is described in one of the most tender stories in the New Testament: "People were also bringing babies to Jesus to have him touch them. When the disciples saw this, they rebuked them. But Jesus called the children to him and said, 'Let the little children come to me, and do not hinder them, for the kingdom of God belongs to such as these'" (Luke 18:15, 16 NIV). If a client struggles with letting God into his or her life, that person, like these little children, may have been hindered from getting close to God by some well-intentioned people who did not understand the breadth and depth of God's acceptance. Such people may need to experience not only a loving and accepting counselor or pastor, but also a church that understands what they need if they are to claim, "For my father and my mother have forsaken me, but the Lord will take me up" (Ps. 27:10). People who experience God's love in the context of a Sunday school class, Bible study group, or other support group, grow toward wholeness in their views of themselves and God. Feeling God's love, then, is seldom experienced apart from the presence of loving people in our lives.

To act on God's love is a response of obedience that springs from hearing, seeing, and feeling God's love. He does not ask us to act obediently before we have experienced his mercy. The Bible makes it clear that we are to act on what we have heard. "But prove yourselves doers of the word, and not merely hearers who delude themselves" (James 1:22; see also

Matthew 7:24–27, Luke 6:46–49, Romans 2:13, and James 2:14–20).

Therapeutically, it is also important for counselors to remember to take counselees through the process of hearing, seeing, and feeling before instructing them to act differently. Hearing an interpretation, seeing an insight, and feeling an emotion are necessary steps to acting on the truth if behavioral change is to be integrated into a person's lifestyle. A biblical illustration of this process is found in Mark 6:52: "For they had not gained any insight from the incident of the loaves, but their heart was hardened." The disciples were unable to respond in faith to Jesus' walking on the water because they had not gained any insight from the miracle of the loaves and fishes. Their minds were closed to learning. They did not see what they had seen, hear what they had heard, feel what they had felt during the miracle; so when they witnessed another miracle, they were unable to act in faith.

Here is how I would diagram and summarize the sensory sequence in the process of experiencing God as nurturing parent:

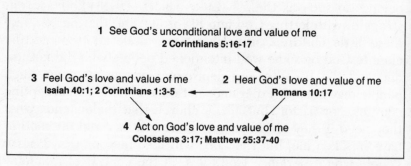

1 See God's unconditional love and value of me
2 Corinthians 5:16-17

3 Feel God's love and value of me
Isaiah 40:1; 2 Corinthians 1:3-5

2 Hear God's love and value of me
Romans 10:17

4 Act on God's love and value of me
Colossians 3:17; Matthew 25:37-40

People in counseling will begin their process of experiencing God as nurturing parent at one of these four points. Usually the beginning point is either auditory or visual. If they have an intense emotional conversion or religious experience, they may be aware only of the kinesthetic modality. When they are unable to maintain the emotional sense of closeness with God or acceptance of God, they will experience frustration and doubt. As counselor, keep in mind that the process actually begins for them at one of the other sensory modalities. Assist them in recovering what precedes the affective experience so they can recreate and maintain the positive experience for themselves. Their sensory processes can be recovered by asking what they say or see before they feel close to God. If they say they do not know or cannot remember, ask them to guess or make up something. This creative experience frequently identifies the lost auditory or visual experience.

In the event this exploration is unproductive, ask what they were doing before they felt close to God. It may be they were reading the Bible or devotional literature, singing, listening to a religious radio program or taped message, or watching a television program. When some behavior precedes the feeling experience, explore what they say to themselves or think about, or how they look at the world or themselves. Going after their interpretation or perception of the behavior will give you missing parts to their sensory sequence.

When your explorations seem to produce no auditory or visual information, ask them to imagine what they need to say to themselves, or hear and look at, or be shown, in order to begin feeling close to God. You may also ask them to tell you what they think about when they feel close to God. Another productive strategy is to ask them to tell you what they wish they would say/hear or see/look at when they feel close to God. This may give you and them the missing parts to their sensory process of experiencing God as nurturing parent. Whatever information they give you, work it into their unique sensory process and have them practice utilizing the process in sessions until they are able to create the experience of God as their nurturing parent without your assistance.

As I reflect on the sensory process described above, I remember 1 Corinthians 13:12: "For now we see in a mirror dimly, but then face to face; now I know in part, but then I shall know fully just as I also have been fully known." This passage suggests to me the following sensory metaphor. In spite of the fact that, as sinful human beings, we *hear* life through cracked speakers (dull ears), *see* life through foggy lenses (dim eyes), *feel* life through broken hearts, and *act out* life through inconsistent behavior, God is our nurturing parent who never leaves us or forsakes us.

Romans 8:31–39 affirms that no one can be against us if

God is for us, that no one can "bring a charge against God's elect," that no one can "separate us from the love of Christ." Our task as Christian counselors is to help people come to this experience for themselves. We teach them to experience God as their nurturing parent by being a nurturing person in their lives and by working with their sensory modalities.

Counseling Illustrations

The testimony of John eloquently describes the above process: "That which was from the beginning, which we have *heard*, which we have *seen* with our eyes, which we have *looked at* and our hands have *touched*—this we proclaim concerning the Word of life" (1 John 1:1).

Counselors have a similar task: proclaiming their relationship with God in terms that describe what they have seen, heard, and touched. Since the reality of clients' relationship with an affirming God often comes first through the relationship with an affirming counselor, the therapeutic relationship can be used to help clients experience God positively. One way that I have facilitated a person's positive experience of God is to paraphrase a Bible story, using it metaphorically.

As Sharon built her self-esteem through positive internal dialogue, she became more willing to face her anger toward and hatred of her parents. Fearing that God would punish her for negative feelings, Sharon hesitated to share with me the intensity of her rage. In childhood, she was not allowed to express anger openly; as a result, she developed secret and self-abusive behaviors like overeating, pouting, locking herself in her room, and acting irritable and oversensitive. She also accused herself of being evil because of her hateful feelings.

Picking up on her self-accusation and fear that God was accusing her, I led her in the following experience, pausing before each new instruction: "Sharon, I wonder if you would be willing to picture yourself in the middle of an arena." She closed her eyes and listened intently for the next instructions. "Although you are alone, notice people are sitting in bleachers all around you. Watch them stand up, and see them point their fingers at you. Hear them yelling, YOU, YOU, YOU, YOU, YOU! Feel the embarrassment and humiliation. Feel yourself trying to get up and run out of the arena before you are stopped by guards. Notice that the people have rocks in their hands and have them raised over their heads ready to throw them at you.

"Listen as all of a sudden the crowd becomes quiet. As you wonder what is happening, you see a man walk into the arena. He walks toward you, smiles, and greets you by name. 'Hello, Sharon. You must be pretty scared. I have come to help you.' See him sitting down next to you. This man looks familiar, but you cannot quite place him.

"As you try to figure out who he is, the crowd begins to yell accusations about you to the man. When they call him by name you remember who he is. 'Jesus, she is a silly, stupid, sinful, and crazy woman,' they yell. 'She does not deserve happiness or love. She deserves a life of loneliness and self-hate. Teacher, this woman has been caught in the very act of many sinful deeds. The law says she should be stoned. What do you say?'

"Without looking at the crowd, he doodles in the dirt for several minutes. A hush falls over the arena as the man stands and addresses the crowd. 'You who are innocent and have never said anything silly or stupid, nor lived sinfully or acted crazy, throw the first stone.' He then sits down and continues to doodle. Notice the crowd laying down their stones, hanging their heads, and walking quietly out of the arena, leaving you alone with Jesus.

"When the crowd is gone, this Jesus, who is the Christ,[4] turns to you, looks you in the eyes, and asks, 'Where are your accusers?'

"Astonished, you say softly and hesitantly, 'They are gone.'

"Jesus Christ says, 'Neither do I accuse you. Stop accusing yourself and go live with my love, grace, and mercy, careful to process your anger, hurt, and rejection each day.'

"You feel relief that you are not accused. Jesus asks whether he can hug you. Longing to be touched without being taken advantage of, you agree. You cling to Jesus until you feel ready to let go. As you release your hug, the Lord Jesus releases his hug. Listen to him say good-bye and watch him walk out of the arena. You are crying softly, cherishing this moment. You linger for as long as you need.

"When you are ready to leave, you notice the many rocks that were not thrown at you. Wanting a souvenir of your encounter with Jesus, you select a rock and write Romans 8:1 on one side, 'There is therefore now no condemnation for those who are in Christ Jesus,' and John 8:11 on the other side, 'Neither do I condemn you.' When you are ready, see yourself walk out of the arena toward home. Ponder the experience you have just had with Jesus, and feel the relief of being understood and accepted. Notice how light your body feels. Feel the freedom to be you. See that you are approaching your home. Walk in and go to your bedroom. Place the rock on your dresser where you can see it every day as a reminder of the freedom and forgiveness you have in Christ.

"Now see yourself walking out of your room and house and entering this room with me. Take as much time as you need to get here. As you return, feel clean, affirmed, awakened, and refreshed."

I waited as Sharon wiped her eyes, breathed deeply, and squeezed my hand. She looked at me and smiled.

"Sharon, can you describe what you are experiencing?"

"Dave, this is wonderful. I need to hold on to this experience. I feel okay to be just who I am."

"Well, Sharon, what I would like you to do when you leave here today is to find a hand-sized rock, write on it Romans 8:1 and John 8:11, and place it on your dresser just as you did it in your imagination. Are you willing to do this?"

Sharon agreed. "You know, I have read the Bible many times, but I have never thought of it applying to me this way."

I responded, "Yes, I hear you. What a wonderful experience to have Scripture come alive and personal."

Notice that I have used all four sensory modalities in telling Sharon this story. She is invited into the experience of imagining with her ears, eyes, heart, and actions. Her negative life-experience is woven into the Bible story to assist her in making a personal application. Although she has heard of or read this story many times, its personal application becomes real for her as she imagines herself in the story.

The following week, Sharon brought a stone with Romans 8:1 and John 8:11 written on it. I reinforced the above experience by asking her to report what she was saying to herself about being silly, stupid, sinful, and crazy. When her internal dialogue became negative, hearing herself or her parents putting her down, she took herself to the arena and heard Jesus tell her, "Neither do I condemn you." Picking up on her experience, I wrote on a piece of paper. "*God says, 'I love, value, and affirm your capability even when you are silly, stupid, sinful, or crazy'*" (a paraphrase of Rom. 5:8). I then asked Sharon to hang the paper on her refrigerator or mirror to remind her that God really does love, value, and want her.

The story of Jesus inviting himself to Zaccheus's house is another Bible story I have used to help people experience God's affirming love and value.

"I want to tell you a story," I begin. "Can you imagine yourself wanting to see someone a great deal, but feeling reluctant and afraid to approach him because of who you are and the bad things you have done?" I wait for some sign of acknowledgment. "Okay, what I would like you to do is see yourself hiding behind a bush. You do not want to be noticed, so most of your body is hidden behind the bush; and you are poking your head through the branches and peeking. You are here because you want to see Jesus and listen to him without being seen.

"Hear the crowd walking down the street toward the bush where you are hiding. See them coming closer and closer. Your heart begins to race and pound. You are not sure whether you are more excited or scared.

"Peek out a little further to look for the man whom you are so anxious to see. Notice that he stops right in front of the bush where you are hiding, looks right at you and says, '_____ (counselee's name), come out from behind the bush. I want to come to your house for lunch.' Part of you wants him to keep walking and ignore you, but another part is glad he wants to talk to you. You feel scared because you are afraid he is going to criticize you for how you are living. And yet you feel excited that he is taking the time to talk with you. Not many people take time to talk with you because they do not trust or understand you. They feel that you have treated them unfairly and cruelly.

"Notice how astonished the crowd is that Jesus Christ is taking time for and showing interest in you. Hear them murmur, 'What does Jesus see in him? I am a better person than he is. Why doesn't Jesus come to my house?'

"Hesitantly, you walk out from behind the bush and show the Lord Jesus where you live. You are amazed at how gentle his voice sounds and his face looks. You begin to relax, sensing that whatever your house looks like and whatever you have to serve will be acceptable to Jesus. You are the only person who knows what you and Jesus talk about over lunch because this is a private meeting. You take this opportunity to tell Jesus how lonely and guilty you feel. He listens and offers encouragement to face who you are and what you have done that makes you feel that way.

"Jesus, God's son, offers you his love and forgiveness. You are having difficulty believing that you can be okay after all the horrible things you have done and said. He assures you that he is bigger than any sin you have committed. He tells you that he has paid the price of your sin. In response, you confess even more of your negative thinking, covetous imaginations, and behavior. Jesus accepts whatever you tell him, offering forgiveness. Jesus' response seems almost too good to be true, but you are feeling so relieved and free that you begin to believe you are forgiven.

"As you finish the meal, Jesus announces that he needs to move on. You feel grateful for the personal audience you are having with him. You shake his hand firmly and warmly, thanking him for spending the time with you and making you feel clean and free. As he leaves, you vow that with his help you will change your behavior and thoughts to be more like his.

"See yourself several days later walking down the street. The people seem to be responding to you differently. Notice how puzzled they look. Hear them asking each other, 'What has happened to _____ (client's name) that he (or she) seems so different?' Take in their response and enjoy your new image as you imagine how Jesus looks at you. Keep that image in mind as you find yourself walking out of this encounter with Jesus and back to this office with me. Take all the time you need to be oriented into this office. When you are ready, report what you are experiencing."

Remember to take time to process the individual's experience. This deprograming phase will inform you of the counselee's experience of the metaphor and give you specifics to add to the process; and, frequently, it will remind both of you of unfinished issues that need to be worked on in counseling.

Jesus and the woman at the well (John 4) is another Bible story I use in counseling. I tell my students that I pray to become a more talented therapist who, like Christ Jesus, tells a person everything he has done in such a way that the person feels affirmed as a worthwhile human being, not condemned as a sinner; drawn to God, not threatened with punishment and rejection; invited to face himself or herself, not encouraged to hide.

I am convinced that what I say has positive impact both because of who I am as a person and because of how I relate to others. Words in and of themselves have little power. When Jesus treated the woman at the well with respect, although the disciples marveled that he was speaking with an outcast, she felt Jesus' approval.

How do counselors confront clients with their sinfulness without their feeling condemned? First, they must be loving, accepting, understanding, nurturing persons who remember that they are daily experiencing God's love, nurture, mercy, and forgiveness. Then they must speak the truth in love, kindness, and gentleness (Ephesians 4:32; 2 Timothy 2:24–26).

When I believe that clients need to hear "bad news," I will often introduce it by saying, "I want to tell you something that might seem harsh and make you feel uncomfortable. Are you ready to hear it?" Usually I get an invitation even though they are scared. Frequently counselees will receive the bad news without too much difficulty. I have even had some ask me at the end of a session, "When are you going to make me uncomfortable?" Their reaction attests the positive power of confronting people in love and understanding. At times I will ask a client to teach me how I can tell him or her something negative. "If I need to say something negative to you, how can I tell you in a way that does not make you feel rejected or misunderstood?"

But it is not always possible to tell people what they need to hear in a way they will accept. The rich young ruler's encounter with Jesus is one such story. I tell them this story when counselees ask me for advice, but reject it when I give it to them. Rejection gives me another opportunity to affirm that although I am giving them what they are asking for, they, for whatever reason, are not ready to hear it. Notice that this is not said in anger, but as a statement of fact. Jesus' response to the rich young ruler's rejection of his answer is a demonstration of the desired therapeutic attitude and emotion. It also teaches counselors that it is acceptable to let persons go their way without making heroic attempts to save them, even if they are on a sinful or self-destructive course.°

I also remind my students that Jesus was not 100 percent successful in his encounters with people. Shortly before his trial, Jesus was teaching in the synagogue, lamenting the hypocrisy and hardness of heart of the scribes and Pharisees. "'O Jerusalem, Jerusalem,'" he cried, "'who kills the prophets and stones those who are sent to her! How often I wanted to gather your children together, the way a hen gathers her chicks under her wings, and you were unwilling'" (Matt. 23:37). When my students ask me how I keep from becoming depressed over clients who will not listen to me, I say, "I look at my hands three times a day. When I see no nail prints, I remind myself that I am a shepherd, not a savior." Then I repeat the rich young ruler and synagogue stories to them.

Christian counselors need to keep in mind the human longing for acceptance that the above Bible stories affirm. "Lament," the following poem, cries out the low self-esteem person's longing for our affirmation of his or her significance:

°When people are suicidal, homicidal, self-destructive or dangerous to others, counselors and pastors do have a moral and legal responsibility to intervene. My point here is to caution against our temptation to be rescuer and savior at a time when we have reached our limits and/or when the people seeking our help have decided, like the rich young ruler, they do not want or need our help.

Lament

Oh, Lord, I feel so worthless, inadequate, a nothing!
   Prove me wrong!
Lord, I feel so unloved, unlovable.
   Send me someone who will love me deeply,
   So deeply that I can believe otherwise!
I feel so alone, so lonely, so empty.
   Fill me up; surround me with Your presence.
I feel no one cares, no one needs me, no one wants me.
   Please, God, prove to me that I am wrong.
I feel forsaken, blocked off, locked out of joy.
   Oh, Lord, Lord, don't You have the key?
Words seem so empty, no weapon against the lonely pain.
   Lord, make Your promise of love come alive for me!
I cannot see You;
You are so distant, so omnipotent, so supreme.
I cannot believe that You could care
For such an insignificant me!
   Please God, show Yourself to me
   So I can really see
   And feel and touch and hold You.
   Show me You in a human, so I may know the reality
   That I can see and touch and hold.
I want to hurt myself, ridicule myself,
Wound myself in their presence
   So they—and You—may pick me up,
   And soothe me and comfort me and make me feel loved.
I want to scream and cry and catch someone's attention
   So others will start to care,
   So others will want to stop me,
   So I can see that it makes a difference . . .
   NO! . . .
   That *I* make a difference in their lives.
Oh God, I hurt so, I want so:
I hunger and thirst to be Somebody
To Somebody who is important to me.
You are sometimes not real enough,
Not tangible enough to hold on to.

Then Your promises seem like whispers lost on the wind.
And the blessings I have felt seem to melt
From my memory and from my assurance,
And are mere illusions, no longer a foundation for faith.
Oh Lord, I feel lost.
   Please find me.
   Search for me and seek me
   So that I can really believe that You want me!
Oh God! Is it only a dream that I felt loved?
I can't feel it now!
I can't touch it now!
Love is the only life-line that will save me;
Yet I sink deeper down the abyss.
Oh God, reach out, with human hands and human
   words and human love
And hold on to me with divine love
And don't let me go!
I'm so afraid of never having had it all.
   Oh Lord, my God, please prove me wrong!

—Marcia Esther Allen

Summary

Teaching people to experience God as nurturing parent is a process that uses their sensory sequence. They build self-esteem through hearing God's message, seeing God's action, and feeling God's touch. The helper has been encouraged to become a representative of God in clients' lives, providing a human relationship that facilitates accepting God as father. The sensory process to build self-esteem was presented as: hearing God's love and value of me, seeing God's unconditional love and value of me, acting on God's love and value of me, and feeling God's love and value of me.

CHAPTER TEN

TEACHING THE CHURCH TO BUILD ESTEEM IN ITS TROUBLED FAMILIES

"GOOD MORNING, THIS IS DAVE CARLSON." "Good morning. This is Phyllis."

"Well, hello Phyllis. Good to hear from you. How are you today?"

"Oh, fine." Then she burst into tears and said, "I'm not fine. Doug left me last night."

I was taken by surprise because I hadn't known this couple was having marital trouble. Her husband's leaving had also taken Phyllis by surprise, because their life together had seemed to be going well. Despite difficulties two years before, she was confident they had worked through their problems.

Phyllis cried softly as we talked. I wondered how I could help. Doug would not talk to any of his friends, or family, she said. He seemed to be angry at everyone, blaming his marital problems on parents, in-laws, and the church. Nevertheless, I assured her I would try to call Doug at work anyway.

Because Phyllis was several hundred miles away, my contact with her would be by phone. Before we concluded the first of what turned out to be many calls, I promised to call her every day, unaware of what a commitment and emotional drain that was going to place on me. I inquired about food and rent money and the availability of other supportive people close to her geographically. From what she told me, I was satisfied that she could provide for her physical needs in the immediate future. But the fact that she was calling me, a person not physically available, made me wonder how comfortable she felt about sharing her turmoil with family and friends more immediately available. I assumed that my phone contact with her would be an important source of comfort, but I knew that would not be enough. She needed people she could see and touch. Phyllis named several people she was going to call after our conversation. I affirmed the need for her to reach out to family and friends, and to her pastor, and told her my wife and I would pray for her. We set up a time for me to call her the next day.

IMAGINING: PRACTICING EMPATHY

Imagine that you are Phyllis, a woman with three school-age children, calling to share the news that your spouse is leaving you. You probably are feeling numb, panicky, scared, saddened, and angry. At times you may be feeling overwhelmed, unable to cook, clean, and take care of yourself or your kids. Helplessness and depression may dominate you. You may be wishing it were only a dream that your husband had left, hoping you will wake up to find you are having a nightmare. No doubt you are feeling humiliation and embarrassment. And there is the possibility that you are feeling guilt and shame.

Also imagine what you are saying to yourself. *Why is this happening to me? What did I do wrong? I am a failure. How can he treat me this way? I don't deserve this kind of treatment.*

How am I going to survive? I want to die; that would be easier than his leaving me.

Imagine how you are looking at yourself. You may be thinking how old you look or believing that you are still attractive. You may see yourself as a good mother and homemaker and wonder how Doug could not see your faithfulness and commitment to him and to the children. Are you imagining ways to hurt him back?

Now imagine how you are acting. Are you crying hysterically, or being brave and putting up a good front? Are you falling apart, or carrying on as though nothing serious has happened? Are you reaching out for help, or hiding from your family and friends? Are you calling your spouse, begging and pleading with him to return, or are you ignoring his absence in the hope that he will return?

Take a moment to think of the challenges you are now facing as you try to survive without your spouse, alone with the kids. This is an exercise in empathy. Your responses may be similar to these: *Will we have to move? How will I pay the rent? What kind of job can I get? I haven't worked since college. How am I going to face my family and friends? What will I tell the children? I don't want to be single or divorced.*

Now take a moment to put yourself in my place as the receiver of this phone call. In what ways do you empathize with me? Are you experiencing sadness? Fear? Anger? Helplessness? What are you saying to yourself? *I don't believe my friend is doing this to his wife and kids. I wish I were there to shake some sense into him. How can I help them when I live so far away?*

Pause for a moment to consider what you would be feeling if these people were members of your congregation. When you are ready, shift your thinking to Phyllis and Doug as your friends. What feelings are you experiencing? Now imagine that Phyllis and Doug are part of your immediate family. Are your feelings easier to identify? Different? More or less intense?

THREE CHALLENGES WHEN FAMILIES ARE IN TROUBLE

The first challenge people face when their families are in trouble is to talk, view, feel, and act positively toward themselves. People tend to blame themselves, or assume that others are blaming them or holding them responsible. Yet, to love and value themselves in the midst of family turmoil is necessary for their own survival, growth, and successful coping.

After loving, valuing, and forgiving themselves, the second challenge is for family members to love the "hurter." To talk, view, feel, and act lovingly toward the person causing or having trouble may be the greatest challenge. If family, friends, or counselors are to help restore the person and his or her relationships, they must act loving, valuing, and forgiving toward the sinner. Because human love is fickle and conditional, drawing upon God's grace to love and forgive the person causing the trouble is the only way helpers can maintain a positive relationship with the person in the midst of turmoil. Remembering God's mercy and forgiveness toward themselves enables them to monitor and control anger and resentment toward the person causing trouble. This awareness also helps the family and counselors give up the human tendency toward vengeance and be more concerned for the sinner than for themselves, or for justice.

Loving and valuing family members who are hurting pose the third challenge. To support and encourage them as they go through a dark valley is to give them a gift of immeasurable worth. When people are hurting is not the time for blaming, condemning, or finding fault. Nor is there any benefit in those responses. It is not a time for rejecting or criticizing. Rather, it is the time for listening to their pain; for caring, not correcting; for accepting them, not for handing out the "right" biblical and/or theological answers. Speaking in terms of *should, ought, must,* and *have to*—even if each is true—is to act like Job's friends, who broke their seven days of comforting silence to offer useless counsel. Questions such as "Why didn't you . . . ?" are not helpful at this time. And statements like "If I were you, I would . . ." are frequently premature if not arrogantly self-righteous. And even when people speak with positive intent, they often lack sufficient information or empathy to be credible and caring.

Is There an Ideal Family?

You can find an ideal family every Sunday morning, getting out of their car just before Sunday school or church. They are always dressed well, smiling as if they were happy to be coming to church. Mom and Dad frequently hold hands if the child is not too small and the Bible too big.

Everyone envies the ideal family. Everything seems to be going well for them. The wife is attractive and capable, a Proverbs 31-type woman. The husband is handsome and accomplished, working his way up the corporate ladder. The kids are cute, bright, and successful at everything they attempt. The ideal family sends a Christmas card every year, usually accompanied with their family picture and a letter informing friends of just how wonderful their life and family are. As the recipients read these letters and cards, they experience envy, sadness, and anger because their families, spouses, and children do not measure up to those of the sender's. What is really ironic is that the family sending this greeting may see someone else's family and marriage as the ideal and feel envious, sad, and angry that their family is not like that one.

Is there an ideal family? Sure there is, existing in our imaginations and hopes. It is portrayed in television programs, movies, books, articles, sermons, and Christmas letters. But the real family is very much like the pastor's, counselor's, parishioner's, and neighbor's—it is the family that no one can see or hear or feel because it hides behind closed doors and so protects itself from being exposed to the world.

The real family has spots, wrinkles, and warts. It has frustrations, failures, and disappointments. Only rarely does the real family dare show its troubled reality to the church, or to friends, or to themselves. Recently, I was at an anniversary celebration where an adult daughter read a poem conveying to her parents her appreciation for their love, patience, and understanding during her teenage struggle with Christianity. It was a courageous and transparent admission, surprising—if not shocking—the parents and audience by its honesty of confession. This was a rare example of a real family sharing what was going on in their lives.

Having the privilege of counseling people from within the church to which my family and I belong, I know many stories of heartache that are not public knowledge. Following a church service, a woman approached me with her family's pain. She said, "Don't any people in this church have trouble with their kids?"

I responded, "I can tell you that many people have had or are having the same struggle with their children that you are experiencing. I cannot tell you who they are because confidentiality is their privilege, but I can ask one of them to call you and help you through this trial." (I wrote earlier that it is a privilege to counsel people from my own church. It is also a burden, at times, because it interferes with my worship as I see hurting Christians singing in the choir or sitting in front of me, and I am reminded of their pain.)

A Christmas Letter from a Real Family

The real Christmas letter which follows is unusual because most families do not communicate as honestly and transparently. Notice the pain and anguish as this mother writes about her son's death. Also pay attention to her search for meaning and purpose, and see how she interprets the events to bring herself consolation and comfort. She writes this letter for herself as much as for her friends. Read this letter as though you were receiving it from one of your friends, allowing yourself to feel whatever emotions it triggers. I share it with the family's permission.

Dear Friends and Loved Ones:

Never did we think that we would have to write a letter like this, but we feel that it will be one of hope and one that Tim would be pleased to see done. In Tim's twenty-second year, with two and one half years of college and an analytical mind that wanted to become a systems analyst, our son died by his own hand on November 8, 1983, a victim of depression, compounded by catastrophic anxiety and panic which could not be controlled. Life for us will never be the same.

[The writer relates the events of the weekend up to the night before his death.] On Sunday evening Art, Tim and I were watching TV and Tim said out of a clear blue sky, "Mom and Dad, I just want you to know that I love you both very much." We assured him of our love for him too. This was unusual for Tim because he was not a wordy person, but he asked for special prayer and then we all prayed for special healing. On Monday he went to work as usual (he had to drop out of school because of anxiety). On Monday night I said I had to go to Sears to pick up two bedspreads and he was so concerned that it would be too heavy for me, so he went along and carried them home for me. When we got home, he was beside himself with anxiety, so Art and I laid hands on him and we literally cried out to God. Tim even said, "God, did you forget I'm here suffering so much? Please, please help me." We stayed up late that night and just talked, but finally Art and I went to bed and we told Tim we loved him. I then knelt by my bed and prayed like never before for my precious son, whom I knew God loved but who could not understand why he had to endure so much. That was the last time we saw Tim alive. Sometime during the night, apparently the panic was too overwhelming and he did what he felt he had to do.

[Following a discussion of the funeral, the letter continues:] Do we feel anger for Tim? No, only some anger for some doctors who refused to consider the bio-chemical aspects of his physical condition. He is no longer suffering as we saw him suffer for three years. Some people have said, "How could such a nice Christian boy do this to you?" By the time a person gets to the desperate straits of suicide, he is not thinking of the consequences his act will have for others, only of his own intolerable situation. We ask ourselves, could we have loved him more, encouraged him more, given him more direction? Yes I suppose we could have; however, that love couldn't have kept him alive. When we read his letter to us, we feel at peace. He said, "Dear Mom and Dad, I love you very much. I want you to know that my death was not the result of you in any way. You were both the greatest positive influences in my life during the most difficult time in my life. You supported me with your prayers and by what you said through the whole time. I died being right with the Lord and at peace about the afterlife. I will definitely see you in Glory. I finally decided to quit being strong and struggling against impossible odds. I love you very much. May God comfort your hearts with His peace." His Bible was with him and we saw how underlined it was. That is unusual for a young man of 21. We have an aching sense of loss. If only the phone would ring and we could hear his voice. His easy-going personality was always a pleasure.

How does one survive the death of a loved one by suicide? By the Grace of God, by our dear daughters and their families, and by loved ones and friends. . . .

Thanks to you all for your concern and love for us, and may your Christmas be one of joy. We will spend Christmas with our family, and the grandchildren will help to make it a happy time. Somehow I felt compelled to write this letter this year instead of a card. Many of you have not known the whole situation. For those of you who have, please excuse us.

How to Live with Being a Real Family

If an ideal family is not possible to achieve, then how do we live with being a real family? Challenging the assumption that ideal families do exist is an excellent starting place.

The Scriptures will help us understand that the Bible does not present ideal families. Take a moment to read Colossians 3:18–21; Ephesians 5:21–6:4; and the book of Proverbs. Notice the difficulties in the New Testament church and in Old Testament families. These words were written for our encouragement, edification, and instruction. Husbands, wives, children, employers, fathers, and mothers had trouble. The apostle Paul writes to correct and prevent problems in Christian families. Certainly the writer of Proverbs has prevention of trouble in mind.

People who want to learn how to deal with their families

also can receive encouragement from knowing that *God had trouble with his family, too.* The following names serve to remind us of God's conflict with his children: Adam and Eve, Noah's generation, Abraham, Sodom and Gomorrah, Hosea, Moses, and the children of Israel—who forgot God's rescue and worshiped a golden calf, asked for a king, and lost the Scriptures.

Human history had barely begun when Adam and Eve had trouble obeying God and so fell into temptation, blaming each other rather than accepting the responsibility for their decisions. Cain and Abel represent sibling rivalry. Noah and Ham, and David and Absalom illustrate father-son conflict. Abraham and Lot demonstrate brother-in-law difficulties. Lot and his daughters introduce incest as a problem in biblical families. Potiphar's ignoring of his wife and her lusting after Joseph remind us of marital strife. In the New Testament, Mary, Jesus' mother, illustrates the problem of unmarried pregnancy. Joseph's struggle over his forthcoming marriage to Mary illustrates engaged-couple conflict. Given evidence in Scripture that there are no ideal families and given the evangelical Christian belief in the depravity of man, I would think we would have no problem accepting this truth: Christian families have trouble, too. Unfortunately, this acceptance does not predominate in many churches.

The fact that God had trouble with his family teaches us that God knows what it feels like to have family difficulty. He can empathize with our struggles and pain, imagining and identifying what we are going through. He does not feel pity for us because recipients see pity as depreciation and lack of respect. Nor does God feel sympathy for us, feeling what we feel in the sense that he loses his objectivity and sense of identity.[1]

Rather, he teaches us how to deal with blaming ourselves. God didn't blame himself for his family trouble because he was not responsible for his children's sinful decisions.

Human families may not be able to comfort themselves with this knowledge when the parenting they have provided has been inadequate, neglectful, or abusive. People ask two common questions when their family is in trouble: "Whose fault is it?" and, "Where did I fail?"

A human tendency is to look for someone to blame. Establishing fault, however, has no redemptive value. It may relieve family members of guilt, but it does not restore the damage or repair the hurt. Blaming, shaming, and condemning help people feel innocent and so may lead to self-righteousness and the appearance of arrogance. Blaming may also help people feel self-confident: "I knew better. If only he had listened to me!" And blaming may help people feel comfortable or relieved: "It's not me or my family."

Because God understands the destructive force of blaming, he asks us to consider our wicked ways. He describes our sin and points out a way of redemption through confession and repentance. God does ask us to take responsibility for our sinfulness, but he does not humiliate us. He asks us to be humble, to see who we really are—sinful creatures whom he desires to redeem. His loving care toward us and his gentle message to us provide the relational environment that enables us to respond positively to him and admit that we need him and his redemption. Blaming, on the other hand, is destructive because it encourages the one blamed to wallow in self-pity or create self-punishment as a way of atoning for his or her sin. It also encourages self-condemnation, self-rejection, and self-hate. The self-blamer will ask: "Was I protective or helpful enough? Did I give or love enough? What more could I have done that would have helped my child avoid the trouble he is in?" Blaming accomplishes nothing good, but it builds up guilt, shame, depression, anxiety, and defensiveness. The Bible is full of illustrations of the destructive power of blaming: Adam and Eve blaming each other and the serpent, Cain blaming Abel, Job's wife blaming Job and God, the crowd asking Jesus "who sinned?" when the tower collapsed (Luke 13:4). Judas's killing himself is one of the saddest stories of self-blame when compared to the forgiveness that was available to another betrayer, Peter.

"Where did I fail?" is also an unproductive and unredemptive question, because finding the answer, if there is one, does not solve or correct the problem.[2] It does lead to guilt, shame, humiliation, depression, anxiety, and defensiveness. Dwelling on failure is merely another form of blaming. If parents want to take responsibility for family problems, they need to be sure that they are not taking away their children's share. Rather than saying, "Where did I fail?" parents need to ask, "For what am I responsible? What can I do now to be helpful? What can I correct in my ways of relating that will help my child respond positively to me, to God, and to others?"

My emphasis as a counselor is to help parents contribute to the solution instead of blaming themselves or their children. As mothers and fathers we can only carry out parental responsibilities to the best of our ability with the information available. People can read books, attend seminars, and even go to counseling and still have marriages, families, and children that get into trouble. Husbands and wives can increase their chances for a positive marriage and family life by continually giving their attention to two areas of their lives: (1) developing personally by dealing with their individual immaturities, inadequacies, and immoralities, and (2) acknowledging their need for God, his Word, their families, and the body of believers.

Taking Constructive Steps

Church, family, and friends can take constructive steps to help families who are in trouble. First, all involved need to acknowledge and accept that there are natural consequences to human actions, whether or not they originate in sinful behavior. Those experimenting with drugs, accident victims, and diseased persons may all suffer permanent damage. Inappropriate sexual behavior may result in an unwanted pregnancy, disease, or social embarrassment. An affair may cause seemingly irreparable damage to a marriage. A divorce may negatively affect children.

Second, family and friends and the church need to respond to the hurting person or persons with supernatural love, mercy, and forgiveness. The apostle Paul's words of admonition must be heeded: "Let all bitterness and wrath and anger and clamor and slander be put away from you, along with all malice. And be kind to one another, tender-hearted, forgiving each other, just as God in Christ also has forgiven you" (Eph. 4:31, 32). This forgiving requires supernatural love because no human is capable of responding nobly without the empowering of the Holy Spirit.

The Church's Part in Taking Constructive Steps

The church, as belonging to the helping community, needs to be part of the family's solution more than identifier of the family's problems.[3] To do this, the church needs to affirm the importance of the family through sermons, weekend conferences, retreats, films and videos, and books on the family.

The family can also be affirmed through family nights when its members come to church for activities such as sports, picnics, prayer, and Bible study. One church holds communion for each individual family on New Year's Eve. Stressing family nights in the home is another way the church can affirm the importance of the family. Churches may need to provide their families with ideas for how to conduct such nights, including suggested activities and written plans. Modeling a family night during a church service may provide motivation and resources for families.

How to hold a family council and involve children in decision-making can be a topic for a church meeting. Role-playing and written instructions are helpful in introducing new ways of relating. Some churches have family Sunday school classes. Organizing support groups around problems such as alcoholism, substance abuse, anorexia, death, and illness is a helpful resource. Other support groups can assist new parents, teenage mothers, parents of teens and of adult children, divorced and separated people, and singles. How to control children's use of television, helping kids choose the right friends, and telling children about sex are other topics that the church can address and thereby strengthen the family.

Using Christian counselors as consultants to these groups and as assistants to lay leaders is often desirable. The church can also celebrate the family on Sundays other than Mother's Day, Father's Day, and Children's Day. Making helping an integral part of the church's ministry is a crucial way to support family life. "This is pure and undefiled religion in the sight of our God and Father, to visit orphans and widows in their distress, and to keep oneself unstained by the world" (James 1:27). Some churches organize in lay helping groups in order to respond to the needs of widows and children.

Lastly, the church needs to affirm that not all problems can be solved in this life. Strange as it may seem, Christians often need to be reminded that this is not all there is to life. The past cannot be undone; it can only be forgiven and understood. Attempts to undo the negative past result in frustration and failure. Facing its consequences, taking constructive steps to change hurtful behavior that caused problems, making restitution if possible, and asking for forgiveness are possible steps; but they may have little impact on the damage already done. Present circumstances may not be changeable, but they can be viewed positively. If they are to cope adequately with family difficulties, people also need to stop hoping for some magical solution or rescue; the church can help them face the present with courage and honesty.

Parishioners may need to confront reality with the hurting family, or be patient as the family struggles to accept present circumstances. Because the church has years of experience in knowing what people can anticipate in their lives, it can affirm that although the future may be anticipated, it cannot be controlled. Older people in the church are a great resource for younger parents, couples, and singles; and the church can be the bridge that brings older and younger people together. In return, young people can help the elderly get to church activities, as well as visit them, take them to the doctor when needed, and make them feel wanted and useful in the church.

The Friend's Part in Taking Constructive Steps

What can friends do when a family is having trouble?[4] Loneliness, embarrassment, and helplessness often typify the hurting family's emotional experience. By letting them know that they are not alone, by being available to them, by calling to encourage them, by looking for practical ways to help (for example, bringing an evening meal, mowing the lawn, washing the car, doing the wash, helping the children get to their activities), friends can give practical help. Above all, friends will let people talk or cry or rage, and express their questions and fears.

225

At the same time, friends do not have to answer the unanswerable questions, such as why did this happen now, or where is God, or why doesn't God hear their prayers. There will be time to explore such questions later, when the family crisis is less immediate. No carefully thought-out answer or profound theological truth or Bible verse will take away pain or answer questions, because those questions are emotional, not rational.

Nor is it the friend's responsibility to make the trouble seem less serious or embarrassing. This is a time for empathy, for imagining what the family is experiencing; it is not a time for friends to share their own misfortunes. Family members will be ready to hear a friend's troubles after that friend has first listened to them. Listening, more than talking, is a friend's gift in time of trouble. And being physically present without having to talk brings comfort.

Family trouble often produces guilt, self-criticism, and condemnation. Friends, therefore, need to avoid any comments that contribute to blame, criticism, or condemnation. They will want to listen to the self-accusations: "Why didn't we. . . . We should have. . . . What's wrong with us? . . . If only. . . ." And they will want to respond to them as pleas for control from a family feeling suddenly helpless. Telling people what they should have done or could do now is not helpful because they will use the advice to condemn themselves more. Such advice, as well as not being helpful, tends to create self-righteousness and arrogance. Friends need to be humble, admitting to themselves that they could be in the troubled family's place. Acknowledging God's grace and protection and knowing that no family has a guarantee of being "trouble free" will permeate friends' attitudes, whatever they say or do.

It is useful for friends to ask resource questions: "What are you trying?" Or, "What is getting in the way of your attempts working?" Or, "What can you do now to deal with the crisis?" As the family raises questions about the current trouble, friends can think *with* them (not *for* them) empathically. Family members may have a hard time making decisions, but making their decisions and taking over their responsibilities debilitates them further.

Family trouble is also a time for prayer, and friends pray for one another. Before praying with the family, it is courteous to ask whether prayer is desired. Prayer can be offered for strength and wisdom for family members to live through the trouble. Also, a friend may thank God for his comforting presence and friendship, acknowledge questions that seem unanswerable, and request guidance for the family and their friends. Privately, friends can pray for their own families, affirming their own marriages and children and asking for sensitivity to see their children at their best. When friends help friends, they send an esteem message that says, "Even though you or your family are in trouble, we love and care for you. You are worth our time and encouragement." Without friends' support, families have difficulty maintaining self-esteem.

The Family's Part in Taking Constructive Steps

Families in trouble need to focus on "What can I do now?" more than on "Where did I fail?"[5] This is not a time for the family to blame and criticize each other. Rather, it is useful for the family to see that they can take corrective action, and that they can contribute to a solution rather than act in ways that maintain the problem. Family members may need to explore what they need to change about themselves if family problems are to ease. Encouraging each other to take responsibility for various parts of the problem is a positive step when done with humility and empathy.

Exploring the personal meaning of family trouble is often crucial. As a counselor, I encourage clients to ask, "What does the family trouble mean to me?" I am wondering: Does the family expect no difficulties? How do they measure success and failure? How does this trouble affect their sense of esteem? A mother who was sending her son off to college found his bedroom a disaster area after he had packed his belongings. She asked me, "Will he ever learn to clean up his room?" As I explored the meaning of her son's not leaving his room neat, she said, "It means I haven't taught him very well."

Again, a father told me during counseling that his daughter doesn't show him enough affection. His expectation was that she would initiate the hugs and kisses if she really loved him. It had not occurred to him that his daughter might be experiencing similar feelings of neglect. Other parents, whose children are not as accomplished in sports or music or academics as the children of their friends, often feel inadequate or inferior.

Forgiving oneself for not being a perfect spouse, parent, or child is another constructive step family members can take when their family is in trouble. Healthy families expect imperfection in each other because that is the human condition. Christian families can be encouraged to expect imperfection because they have already accepted the fact, at least spiritually, that no one is perfect.

To acknowledge human imperfection emotionally and socially, however, may be more difficult. No family is all-knowing or all-powerful. To expect perfection of oneself or of one's family is to invite depression and despair. And to forgive one's parents, children, and spouse for not being perfect may be even more difficult because, although humans long for perfect relationships, parents, spouses, and children fail each other without exception. No family member is ever adequate for his or her role in the family. No one can ever provide enough love, wisdom, or maturity. This fact means that people will need to give up expecting all their needs to be met in the family and learn how to forgive the family for its limitations. It also means that they will need to acknowledge they cannot produce the perfect marriage or family. But they are able to learn to nurture and discipline better, to develop their ability to love unconditionally and nonjudgmentally, and to live with imperfections while acknowledging their need for God's grace and love. Because the family is imperfect, the members will need to supplement what the family gives them, finding other sources for nurture, affirmation, and esteem, and give up any hope that the family will provide for all needs.

Lastly, the troubled family may need to forgive society for all of its negative influences, particularly if outside influences are directly involved in the crisis. I jokingly tell my audiences that if my children do not turn out all right, their friends and teachers will have to take some of the blame because my children spend more time with them than with me. Society's influence on the family also suggests that the family does not have as much control over what impacts it as people would like to believe. Teaching children at home, monitoring television and radio programs, and joining Christian organizations all testify to the Christian's fear that society will influence negatively more than the family can balance.

God Had Trouble with His Family, Too

He knows what it feels like to have family trouble (Isaiah 1:2). Because he also knows that humans are imperfect, his cross stands in the gap for all human failure and inadequacy. I encourage a troubled family to feel sadness for its hurting family member rather than for itself. Although throwing a pity party is tempting, it is not healing. Instead, families need to distinguish heartache from failure, accepting their own limited ability to help those who hurt. If individuals cannot mediate family tension or alleviate family trouble through their own intervention, they may need to consult friends, or their pastor, their doctor, or professional counselors. Hurting families should be encouraged to share hurt, to carry pain with friends at their side, to recognize that although no one can take away pain, others can help them bear their burdens.

A troubled family can help itself by identifying its struggles as part of the normal life cycle. Pastors, counselors, or friends may provide information that will help the family think about its problems in developmental terms.

- Is the family trouble a mid-life crisis, adolescent crisis, or marital crisis?
- Is it the kind of problem that all families can anticipate going through?
- Is it a normal personal crisis?
- Does the problem involve an issue of trust, independence, initiative, industry, motivation, identity, intimacy?

Erik Erikson's eight stages of life is a brief but comprehensive list of developmental tasks. I use it to help me understand individual and family problems from a developmental perspective and then to aid clients in understanding what they are experiencing. Each stage represents a self-esteem issue which forms a building block for healthy self-love. Thus, most problems brought to the pastor or counselor will reflect one or more of these.

ERIKSON'S EIGHT STAGES OF LIFE

Stage one—Infancy: Trust versus Mistrust. "The cornerstone of a healthy personality" is a basic sense of trust in himself and the social and physical environment. Trust is produced when the child is cared for by people in his life that welcome and want him. He develops a sense of security and goodness that is transmitted by the quality of his care. Mistrust develops when inconsistent or discontinuous care causes the child to experience normal separateness from his mother as loss.

Stage two—Early Childhood: Autonomy versus Shame and Doubt. The child's muscular capacity to hold and let go of his body functions, urinating and defecating, matures. He begins to attach value to his sense of independence, control, and willpower. When he is deprived of the opportunities to develop his will, is forced to do his "duty," is defeated in the battle of the wills with his parents or those who are bigger and stronger than he, then the possibility develops that he will feel shame and doubt.

Stage three—Play Ages: Initiative versus Guilt. With the child's ability to move around freely and communicate, his imagination has few boundaries. This age includes intrusive activity, avid curiosity, and consuming fantasies which may lead to destructive guilt and anxiety when they are restricted and punished inappropriately. His conscience, which develops during this stage, may be so overwhelmed by critical parents that he develops a deep-seated conviction that he is essentially bad. Results are inhibition, preoccupation with morality, and/or vindictiveness.

Stage four—School Age: Industry versus Inferiority. Having permission to be curious and to initiate, the child now moves into a stage of doing, learning how to do, and making things with others. As he learns to accept instruction and win recognition by producing "things," he begins to develop the capacity to enjoy work. When the child does not receive encouragement and recognition for what he does and makes, he may develop a sense of inadequacy and inferiority. Some children give up and become lethargic; others try harder and become perfectionists.

Stage five—Adolescence: Identity versus Identity Diffusion. "Who am I?" is the question the child has been working on since birth. This is the stage at which all his experiences of himself come together to form a basic answer to his identity questions. Knowledge of his biological drives, native endowments, social roles, successes, and failures begin to shape a firm sense of who he is. Some identity diffusion or confusion is unavoidable during adolescence because of the tremendous physical and psychological upheaval characteristic of this period. Inability to "take hold" of his identity results in identity confusion. Failure to live up to expectations of his parents, class, or community may encourage the child to form a negative or anti-social personality.

Stage six—Young Adulthood: Intimacy versus Isolation. Intimacy with others is possible only as a person begins to feel secure in his identity and able to be intimate with himself. Many marriage and family problems can be traced to the spouses' and parents' undeveloped sense of knowing who they are. A person who cannot enter wholly into an intimate relationship because of the fear that he will lose his identity will find it difficult, if not impossible, to form a love-based, mutually satisfying sexual relationship with a member of the opposite sex. Nor will he be able to let his children into his emotional world.

Stage seven—Adulthood: Generativity versus Self-Absorption. A capacity for intimacy allows the person to establish and guide the next generation through the development of his own family or by relating to and teaching others. Failure to move into this stage often results in self-absorption and a "pervading sense of stagnation and interpersonal impoverishment."

Stage eight—Senescence: Integrity versus Disgust/

Despair. Integrity involves a person's accepting responsibility for what his life is and was and of its place in the flow of history. It becomes possible when a person achieves a satisfying intimacy with others and adapts to triumphs and disappointments in his attempts to be himself. A person who can look back on his life without a sense of accomplishment develops despair, marked by feelings of displeasure and disgust with himself.[6]

IT IS NOT TOO LATE TO START OVER

The troubled family can acknowledge the possibility of new beginnings. It is seldom too late to start over. It is never too late to have a delightful childhood or adulthood. It may be too late to have a loving marriage or a caring family in the event that those relationships may not be restorable. But each family member has time to create a good life for himself or herself even if other family members refuse to cooperate. The Bible is full of stories of people who knew the truth that it is not too late to start over. (See, for example, the Prodigal Son, Noah, the children of Israel in the Promised Land, Job, Peter, Jesus' mother, and John.)

Troubled families gain comfort when they remember that the church is a collection of failures. They need to be reminded that no matter what problems the family has, the church has helped with these kinds of problems throughout history. Elton Trueblood says, "The church is a hospital for sinners, not a museum for saints." The church may need to be reminded of this truth if it hopes to give hurting families comfort and solace.

Focusing on the future more than on the past is another way the troubled family can have a new beginning in the midst of turmoil. Looking at the past has limited value unless the family can learn what to do differently; but focusing on the present can help it to get through the problem. Since not all problems are solvable in this life, the family's hope may need to be in the life Christ is preparing for all of God's people.

Things the family can do in the present are summarized by an unknown author in "The Practical Parents' Creed":

I Can and Will . . .

Look for ways to expand my understanding of children.

Listen patiently to what children have to say and try to answer the questions they ask.

Resist impulses to interrupt or contradict children when they try to share their ideas and opinions.

Seek to be as courteous, fair, just and kind to children as I would have them be to me.

Refrain from laughing at children's mistakes or resorting to shame and ridicule when they displease.

Avoid tempting children to lie or steal. I can try to demonstrate by all I say and do that honesty is the policy that produces happiness.

Hold my tongue when I am out of sorts instead of irritably lashing out at children.

Remember that children are children, and not expect of them the judgment of adults.

Provide all possible opportunities for children to learn to make their own decisions and to wait on themselves.

Grant children all their reasonable requests, but have the courage to deny them privileges I know will do them harm.

Strive to be a leader and a teacher of children instead of a dictator.

Think and act in ways that will make me deserve to be loved and respected and imitated by children.

I conclude this chapter with a prayer, by an unknown author, that summarizes what I have written in these pages. Through it, I ask the Lord not only to make me a better parent, but also to help me treat myself the way I pray to treat my children. I ask counselees to read it both as the parent of their children and as the parent of themselves.

A Parent's Prayer

O Heavenly Father, Make me a better parent. Teach me to understand my children, to listen patiently to what they have to say, and to answer all their questions kindly. Keep me from interrupting them and contradicting them. Make me as courteous to them as I would have them be to me. Forbid that I should ever laugh at their mistakes or resort to shame or ridicule when they displease me. May I never punish them for my own selfish satisfaction or to show my power. Let me never tempt my child to lie or steal. And guide me hour by hour that I may demonstrate by all I say and do that honesty produces happiness. Reduce, I pray, the meanness in me. And when I am out of sorts, help me, O Lord, to hold my tongue. May I ever be mindful that my children are children and I should not expect of them the judgment of adults. Let me not rob them of the opportunity to wait on themselves and to make decisions. Bless me with the bigness to grant them all their reasonable requests and the courage to deny them privileges I know will do them harm. Make me fair and just and kind. And fit me, O Lord, to be loved and respected and imitated by my children. *Help me remember when I have trouble with my children that You had trouble with Your children, too* (italics mine). Amen.

Summary

Since ideal families do not exist in real life, this chapter focused on helping families accept their limitations and reject their idealizations. Empathy for hurting families develops when we remember that God had trouble with his family, too. This chapter gave suggestions for how churches, friends, and families can take constructive steps in dealing with troubled families.[7]

Helping families in trouble is a way to help them bear their burden, affirm their worth to the body of Christ, and value themselves in spite of their family trouble. It also creates humility in helpers when they recognize that there are no guarantees for their marriages or families being problem-free. When we understand that our value and love are not dependent on the absence of problems, we are freed to admit our difficulties and seek out help without embarrassment, shame, or humiliation. Likewise, we are freed to give help without judgment or condemnation.

CHAPTER ELEVEN

HELPING PEOPLE CHANGE
THE ANSWER IS NOT THE SOLUTION

THERE IS NO PHILOSOPHICAL SYSTEM or scientific knowledge that does not involve oversimplification, says Paul Tournier.[1] My challenge in writing this book on the process of building self-esteem has been how to make the complex process understandable without oversimplifying it and realistic without its being overwhelming. How to present a counseling process that motivates other helpers to experiment and integrate these strategies with what they are already doing—that, too, has been challenging. As a seminary professor, therapist, and speaker, I have learned that the answers are usually simple to me and difficult to students and clients. This dichotomy is understandable inasmuch as I have developed the process of building self-esteem in myself and in my clients out of my own need. Much of what I have presented comes out of my own struggles with low esteem.

What I have described here is a map. My fear is that the reader will confuse it with the territory. The map is not the territory; rather, it represents the real counseling process. I have obviously chosen illustrations of counseling sessions that worked. I wish every session with every person I see could result in a positive outcome. I do not claim that. When people do not respond positively to my attempts to help, I draw comfort from Jesus' experience of crying over Jerusalem, wishing he could tuck its citizens under his wings like a mother hen. But they would not let him.

Inability to help everyone, however, does not negate our attempts to help or the strategies we use. What I teach in these pages will not make you, a helper, 100 percent effective; but these strategies will help you become more effective as a helper. My own counseling has been enriched by utilizing the sensory modalities, predicates, and eye scan; and because of my success, I recommend this counseling process to others.

SELF-ESTEEM: THE BASIC PROBLEM

My clinical and youth-pastor experience affirms that I

> . . . cannot think of a single major psychological problem—from fear of intimacy or of success, to underachievement at school and work, to anxiety or depression, to alcohol abuse or drug addiction, to child molesting or spouse battering, to suicide or crimes of violence—that is not traceable to a poor self-concept. Of all the judgments we pass in life, none is as important as the one we pass on ourselves. Our self-concept tends to be our destiny.[2]

I consider self-esteem, then, to be a basic issue in people who come to me for counseling, and to my students who come for instruction in how to counsel. How I respond to my clients and students sends them a message that shows and tells them what they are worth. My warmth, compassion, understanding, integrity, and consistency are important characteristics that communicate self-esteem messages to them. Being on time for my appointments and classes, my verbal and nonverbal responses—these send affirming or discounting messages.

Self-worth is influenced by the messages we actually hear or think we hear, by the way people treat us, or by our perceptions of what others are feeling toward us. As a child, when humiliated by a teacher in a third-grade arithmetic class because I couldn't solve a problem in front of the class, I learned Erik Erikson's observation: "The most deadly of all sins is the mutilation of a child's spirit." My experience as a therapist reaffirms this truth daily. *Be respectful of how you relate to the people in your world because you have the power to create or to destroy another's spirit.* That is the message I am sending ministers, counselors, parents, and everyone who reads this book.

SELF-ESTEEM: A BASIC HUMAN NEED

I have presented self-esteem as a basic human need that is developed or destroyed in relationships with the most important people in our lives. Our desire for self-esteem, like all other human needs and desires, is insatiable (Proverbs 27:20). But it is moderated, curbed, and civilized by caring people who accept our limitations and idiosyncrasies, or by cruel ridicule and social ostracism.

When others know and accept our boundaries—our bodies, minds, feelings, needs, values—we learn that we can expand some of what we are and still accept our limitations, compensating for them in healthy ways. A personal sense of self-worth is the product of others recognizing our worth. Then *we* appreciate our worth. And this, in turn, helps us recognize and appreciate the worth of others.

The clients in these pages teach us that persons who value, prize, and affirm them help them value, prize, and affirm themselves and then enable them to build the esteem of others. Their stories also teach us that negative relationships damage people's esteem to such a degree that they cannot build their own esteem without professional help. It is difficult for them to acknowledge and accept their positive or negative thoughts, feelings, and behaviors without a helper who accepts them as they are. Many people think they are bad because of the rejection they received as children. Accepting God's love and forgiveness is difficult or impossible until they experience human love and affirmation.

Accepting People in Spite of Pretensions and Depravity

It is true that humans tend to defend against the perception of their own urges, desires, thoughts, and behaviors that are incompatible with their ideal selves. Any distressing insight that arouses feelings of shame, anger, or fear; any thoughts of self-reproach; any pictures of inadequacy are usually repressed. Because our human nature is sinful, we tend to deceive ourselves, interpreting or excusing our behavior positively, enhancing or disguising our self-image, and numbing our feelings. I have stressed, however, the therapeutic importance of acknowledging and accepting a person's failure, faults, and sinfulness rather than judging and condemning because this response enables the person to change positively. Such persons then can accept and confess their own problems and begin to act appropriately.

> To give up pretensions [of being who you are not] is as blessed a relief as to get them gratified; and where disappointment is incessant and the struggle unending, this is what men will always do. The history of evangelical theology, with its conviction of sin, its self-despair, and its abandonment of salvation by works, is the deepest of possible examples. . . . There is the strangest lightness about the heart when one's nothingness in a particular life is once accepted in good faith. . . . How pleasant is the day when we give up striving to be young—or slender! Thank God! we say. Those illusions are gone. Everything added to the self is a burden as well as pride.[3]

The lesson taught: As people experience that they are loved and valued regardless of their behavior, thoughts, and feelings, they can then own their weaknesses, accept their defenses, acknowledge their sinfulness, and accomplish what seems so elusive to themselves—change their self-talk, self-image, self-actions, and self-feelings. They can then become whom God calls and creates, the representations of God's image.

The client's dominant motivation is no longer the desire for self-esteem because that need has been met through God's words, views, actions, and feelings that demonstrate he or she is loved, valued, and affirmed as a person, "We love, because He first loved us" (1 John 4:19). Any motivation now is the desire to love, obey, and glorify God. Christians, therefore, are freed to serve God rather than themselves when they realize that God is for them, when they realize that to serve God is not to annihilate self, and when they realize that God has called them to be his representatives in others' lives. God esteeming humans, then, is the prelude to humans esteeming God.

Self-Love and Self-Esteem Defined

Self-love is: accepting oneself as a child of God who is lovable, valuable, and capable, giving up considering oneself to be the center of the world, and recognizing oneself in need of God's forgiveness and redemption.

Self-esteem is thoughts, pictures, feelings, and behaviors that people have toward themselves. It is not pride and arrogance that one human is better than another, nor is it the belief that humans are equal to God. Self-esteem as defined in this book is a feeling of being happy with myself, a positive and accurate picture of myself, a confidence that I am okay as I am—an American, a woman, a sinner, Polish, black, Indian, Canadian—whatever.

I possess self-esteem when I think about what I am doing, saying, and believing with discernment, not with condemning judgment. I allow myself to recognize and admit deception and dishonesty to myself and correct them. I act with integrity, saying no when I want to say no and yes when I want to say yes. I take full responsibility for what I say, think, feel, and do, accepting the consequences of my behavior without denial, rationalization, or attempts to escape. I see with my own eyes, not what I am told is there. I hear with my own ears, not what I am told to hear. I feel with my own heart, not what I am told to feel. I ask with my own mouth, not what I am told to ask. I act with my own intentions, not just doing what I am told to do. I trust myself as the final arbiter and decision maker, not letting others decide for me. I use others as a resource and have the courage to make my own decision. I explore, discover, understand myself, not criticizing, putting down or chastising myself. I accept God's love, his value affirmations, and his forgiveness of me, not wanting God to tell me I am better than others.

Self-esteem is the result of facing my pretensions, and acknowledging my longing to grow beyond the need for repentance. It is accepting my mortality, limited wisdom, and power, and groaning for what I am—a sinner in need of God's grace and mercy each day.

Self-esteem is the product of hearing the truth of God's revelation in stereo. In one ear I hear God say, "You are a sinner"; and in the other ear I hear him say, "I am merciful and willing that no one should perish. I love and forgive you." Self-esteem, from a biblical viewpoint, is acknowledging and rejecting my grandiosity. It is not religious or moral superiority or pride in being better than others. It is pride in being God's adopted child. It is humility in being chosen and called by God.

Self-esteem is a relationship issue for humans. First, it is an issue for persons in relation to their Creator and Redeemer. Second, it is an issue for persons in relation to their parents, siblings, peers, teachers, and other significant others as accepters not rejecters, as adopters not abandoners. And third, it is an issue for persons in relation to themselves. To know themselves as sinners, rebels against God, with deceitful hearts, is to produce anxiety, forcing them to accept aspects of themselves that are deeply threatening to their self-esteem. To know that God loves us, even when we are his enemies, reduces anxiety, creates peace, and allows us to face who we are without judgment and condemnation. For "to hear the gospel is to embrace the judgment God pronounced over the world in Christ—to embrace it not as condemnation, for there is now no condemnation, but as mercy and as witness to the One who is greater than ourselves."[4] The reader will find self-esteem further defined in the Appendix.

Turning a Helping Event into a Process

Helping people change is a process. It is not an event that takes place with one counseling session, one sermon, one Sunday school class, or one book. Helpers need time to process what they are learning about counseling. For the readers of this book, the perspectives and skills that are crucial to the process include:

- the capacity to distinguish psychologically healthy and biblically accurate definitions of self-esteem from psychologically unhealthy and biblically inaccurate definitions;
- the ability to listen for sensory predicates, watch eye movements, and identify the client's sensory process;
- the skill to utilize the outcome questions;
- the skill to identify and express feelings and needs;
- the patience and skill to teach clients these skills.

But time is not enough. Repetition and practice in observing these four—self-talking, self-picturing, self-acting, and self-feeling, both of the helper and the counselee—are needed to internalize what is being learned and make it a "natural" part of the helper's counseling process. This means that failure is inevitable, and that will be discouraging. I challenge failure by reminding myself that I have not successfully accomplished anything on the first try; I did not roll over, crawl, walk, talk, run, ride a bicycle, throw a ball, write, spell, give a speech, teach, call for a date, or counsel with my first attempt. Try to complete the first reading of this book with the following encouragement: *I can learn to be an effective counselor. It is okay for me to fail, to make mistakes, to learn, to do it a second, third, or hundredth time until I learn. It is okay for me to ask for help. I do not have to learn how to counsel all by myself.*

Counseling is a process, not an event. The challenge of counseling lies in the fact that giving an answer to a person's problem is not the solution. A helper's answer to a person's question remains the helper's answer until the person can make it his or her own. An answer, therefore, is no more a solution than a prescription is a cure.

My hope is that this book teaches not only answers, but also a process to assist ministers and counselors as they help people change.

APPENDIX

DEFINITIONS OF SELF-ESTEEM

In order that the counselor may understand something of the many-sided nature of self-esteem, and the key role it plays in one's life, this listing of definitions and related quotations is provided. Most of these are reproduced from the excellent discussion by Robert Campbell in *The New Science: Self-Esteem Psychology* (Lanham, Md.: University Press of America, 1984), pages 6–30.

Alfred Adler: "All our functions follow its (self-esteem's) direction."

William McDougall: "Self-regard is the master sentiment."

Nathaniel Branden: Self-esteem is the "single most significant key to human behavior." Also see Nathaniel Branden, *To See What I See and Know What I Know: A Guide to Self-Discovery* (New

York: Bantam, 1986), 249. Self-esteem is "our experience of being competent to deal with the challenges of life and of being deserving of happiness. [It] is a function of our deepest feelings about ourselves; it is not a matter of particular skills or particular knowledge. It is certainly not a matter of how well liked we are. It is a matter of the extent to which we experience ourselves as appropriate to life and to the requirements of life. [It is an] experience that we are competent (to understand, to think, to judge) to live and worthy of happiness (right to joyful existence, right to wants and needs, right to self-acceptance and respect)."

Robert H. Schuller: Self-esteem is the "alternate will of man."

Arthur Combs and Donald Snygg: Self-esteem is the "most crucial, if not the only task of existence."

George McCall and J. L. Simmons: Self-esteem is "man's main concern."

Ernest Becker: "The basic law of human nature" is self-esteem.

Edith Jacobsen: "Self-esteem is the expression of the harmony or discrepancy between the self representations and the wishful concept of the self."

Stanley Coopersmith: Self-esteem is "a personal judgment of worthiness that is expressed in the attitudes the individual holds toward himself."

Robert Campbell: "Self-esteem is increased or maintained by any good, actual or potential, that one can consider as his own: his ancestry, nationality, competencies, intelligence, achievements, material possessions, virtues, aspirations, talents, friends, and loved ones (and any good that they possess, inasmuch as identification with them can lead to take pride in their excellences), social status, attention and acceptance and love from others, one's standard of values, his beliefs, profession, chances for achievement—the list is endless. . . ." Human beings have two basic motivations. The "desire for self-esteem—excellence and the desire for sensual pleasure." . . . "What can give a person a more secure and exalted self-esteem than to receive honor from the one who knows all and judges justly? What can give a person a greater sense of his own worth than to be united to the Supreme One—a worth not independent of God but totally dependent upon him, and even more desirable and triumphant for that very reason? Such noble exaltation of self-esteem, from sharing in God's nature and gifts, can go hand in hand with a deep realization of one's own viciousness, misery, and nothingness, by one's own nature apart from God. Testimony to this paradox of deep self-contempt accompanied by an inner peace and buoyant joy is frequent in the writings of Christian believers."

Pat Berne and Lou Savary (*Building Self-Esteem in Children;* page xv. See Bibliography): Self-esteem "means having a realistic awareness of oneself and of one's rights; . . . to honor one's uniqueness; to accept one's life as a gift from God; to build healthy relationships; to see and feel one's self as successful; to act toward others in non-threatening ways; to be self-confident; to express their assertiveness; to deal with fear and other strong emotions; to share their love with others."

William James (*The Principles of Psychology* [London: Macmillan, 1910], 310): Self-esteem equals success divided by pretensions (aspirations, ideal self-image, ambitions, and expectations). "My deficiencies give me no sense of humiliation when I measure myself against my abilities not my aspirations, my successes not my ambitions, my accomplishments not my failures, by comparing myself with myself not with others, by competing against me not others."

BIBLIOGRAPHY

Adams, Jay. *The Biblical View of Self-Esteem, Self-Love, Self-Image* (Eugene, Ore.: Harvest House, 1986).

Ahlem, Lloyd H. *Do I Have to Be Me? The Psychology of Human Need* (Glendale, Calif.: Regal, 1973).

Augsburger, David. *Be All You Can Be* (Harrison, Pa.: Choice Books, 1970).

———. *Caring Enough to Hear and Be Heard* (Ventura, Calif.: Regal, 1982).

Aycock, David W., and Noaker, Susan. "A Comparison of the Self-Esteem Levels in Evangelical Christian and General Populations," *Journal of Psychology and Theology* 13 (1985): 199–208.

Backus, William, and Chapian, Marie. *Telling Yourself the Truth* (Minneapolis: Bethany Fellowship, 1980).

Baird, Clifford. *The Power of a Positive Self-Esteem* (Wheaton, Ill.: Victor Books, 1983).

Bandler, Richard, and Grinder, John. *Frogs into Princes* (Moab, Utah: Real People, 1979).

———. *The Structure of Magic* 2 vols. (Palo Alto, Calif.: Science and Behavior Books, 1976).

Berne, Pat, and Savary, Lou. *Building Self-Esteem in Children* (New York: Crossroad, 1985).

Birkey, Verna. *You Are Very Special: A Biblical Guide to Self-Worth* (Old Tappan, N.J.: Revell, 1977).

Blanchard, Kenneth, and Johnson, Spencer. *The One-Minute Manager* (New York: Berkley, 1984).

Bloomfield, Harold and Felder, Leonard. *Making Peace with Your Parents* (New York: Random House, 1983).

————. *Making Peace with Yourself* (New York: Ballantine, 1985).

Brand, Paul, and Yancey, Philip. *In His Image* (Grand Rapids: Zondervan, 1984).

Branden, Nathaniel. *How to Raise Your Self-Esteem* (New York: Bantam, 1987).

————. *To See What I See and Know What I Know: A Guide To Self-Discovery* (New York: Bantam, 1986).

————. *Honor Thy Self: The Psychology of Confidence and Respect* (New York: Bantam, 1985).

————. *The Psychology of Self-Esteem: A New Concept of Man's Psychological Nature* (New York: Bantam, 1971).

Briggs, Dorothy Corkille. *Your Child's Self-Esteem: The Key to His Life* (Garden City, N.Y.: Doubleday, 1970).

————. *Celebrate Yourself* (Garden City, N.Y.: Doubleday, 1977).

Brownback, Paul. *The Danger of Self-Love* (Chicago: Moody Press, 1982).

Burwick, Ray. *Self-Esteem: You're Better Than You Think* (Wheaton, Ill.: Tyndale, 1983).

Buscaglia, Leo. *Personhood: The Art of Being Fully Human* (New York: Fawcett Columbine, 1978).

Butler, Pamela E. *Talking to Yourself: Learning the Language of Self-Support* (New York: Harper & Row, 1983).

Campbell, Charles A. *On Selfhood and Godhood* (New York: Macmillan, 1957).

Campbell, Robert N. *The New Science: Self-Esteem Psychology* (Lanham, Md.: University Press of America, 1984).

Cirese, Sarah. *Quest: A Search for Self* (New York: Holt, Rinehart and Winston, 1985).

Clarke, Jean, I. *Self-Esteem: A Family Affair* (New York: Harper & Row, 1980).

Cole, James Preston. *The Problematic Self in Kierkegaard and Freud* (New Haven: Yale University Press, 1971).

Coleman, William. *Bouncing Back: Finding Acceptance in the Face of Rejection* (Eugene, Ore.: Harvest House, 1985).

Coopersmith, Stanley. *Antecedents of Self-Esteem* (Palo Alto, Calif.: Consulting Psychology, 1981).

Daniels, Victor, and Horowitz, Laurence. *Being and Caring* (San Francisco: San Francisco Book Co., 1976).

Dawn, Dean C. *Increasing Your Self-Esteem: How to Feel Better About Yourself* (Prospect Heights, Ill.: Waveland Press, 1980).

Devines, John. *How Much Am I Worth?* Great Britain: Bibles for India, n.d.

Dobson, James C. *Hide and Seek* (Old Tappan, N.J.: Revell, 1979).

Elkins, Dov P., ed. *Twelve Pathways to Feeling Better About Yourself* (Rochester, N.Y.: Growth Associates, 1980).

——. *Glad to Be Me: Building Self-Esteem in Yourself and Others* (Rochester, N.Y.: Growth Associates, 1985).

Ellison, Craig W. *Your Better Self: Christianity, Psychology and Self-Esteem* (San Francisco: Harper & Row, 1983).

Erikson, Erik, H. *Childhood and Society* (New York: Norton, 1986).

——. *Identity and the Life Cycle* (New York: Norton, 1968).

George, Betty, et al. Kid Skills: Interpersonal Skill Series. *Wonderful You. Self-Awareness. Accepting and Knowing Myself* (Dallas: PLB Family Skills, 1986).

Greenwald, Jerry A. *Be the Person You Were Meant to Be* (New York: Simon and Schuster, 1973).

Guntrip, Harry. *Psychoanalytic Theory, Therapy, and the Self: A Basic Guide to the Human Personality* (New York: Basic Books, 1973).

Harvey, Joan C. and Katz, Cynthia. *If I'm So Successful, Why Do I Feel Like A Fake?* (New York: St. Martins, 1985).

Haught, John F. *Religion and Self-Acceptance: a Study of the Relationship Between Belief in God and Desire to Know* (Washington, D.C.: University Press of America, 1980).

Holmes, Marjorie. *How Can I Find You, God?* (New York: Bantam: 1975).

Jabay, Earl. *Search for Identity: a View of Authentic Christian Living* (Grand Rapids: Zondervan, 1976).

——. *The Kingdom of Self* (South Plainfield, N.J.: Bridge, 1974).

James, Muriel, and Savary, Lois. *A New Self: Self-Therapy with Transactional Analysis* (Reading, Mass.: Addison-Wesley, 1977).

Joseph, Paula O. "An Examination of Self-Love from Biblical and Psychological Perspectives" (Deerfield, Ill.: Trinity Evangelical Divinity School master's thesis, 1975).

Kagan, Jerome. *The Second Year: The Emergence of Self-Awareness* (Cambridge, Mass.: Harvard University Press, 1981).

Kennedy, Eugene. *Free to Be Human* (Chicago: Thomas More Press, 1979).

Kinzer, Mark. *The Self-Image of a Christian: Humility and Self-Esteem* (Ann Arbor, Mich.: Servant Books, 1980).

Kohut, Heinz. *The Restoration of Self* (New York: International University Press, 1977).

Landorf, Joyce. *Balcony People* (Waco, Tex.: Word, 1984).

Lankton, Steve. *Practical Magic: A Translation of Basic Neuro-Linguistic Programming into Clinical Psychotherapy* (Cupertino, Calif.: Meta, 1980).

Larson, Bruce. *The One and Only You* (Waco, Tex.: Word, 1974).

Lasch, Christopher. *The Minimal Self: Psychic Survival in Troubled Times* (New York: Norton, 1984).

Lazarus, Arnold A., and Allen, Fay. *I Can if I Want to* (New York: William Morrow, 1975).

Lee, Dorothy. *Valuing the Self: What We Can Learn from Other Cultures* (Prospect Heights, Ill.: Waveland Press, 1986).

Levin, Pamela. *Becoming the Way We Are* (self-published, 1974); author may be contacted at 1772 Vallejo St., San Francisco, CA 94123.

Lovlie, Anne-Lise. *The Self: Yours, Mine, Ours?* (Oslo: Universitetsforlaget, 1982; distributed by Columbia University Press, New York).

Lowen, Alexander. *Narcissism: Denial of the True Self* (New York: Macmillan, 1983).

Masterson, James. *The Real Self: A Developmental, Self and Object Relations Approach* (New York: Brunner-Mazel, 1985).

May, Rollo. *Man's Search for Himself* (New York: Signet, 1953).

McDowell, Josh. *His Image . . . My Image* (San Bernardino, Calif.: Here's Life, 1984).

Miller, Emmitt E. *Self-Imagery: Creating Your Own Good Health* (Berkeley: Celestial Arts, 1986).

Miller, William A. *You Count—You Really Do!* (Minneapolis: Augsburg, 1976).

Missildine, Hugh W. *Your Inner Child of the Past* (New York: Simon and Schuster, 1963).

Morris, Frank R., and Morris, Dixie G. *The Recognition and Expression of Feelings* (South Bend, Ind.: TACM, 1985); address—52136 Lilac Road, South Bend, Ind. 46628.

Narramore, S. Bruce. *No Condemnation: Rethinking Guilt Motivation in Counseling and Parenting* (Grand Rapids: Zondervan, 1984).

O'Connor, Elizabeth. *Our Many Selves* (New York: Harper & Row, 1971).

Osborne, Cecil G. *The Art of Learning to Love Yourself* (Grand Rapids: Zondervan, 1976).

———. *Self-Esteem: Overcoming Inferiority Feelings* (Nashville: Abingdon, 1986).

Packer, J. I. *Knowing God* (Downers Grove, Ill.: InterVarsity, 1973).

Pierce, Robert A., Nicholes, Michael, and DuBrin, Joyce R. *Emotional Expression in Psychotherapy* (New York: Gardner, 1983).

Powell, John. *Why Am I Afraid to Tell You Who I Am?* (Chicago: Argus Communications, 1969).

Rainey, Dennis and Barbara. *Building Your Mate's Self-Esteem* (San Bernardino, Calif.: Here's Life, 1986).

Ringer, Robert J. *Looking Out for #1* (Los Angeles: Funk and Wagnalls, 1977).

Rogers, Carl. *On Becoming a Person* (New York: Houghton Mifflin, 1961).

Rubin, Theodore Isaac. *Compassion and Self-Hate* (New York: Ballantine Books, 1976).

Satir, Virginia. *Peoplemaking* (Palo Alto, Calif.: Science and Behavior Books, 1972).

Schmidt, Jerry A. *Do You Hear What You're Thinking?* (Wheaton, Ill.: Victor Books, 1983).

Schuller, Robert H. *Self-Esteem: The New Reformation* (Waco, Tex.: Word, 1982).

Seabury, David. *The Art of Selfishness* (New York: Simon and Schuster, 1974).

Skoglund, Elizabeth. *Growing Through Rejection* (Wheaton, Ill.: Tyndale, 1983).

Smith, M. Blaine. *One of a Kind: A Biblical View of Self-Acceptance* (Downers Grove, Ill.: InterVarsity, 1984).

Tournier, Paul. *The Healing of Persons* (New York: Harper & Row, 1983).

Viscott, David. *The Language of Feelings* (New York: Arbor House, 1984).

Vitz, Paul C. *Psychology as Religion: The Cult of Self-Worship* (Grand Rapids: Eerdmans, 1977).

Wagner, Maurice. *The Sensation of Being Somebody: Building an Adequate Self-Concept* (Grand Rapids: Zondervan, 1975).

Wegner, Daniel M., and Vallacher, Robin R., eds. *The Self in Social Psychology* (New York: Oxford University Press, 1980).

Wheelis, Allen. *How People Change* (New York: Harper & Row, 1973).

Wilson, Earl D. *The Undivided Self: Bringing Your Whole Life in Line with God's Will* (Downers Grove, Ill.: InterVarsity, 1983).

———. *The Discovered Self: The Search for Self-Acceptance* (Downers Grove, Ill.: InterVarsity, 1985).

Wright, H. Norman. *Self-talk, Imagery, and Prayer in Counseling,* Resources for Christian Counseling, vol. 3 (Waco, Tex.: Word, 1986).

Wylie, Ruth C. *The Self-Concept: A Review of Methodological Considerations and Measuring Instruments* (Lincoln: University of Nebraska, 1974).

Yankelovich, Daniel. *New Rules: Searching for Self-Fulfillment in a World Turned Upside Down* (New York: Random House, 1981).

NOTES

Chapter 1. Self-Esteem: A Psycho-Theological Definition

1. Alice Miller, *Prisoners of Childhood: the Drama of the Gifted Child and the Search for the True Self* (New York: Basic Books, 1981), 16.

2. Ibid., 45.

3. Ibid., vii, viii.

4. Adapted from Norman Wakefield, *Building Self-Esteem in the Family* (Elgin, Ill.: David C. Cook, 1977), 3.

5. Heinz L. Ansbacher and Rowena R. Ansbacher, eds. *The Individual Psychology of Alfred Adler* (New York: Basic Books, 1956), 103.

6. For further theological considerations of self-esteem, see S. Bruce Narramore, *No Condemnation: Rethinking Guilt Motivation in Counseling and Parenting* (Grand Rapids: Zondervan, 1984); Paul Brand and Philip Yancey, *In His Image* (Grand Rapids: Zondervan, 1984); and Josh McDowell, *His Image . . . My Image* (San Bernardino, Calif.: Here's Life, 1984).

7. Ideas for identity questions come from Frank and Dixie Morris, *Charts: The Whole Person Workbook* (South Bend: TACM, 1982) and *Maps* (South Bend: TACM, 1980).

Chapter 2. Self-Esteem: A Psycho-Theological Process

1. See the classic studies of John Bowlby, *Attachment and Loss*, Vol. 1, *Attachment* (1969), Vol. 2, *Separation: Anxiety and Anger* (1973), Vol. 3, *Loss, Sadness and Depression* (1973) (New York: Basic Books). Also, see Howard Gardner, *Development Psychology* (Boston: Little, Brown, 1982), 27–56; Michael R. Jackson, *Self-Esteem and Meaning: A Life Historical Investigation* (New York: State University of New York Press, 1984); Robert Kegan, *The Evolving Self* (Cambridge: Harvard University Press, 1982); and R. A. Spitz and K. M. Wolf, "Anaclitic Depression," *Psychoanalytic Study of the Child* 2 (1946), 313–42.

2. See Robert Langs, *Madness and Cure* (New York: New Concept Press, 1985).

3. Ideas for these questions came from a Neuro-Linguistic Programing seminar in Chicago, Fall 1980 through Spring 1981.

Chapter 3. Teaching People to Build Self-Esteem: A Twelve-Step Process

1. See Alan Wheelis, *How People Change* (New York: Harper & Row, 1973).

2. For another perspective on the change process see Paul Watzlawick and John Weakland, *Change: Principles of Problem Formation and Problem Resolution* (New York: Norton, 1974).

3. See Joyce Landorf, *Change Points: When We Need Him Most* (Old Tappan, N.J.: Revell, 1981).

4. Although Mowrer's work is currently out of print, he presents an interesting view of helping by taking Christian and biblical principles regarding confession of sin and applying them in a group/community mode. Even though he is not a Christian, he can teach us something about helping, having borrowed many of his ideas from the church. See O. Hobart Mowrer, *The Crisis in Psychiatry and Religion* (Princeton, N.J.: Van Nostrand, 1961), *The New Group Therapy* (Princeton, N.J.: Van Nostrand, 1964), (1960), "Sin, the Lesser of Two Evils," *American Psychologist* 15 (1960): 301–04. "Some Constructive Features of the Concepts of Sin," *Journal of Counseling Psychology* 7, 185–88.

5. For a secular discussion of self-esteem and the problems low self-esteem creates see: James A. Beane and Richard P. Lepha, *Self-Concept, Self-Esteem and the Curriculum* (New York: Teacher's

College Press, 1986); Robert Burns, *Self-Concept Development and Education* (Philadelphia: Taylor and Francis, 1986); Harris Cleme and Reynold Bean, *Self-Esteem: The Key to Your Child's Well-Being* (New York: Zebra, 1982); Michael Krawetz, *Self-Esteem Passport* (New York: H. Holt, 1984); Wyndam Lewis, *Self-condemned* (Santa Barbara, Calif.: Black Sparrow, 1983); Mervin D. Lynch, et al., *Self-Concept: Advances in Theory and Research* (Cambridge, Mass.: Ballinger, 1981).

6. Two helpful books that I have my clients read are: Ray Burwick, *Self-Esteem: You're Better Than You Think* (Wheaton: Tyndale, 1983) and Cecil Osborne, *Self-Esteem: Overcoming Inferiority Feelings* (Nashville: Abingdon, 1986).

7. See Matthew McKay and Patrick Fanning, *Self-Esteem: The Secret to Accepting Yourself* (Oakland: New Harbinger, 1986).

8. See Dennis Rainey and Barbara Rainey, *Building Your Mate's Self-Esteem* (San Bernardino, Calif.: Here's Life, 1986).

9. Ruth M. Ward, *Self-Esteem: A Gift from God* (Grand Rapids: Baker, 1984).

10. Requesting counselees to read books on gifts of the Spirit is helpful. Ray Stedman's *Body Life* (rev. ed. Ventura, Calif.: Regal, 1979) is one such useful book.

Chapter 4. Teaching People Their Sensory Process in Developing Self-Esteem

1. Theodore Rubin, *Compassion and Self-Hate* (New York: Ballantine Books, 1975), 177.

2. Learning and communicating styles are now being taught to teachers in "modality-based instruction." See Zaner-Bloser, *Teacher's Guide for Modality Alphabet Cards* and *Zaner-Bloser Modality Kit* (Columbus, Ohio: Zaner-Bloser, 1981). Teachers are encouraged to observe their students' behavior in order to assess their modality strengths. The three predominant learning styles are *visual*—learning by seeing: watching demonstrations; *auditory*—learning through verbal instructions from others or self; and *kinesthetic*—learning by doing: direct involvement.

Students who are predominantly visual like description, and sometimes stop reading and stare into space, imagining the scene with intense concentration. Auditory learners enjoy dialogue and plays. They tend to avoid lengthy descriptions, are unaware of illustrations, and move their lips or subvocalize. Kinesthetic learners prefer stories where action occurs early. They tend to fidget when reading and are generally not avid readers. Spelling is easier for visual people because they can see the word. They recognize words by sight. Auditory people tend to have difficulty spelling because they sound the word out phonetically. Kinesthetic people tend to be poor spellers because they have to write the word to determine if the word "feels" right.

Memory styles also follow the predominant learning modality. Visual people remember faces, but forget names—unless they write them down. Auditory people forget faces, but remember names. Kinesthetic people remember what was done more than what was seen or heard. Imagination skills are predictable according to the person's learning modality. Communication for visual people is not lengthy. They tend to become impatient when extensive listening is required. Clumsy use of words, underdevelopment of descriptions, and frequent use of visual words (see, look, etc.) characterize the visual person.

Not surprisingly, auditory people tend to be good communicators. They enjoy listening, but often cannot wait to talk. Their descriptions tend to be long and may be repetitive. They like hearing themselves or others talk, and use auditory words like *listen* and *hear*. Kinesthetic people do not listen well. They tend to gesture and stand close when speaking or listening. They quickly lose interest in detailed verbal discourse and use words such as *get, take, handle,* and *grasp.*

3. See Richard Bandler and John Grinder, *The Structure of Magic,* Vols. 1 and 2 (Palo Alto, Calif.: Science and Behavior Books, 1979).

4. Ibid.

5. For additional discussion of the eye scan and sensory predicates, see Byron A. Lewis and R. Frank Pucelik, *Magic Demystified: A Pragmatic Guide to Communications and Change* (Lake Oswego, Ore.: Metamorphous Press, 1984); Stephen Lankton, *Practical Magic: A Translation of Basic Neuro-Linguistic Programming into Clinical Psychotherapy* (Cupertino, Calif.: Meta, 1980); Leslie Cameron Bandler, *Solutions* (San Rafael, Calif.: Future Pace, 1985).

6. Arnold Lazarus has conceptualized human experience in a way that I have found useful in helping counselees describe their sensory experience. The acronym BASIC ID stands for Behavior, Affect (emotions), Sensations, Imaginations, Cognitions Interpersonal Relationships and Drugs/Health. See *The Practice of Multimodule Therapy* (New York: McGraw-Hill, 1980) and *Casebook of Multimodal Therapy*, Arnold A. Lazarus, ed. (New York: Guilford Press,

1985) for a fuller presentation. The BASIC ID can be adapted to the sensory predicates and eye scan by expanding Lazarus's use of imaginations into both auditory and visual imaginations and by defining cognitions as the three eye-scan categories—visual remembered, auditory remembered, and internal dialogue. The eye scan does not explicitly use interpersonal relationships or drugs/health, but they are implied in its counseling application.

7. See the above Lazarus books for a description of "firing order."

Chapter 5. Teaching Counselors the Sensory Process: A Counseling Situation

1. For additional help in basic counseling skills see: Gerard Egan, *The Skilled Helper* and *Exercises in Helping Skills* (both published in 1986, Monterey, Calif.: Brooks-Cole), and Allen E. Ivey, *Intentional Interviewing and Counseling* (Monterey, Calif.: Brooks-Cole, 1983).

2. Andrew's eye scan:

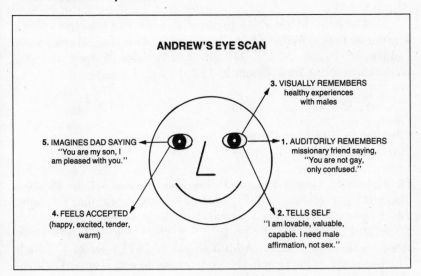

ANDREW'S EYE SCAN

3. VISUALLY REMEMBERS healthy experiences with males

1. AUDITORILY REMEMBERS missionary friend saying, "You are not gay, only confused."

5. IMAGINES DAD SAYING "You are my son, I am pleased with you."

2. TELLS SELF "I am lovable, valuable, capable. I need male affirmation, not sex."

4. FEELS ACCEPTED (happy, excited, tender, warm)

Chapter 6. Teaching Parents to Build Self-Esteem in Their Children

1. See Virginia Satir, *Conjoint Family Therapy* (Palo Alto, Calif.: Science and Behavior Books, 1983), chapters 1–5, especially, for a

discussion of self-esteem as a significant factor in individual, marital, and familial problems.

2. See Jean I. Clarke, *Self-Esteem: A Family Affair* (New York: Harper & Row, 1980); Virginia Satir, *Peoplemaking* (Palo Alto, Calif.: Science and Behavior Books, 1972); Pat Berne and Lou Savary, *Building Self-Esteem in Children* (New York: Crossroad, 1985); Dorothy Corkille Briggs, *Your Child's Self-Esteem: The Key to His Life* (Garden City, N.Y.: Doubleday, 1970); Eugene Anderson, *Self-Esteem for Tots to Teens: Five Principles of Raising Confident Children* (Deephaven, Minn.: Meadowbrook, 1984), as helpful resources in learning to build self-esteem in children.

3. Parents may need to deal with their own parents in their process of building self-esteem in themselves. See Harold Bloomfield and Leonard Felder, *Making Peace with Your Parents* (New York: Random, 1983), and *Making Peace with Yourself* (New York: Ballantine, 1985), for helpful suggestions. When reading alone does not seem sufficient, consulting a counselor to help parents express and forgive their hurt, anger and sadness may be necessary.

4. Erma Bombeck, *At Wits' End* (Garden City, N.Y.: Doubleday, 1983).

5. Abraham Maslow, *Motivation and Personality* (New York: Harper & Row, 1970) and "A Theory of Motivation," *Psychological Review* 50:4 (July, 1943), 370–96, and *Religion, Values, and Peak Experience* (New York: Penguin, 1978).

Chapter 7. Teaching People to Be Their Own Nurturing Parents

1. John M. Dusay, *Egograms: How I See You and You See Me* (New York: Harper & Row, 1977); Mary McClure Goulding, *Changing Lives Through Redecision Therapy* (New York: Grove, 1982); Muriel James and Lois Savary, *A New Self: Self-Therapy with Transactional Analysis* (Reading, Mass.: Addison-Wesley, 1977); James J. Lynch, *The Language of the Heart: The Body's Response to Human Dialogue* (New York: Basic Books, 1985).

2. Some Christians, given their belief in the depravity of man, have objected to the Transactional Analysis idea. While Eric Berne, the creator of TA, was not a Christian and was not writing from a theological perspective, his ideas have stimulated

creative and useful perspectives and tools. Thoughtful Christians can be taught by and use ideas from non-Christians without buying into the whole system. Application of TA to Christian living has been attempted by several authors, among them, Art Greer, *No Grown Up in Heaven: A* Transactional Analysis Primer for Christians (and Others) (New York: Hawthorn, 1975), and Muriel James, *The Power at the Bottom of the Well:* Transactional Analysis and Religious Experience (New York: Harper & Row, 1974).

3. Robert J. Zinger, *Looking out for #1* (Los Angeles: Funk and Wagnalls, 1971), 34.

4. See, for example: Robert H. Schuller, *Self-Esteem: The New Reformation* (Waco, Tex.: Word Books, 1982); William Backus and Marie Chapian, *Telling Yourself the Truth* (Minneapolis: Bethany House, 1980); Jerry A. Schmidt, *Do You Hear What You're Thinking?* (Wheaton, Ill.: Victor Books, 1983), and H. Norman Wright, *Self-Talk, Imagery, and Prayer in Counseling,* vol. 3, Resources for Christian Counseling (Waco, Tex.: Word Books, 1986).

5. Dorothy Briggs, *Celebrate Yourself* (Garden City, N.Y.: Doubleday, 1977), 49, 50.

6. Pamela Levin, *Cycles of Power.* This book may be obtained by writing the author at the following address: 1772 Vallejo St., San Francisco, CA 94123.

7. Paul Tournier, *The Healing of Persons* (London: SCM, 1963), 120–30.

8. Ibid., 125.

9. Clifford Baird, *The Power of a Positive Self-Esteem* (Wheaton, Ill.: Victor Books, 1983), 17.

10. Harry Guntrip, *Psychoanalytic Theory, Therapy, and the Self* (New York: Basic Books, 1973), 11.

11. Eugene Kennedy, *Free to Be Human* (Chicago: Thomas More Press, 1979), 95.

12. Briggs, 4.

13. Kenneth Blanchard and Spencer Johnson, *The One-Minute Manager* (New York: Berkley, 1984), 47.

14. Theodore Isaac Rubin, *Compassion and Self-Hate: An Alternative to Despair* (New York: Ballantine, 1975), 13.

15. Blanchard and Johnson, 15.

16. Lloyd H. Ahlem, *Do I Have to Be Me?* (Glendale, Calif.: Regal, 1973), 73.

Chapter 8. Teaching Counselees to Nurture Themselves
Through Recognizing and Accepting Feelings

1. Adapted from Dixie G. Morris and Frank R. Morris, *The Recognition and Expression of Feelings* (South Bend, Ind.: TACM, 1985), and Sherod Miller, et al., *Alive and Aware Workbook* (Minneapolis: Couples Communication, 1977).

2. For further discussion of Christians and their emotions see Barry Applewhite, *Feeling Good About Your Feelings: How to Express Your Emotions in Harmony with Biblical Principles* (Wheaton, Ill.: Victor Books, 1978); Beverly Beckman, *Emotions in God's World* (St. Louis: Concordia, 1986); James C. Dobson, *Emotions, Can You Trust Them?* (Ventura, Calif.: Regal, 1984); Timothy J. Gannon, *Emotional Development and Spiritual Growth* (Chicago: Franciscan Herald, 1965); Bert Ghezy and Mark Kinzer, *Emotions as Resources: A Biblical and Pastoral Perspective* (Ann Arbor, Mich.: Servant, 1983).

3. For further help in learning how to help people process feelings, see Robert A. Pierce, Michael P. Nichols, and Joyce R. DuBrin, *Emotional Expression in Psychotherapy* (New York: Gardner, 1983); Leslie S. Greenberg and Jeremy D. Safram, *Emotion in Psychotherapy* (New York: Guilford Press, 1986); Gary Collier, *Emotional Expression* (Hillsdale, N.J.: L. Erlbaum Associates, 1985); Stanley Keleman, *Emotional Anatomy: The Structure of Experience* (Berkeley: Center Press, 1985); Rolland S. Parker, *Emotional Common Sense: Avoiding Self-Destructiveness and Enhancing Personal Development* (New York: Harper & Row, 1981).

Chapter 9. Teaching Counselees to Experience God as
Their Nurturing Parent

1. J. I. Packer, *Knowing God* (Downers Grove, Ill.: InterVarsity, 1973), 184.

2. Packer, *Keep in Step with the Spirit* (Old Tappan, N.J.: Fleming H. Revell, 1984), 222.

3. *Red Flag, Green Flag: A Personal Safety Book* (Fargo, N.D.: Rape and Abuse Crisis Center, n.d.).

4. Jesus is the name above all names, the Christ, Messiah, Savior, and Lord. In this story he is the Jesus of John 8:1–11, speaking to a woman who needs the same encounter with him as did the woman caught in adultery.

Chapter 10. Teaching the Church to Build Esteem in Its Troubled Families

1. See Jacquelyn Small, *Becoming Naturally Therapeutic* (Austin, Tex.: The Eupsychian Press, 1981); Gerard Egan, *The Skilled Helper: A Model for Systematic Helping and Interpersonal Relating*, 2nd ed. (Monterey, Calif.: Brooks-Cole, 1982); and Allen E. Ivey, *Intentional Interviewing and Counseling* (Monterey, Calif.: Brooks-Cole, 1982) for help in learning empathic skills.

2. The series, "We Have a Problem," in *Parents* magazine, beginning February 1987, can be a helpful resource to counselors and troubled families.

3. To help your church take constructive steps, see the following: Don Baker, *Beyond Rejection* (1985) and *Beyond Forgiveness* (1984) (both by Multnomah Press, Portland, Ore.); John C. Howell, *Church and Family: Growing Together* (Nashville, Broadman, 1984); J. D. Middlebrook and Larry Summers, *Church and Family* (Springfield, Mo.: Gospel Publishing House, 1980); Charles M. Sell, *Family Ministry: Family Life Through the Church* (Grand Rapids: Zondervan, 1981); and David M. Thomas, *Family Life Ministry* (St. Meinrad, Ind.: Abbey, 1979).

4. Friends can learn to help friends through lay counseling books and seminars. These books are helpful: Gary R. Collins, *How to Be a People Helper* (1976) and *Helping People Grow* (1980) (both by Vision House, Ventura, Calif.); Everett L. Worthington, Jr., *When Someone Asks for Help* (1982) and *How to Help the Hurting* (1985) (both by InterVarsity, Downers Grove, Ill.).

5. Joy P. Gage, *When Parents Cry* (Denver: Accent Books, 1980).

6. See Erik H. Erikson, *Identity and the Life Cycle* (New York: Norton, 1968).

7. Pastors and counselors who want more information on family counseling will want to consult Vol. 14 in the Resources for Christian Counseling series, George A. Rekers, *Counseling Families* (Waco, Tex.: Word, 1988).

The following books on family counseling will also be useful references: Michele Baldwin and Virginia Satir, *The Use of Self in Therapy* (New York: Haworth Press, 1987); John Bandler, Richard Grinder, and Virginia Satir, *Changing with Families* (Palo Alto, Calif.: Science and Behavior Books, 1976); Robert Beavers, *Successful Marriage* (New York: Norton, 1985); Elizabeth A. Carter and Monica M. Goldrick, *Family Life Cycle: A Framework for Family Therapy*

(New York: Garner Press, 1980); Walter Kempler, *Experiential Psychotherapy Within Families* (New York: Brunner-Mazel, 1981); and Daniel Wile, *Couples Therapy: A Non-traditional Approach* (New York: Wiley, 1981).

Chapter 11. Helping People Change: The Answer Is Not the Solution

1. Tournier, *The Healing of Persons*, 124.

2. Nathaniel Branden, *Honor Thy Self: The Psychology of Confidence and Respect* (New York: Bantam, 1985), 249.

3. William James, quoted in Robert Campbell, *The New Science: Self-Esteem Psychology* (Lanham, Md.: University Press of America, 1984), 2, 3.

4. Douglas Frank, *Less Than Conquerors* (Grand Rapids: Wm. B. Eerdmans, 1986), 91.

INDEX

David E. Carlson

David Carlson, C.S.W., A.C.S.W., president of Arlington Counseling Associates, Ltd., in Arlington Heights, Illinois, received graduate degrees in sociology, theology, and social work from Northern Illinois University, Trinity Evangelical Divinity School, and the University of Chicago, respectively. He has earned a diplomate in clinical social work and has trained at the Family Institute of Chicago, the Family Learning Center of South Bend (Ind.) and the Experiential Family Therapy Program in affiliation with the Department of Preventive Medicine and Community Health, University of Illinois at Chicago. He has twenty-seven years of counseling experience in a variety of settings, dealing with delinquent and dependent youth and with parent-child conflicts, marital discord, death, divorce, depression, and substance abuse.

Formerly, Carlson was chairman of the department of sociology at Trinity College before joining the Divinity School as visiting professor of counseling psychology. He is also professor of counseling psychology at the Caribbean Graduate School of Theology, Kingston, Jamaica. He is married to Beverly and has two adult children, Todd and Heidi.